Transportation Engineering

About the Author

Beverly Thompson Kuhn, Ph.D., P.E., PMP, is a Senior Research Engineer and Division Head with the prestigious Texas A&M Transportation Institute (TTI), which is part of the Texas A&M University System. She is an expert in the area of transportation systems management and operations and the application of research results to improve traffic operations. She has taught introductory transportation engineering courses at both Texas A&M and Penn State University and has authored numerous papers and publications, including chapters in McGraw-Hill's *Handbook of Transportation Engineering,* and is an active member of the Transportation Research Board (TRB) and the Institute of Transportation Engineers (ITE).

Transportation Engineering

A Practical Approach to Highway Design, Traffic Analysis, and Systems Operations

Beverly T. Kuhn, Ph.D., P.E.

New York Chicago San Francisco
Athens London Madrid
Mexico City Milan New Delhi
Singapore Sydney Toronto

Library of Congress Control Number: 2018948983

Transportation Engineering: A Practical Approach to Highway Design, Traffic Analysis, and Systems Operations

1 2 3 4 5 6 QVS 23 22 21 20 19

ISBN 978-1-260-01957-5
MHID 1-260-01957-8

The pages within this book were printed on acid-free paper.

Sponsoring Editor
Lauren Poplawski

Editorial Supervisor
Donna M. Martone

Acquisitions Coordinator
Elizabeth Houde

Project Managers
Kritika Kaushik,
Cenveo® Publisher Services

Copy Editor
Girish Sharma,
Cenveo Publisher Services

Proofreader
Bhavna Y. Goyal,
Cenveo Publisher Services

Indexer
Cenveo Publisher Services

Production Supervisor
Lynn M. Messina

Composition
Cenveo Publisher Services

Art Director, Cover
Jeff Weeks

Contents

Preface

Transportation—the movement of people, goods, and services in a safe and efficient manner—is a foundational component of society and has been for eons. It is essential to how we live our lives, it drives the economy in countless ways, and it often only comes to the attention of society when it fails to live up to its expectations. Millions of individuals are responsible for keeping this behemoth in working order, and they face challenges at every turn. Professionals with a broad range of skills undertake the cradle-to-grave responsibility of planning, funding, designing, constructing, operating, maintaining, repairing, retrofitting, and upgrading the entire transportation system across all modes to meet society's demands. This textbook focuses on the surface roadway network, which is one aspect of this system with which nearly all travelers across the globe are familiar. It provides information on the critical scientific principles needed to create a safe and efficient system and addresses the interrelated topics of demand and operations, which directly affect the sustainability of the surface network. It also highlights emerging topics that transportation professionals are beginning to face that could revolutionize the way we travel in the future.

Acknowledgments

First and foremost, I would like to thank my husband, Darrell Kuhn, for his unending love and support throughout my entire career and for always being a willing companion on this journey. I also thank my sons, Harrison Kuhn and Parker Kuhn, for their understanding for the many times I was away from home. I extend my thanks to all of the professors, mentors, and colleagues who have guided and supported me over the past 30 years. I would not be where I am without any of you. I would also like to thank Lauren Poplawski at McGraw-Hill for her guidance throughout the publication process. Finally, to my family and friends who have always supported me from both near and far throughout my career, I am humbled and forever grateful to be a part of your tribe.

CHAPTER 1

Introduction

1.1 Introduction

Transportation—the movement of people, goods, and services in a safe and efficient manner—is a foundational component of society and has been for eons. It contributes to the safety, security, and prosperity of global economies and is something that many individuals often take for granted. The action of getting into a car to drive to work on smooth roads with minor interruptions while arriving safely is undertaken millions of times each day without a second thought by the driver. Additionally, passengers take millions of commute trips by bus, train, bicycle, or walking, arriving at their destination without the hassle of driving themselves. Furthermore, they likely conducted business or handled personal issues via telephone along the journey if they were not driving alone in a vehicle. Consumers fill their shopping carts with products without considering how they got from the field, plant, or factory to the shelf in the store, much less how the various components originally arrived at the factory. Their online purchases arrive at their doors in only a few days and, in some cases, hours. Consumers fly around the country or the globe in comfort, passing through major airline hubs with every convenience available. However, when individuals do not have access to affordable transportation, their ability to make a living, to take care of their personal health and that of their family members, and to contribute to society is impaired. As individuals age, their ability to be independent deteriorates, making access to affordable mass transit or other means of mobility even more critical to a high quality of life. The same can be said for those with disabilities that make driving a personal vehicle impractical or impossible. Transportation is an integral part of life in today's rapidly advancing world that must be maintained in terms of affordability, flexibility, and sustainability.

Transportation is essential to how we live our lives, it drives the economy in countless ways, and it often only comes to the attention of society when it fails to live up to its expectations. Millions of individuals are responsible for keeping this behemoth in working order, and they face challenges at every turn. Professionals with a broad range of skills undertake the cradle-to-grave responsibility of planning, funding, designing, constructing, operating, maintaining, repairing, retrofitting, and upgrading the entire transportation system across all modes to meet society's demands. This textbook will focus on one aspect of this system with which nearly all travelers across the globe are familiar: the surface roadway network. While surface transportation is by no means the sole mode of transportation used today, it represents the most common mode with which travelers interact on a daily basis. This text will provide information on the critical scientific principles needed to create a safe and efficient system and address the interrelated topics of demand and operations, which directly affect the

1

sustainability of the surface network. Finally, it will highlight emerging topics that transportation professionals are beginning to face that could revolutionize the way we travel in the future.

1.2   Transportation Engineering

Merriam-Webster defines engineering as the "activities or function of an engineer" in which science and mathematics are applied to matter and energy in nature and are made useful to people.[1] Thus, within the transportation context, transportation engineering is the field of study related to planning, design, operation, and maintenance of any aspect of transportation systems and networks. It is the responsibility of transportation professionals to ensure that the complex transportation facilities, which afford mobility for people and goods, do so in a safe, rapid, comfortable, convenient, and environmentally compatible manner that is sustainable and resilient in the face of numerous challenges and threats such as natural disasters, population growth, and climate change.

Transportation engineering has for decades been included as part of the discipline of civil engineering since transportation networks typically fall within the public domain. They are available for the general public, and their upkeep is typically the responsibility of public agency employees and their contractors. It is important to note that transportation engineering could be considered more of an art than a science. Professionals within the field are required to make many decisions based on society's needs and desires for mobility, and the answers are not always easy given the need to balance needs with the reality of limited resources. The identification of solutions involves the synthesis of different intellectual perspectives and scientific bases to solve transportation problems across the breadth of competing interests: technical, economic, social, and environmental in nature.

1.3   The Surface Transportation System

Since the turn of the previous century, the United States has grappled with the challenge of providing convenient and safe transportation options to its citizens. Over the decades, the national policy on surface transportation has shifted from construction to sustainability as evidenced by the evolution of funding bills passed by the U.S. Congress. The following provides a brief overview of critical federal funding legislation, which has shaped the transportation system in the United States over the past century.

The Federal Aid Road Act of 1916[2] recognized the rise of the automobile and the growing challenge of getting the farmer out of the mud. With this legislation, which was passed by President Wilson on July 11, 1916, Congress formally recognized that the government had the right to fund the construction of interstate highways under the constitutional right to regulate interstate commerce and that these facilities would be the backbone of the country's economic growth. The first federal highway funding legislation in the United States, this act addressed the inadequate roads in the country and the need for an increased federal role in funding.[2] The law required each state to establish and maintain a highway agency, employing engineering professionals to carry out federal-aid projects identified by the federal government. The law focused on rural post roads and illustrated the importance of working to enhance rural life in the United States. The Federal Aid Road Act of 1927[3] amended the 1916 act by expanding the roads eligible

FIGURE 1.1   Vehicle stuck on a muddy roadway. (© *Texas Department of Transportation [TxDOT].*)

for funding from rural post roads to any public road being used or which formed a connecting link with other roads. As shown in Fig. 1.1, many existing roadways became muddy after heavy rains, making travel virtually impossible. These early road acts sought to provide states with the resources to help improve the quality of these roadways so that travelers could use them under a variety of conditions. Improving these facilities would also foster interstate commerce into the future.

Various forms of transportation funding progressed over the next few decades until 1956. With the National Interstate and Defense Highway System Act of 1956,[4] President Eisenhower established the interstate highway system in the United States. The law authorized the expenditure of $25 billion to construct 41,000 miles of interstate highways between 1957 and 1969. This legislation represented a fundamental shift in the country toward a surface transportation system that from that point forward would focus on the automobile. Eisenhower's support of the system was based on the need for economic development, congestion relief, improved safety, and the reduction of lawsuits involving motor vehicles.[5] The interstate highways were also intended to support national defense in the post-war era, though this was not the primary reason for their construction. The interstate system also helped establish uniform geometric design and construction standards that included such features as fully controlled access, design speeds, paved shoulders, and a minimum of two 12-foot travel lanes in each direction. Many of these design criteria still exist today.

The shift toward an automobile-centric transportation system directly impacted the pattern of community development and the transportation network into the future. For example, the interstates were frequently constructed through the rural countryside where only local roads existed previously. Figure 1.2 shows early construction on Interstate 45 (I-45) in the area north of Houston, Texas, which at the time was the rural community of Conroe. The construction of this highway connected Houston and Dallas, greatly reducing the travel time between these cities that are over 200 miles apart. A trip that at the time took the better part of a day became only a few hours in length. The existence of such new transportation facilities in rural areas often attracted development,

Figure 1.2   Early construction of Interstate 45 (I-45), Conroe, Texas. (© *TxDOT.*)

particularly around interchanges with other major roadways and highways. Areas such as Conroe transformed from the rural landscape of a sleepy town to a bustling suburb, as shown in Fig. 1.3. While the concept of selecting a location for an interstate facility through the rural countryside seems straightforward, alignments were often controversial at the local level. Small communities or counties did not always want to have an interstate close by, fearing that the roadway would negatively affect the small town atmosphere they enjoyed. Such local sentiment often impacted the final location of the facility by having the facility bypass the community and sometimes having a detrimental effect on the economic health of the region that rejected it.

The construction of the interstate system also impacted the urban environment, as shown in Fig. 1.4. In many cities, the proposed alignment for the interstates often divided established neighborhoods and created conflict between their residents and the local leaders.[6] Some critics of the system noted that many of these facilities divided lower-income neighborhoods, having them bear a disproportionate burden for the progress brought by the interstate. Additionally, the interstates made the commute from outlying suburbs easier for workers, encouraging suburban sprawl with low-density, affordable development and an ever-increasing reliance on the automobile as a mode of transportation. Many early mass transit services faded from the urban landscape. Air and noise

Figure 1.3   Aerial view of Conroe, Texas. (© *Google Maps*.)

Figure 1.4   Construction of Interstate 45 (I-45) in Houston, Texas. (© *TxDOT*.)

FIGURE 1.5   Early roadway congestion. (© *Texas A&M Transportation Institute [TTI].*)

pollution increased in the urban centers along with growing traffic congestion. In short, the interstate system likely contributed to the transportation-related problems it was intended to solve.

As early as the 1960s, these new interstates were experiencing congestion, as pictured in Fig. 1.5. The commuters from the suburbs traveling to the employment centers in large cities were forced to sit in traffic on a daily basis. Such situations created the ongoing challenge to provide adequate capacity for peak period travel. Early efforts to monitor traffic on the roadway network included such innovative strategies as the construction of towers along the roadway (see Fig. 1.6) to observe traffic behavior and to identify bottlenecks in the system. Motion picture cameras were also installed along interstate corridors to record traffic flow during congested periods. Films were then used by traffic engineers in monitoring the conditions and improving operations (see Fig. 1.7). These scenes were repeated in urban areas across the country. Since the inception of the interstate system, transportation professionals have been striving to determine how best to operate and maintain that investment and tackle the challenge of congestion and growth.

In 1969, Congress passed the National Environmental Policy Act (NEPA),[7] which represented one of the first broad efforts by the government to establish a framework for protecting the environment. This law, which applied to all branches of the government, directed agencies to consider the environment before advancing any major federal action or project that would significantly impact the environment in the United States. It goes without saying that NEPA requirements had a direct impact on transportation-related project such as airports, highways, and other transportation facilities. Among the most visible of impacts, federal agencies were required to conduct environmental assessments (EAs) and develop environmental impact statements (EISs) in advance of major projects.[5] These assessments are designed to identify the likelihood of environmental impacts of projects when compared to other courses of action.

In addition to the NEPA act, Congress passed the 1970 Clean Air Act (CAA) and 1977 Clean Air Act Amendments (CAAA),[8] which shifted the role of government in controlling air pollution. The intent of these acts was to protect public health and public welfare and to regulate emissions of hazardous air pollutants. They authorized

FIGURE 1.6   Early traffic monitoring on Interstate 45 (I-45) Gulf Freeway, Houston, Texas. (© *TTI.*)

FIGURE 1.7   Early traffic monitoring technology, Interstate 45 (I-45) Gulf Freeway, Houston, Texas. (© *TTI.*)

federal and state regulations to limit stationary and mobile source emissions and created four regulatory programs to oversee these regulations. They were the National Ambient Air Quality Standards (NAAQS), State Implementation Plans (SIPs), New Source Performance Standards (NPS), and National Emission Standards for Hazardous Air Pollutants (NESHAPs). The 1977 amendments included provisions for the Prevention of Significant Deterioration (PSD) of air quality in areas attaining the NAAQS and requirements for non-attainment areas. Non-attainment areas are those geographic regions not meeting the federal air quality standards.

The 1990 CAAA[9] amended the original CAA to set new goals (dates) for achieving attainment of NAAQS since many areas of the country were having difficulty meeting the deadlines. Key components of the amendments included the requirement of technology-based standards for major pollution sources and certain area pollution sources, and the establishment and periodic review of emission standards (i.e., maximum achievable control technology) that require the maximum degree of reduction in emissions of hazardous air pollutants.

In addition to environmental legislation related to clean air, Congress focused on disabled citizens with the passage of the Americans with Disabilities Act (ADA)[10] in 1990. This act, which was signed into law on July 26, 1990, by President George H. W. Bush, represented one of the country's most comprehensive pieces of civil rights legislation related to people with disabilities. The primary focus of the legislation was to ensure that citizens with disabilities have the same opportunities as everyone else to participate in all aspects of life, including employment opportunities, the purchase of goods and services, and to participate in state and local government programs and services. The ADA had broad transportation implications including the accommodation of disabilities in surface transportation services such as city buses, public rail transit, and sidewalks.[11]

In 1991, Congress passed the Intermodal Surface Transportation Efficiency Act of 1991 (ISTEA),[12] which continued to focus on authorization for highways, highway safety, and mass transit. Signed by President Bush, the bill authorized expenditures of $155 billion, established the National Highway System (NHS), and gave state and local governments more flexibility in determining transportation solutions for their jurisdictions. Additionally, the legislation highlighted new technologies as potential solutions to improving the efficiency and safety of the transportation network. Key components of the law allowed highway funds to be used for transportation-related environmental projects and emphasized highway safety by establishing a new program to encourage use of safety belts and motorcycle helmets. Other measures established uniformity in state vehicle registration and fuel tax reporting to streamline efforts and improve productivity.

President Clinton signed the Transportation Equity Act for the 21st Century (TEA-21)[13] in 1998, which built on the initiatives of ISTEA. The legislation had four key thrust areas: rebuilding America, improving safety, protecting the environment, and creating opportunity. The guaranteed $198 billion investment included in the bill was intended to balance the federal investment across highways, transit, intermodal projects, and technologies while continuing to encourage state and local flexibility in expenditures. Safety programs highlighted the importance of improving safety belt use, fighting drunk driving, and improving truck safety programs across the country. Other efforts targeted increasing pipeline safety and that of rail-highway grade crossings. Protecting the public health and the environment included the expansion of Congestion Mitigation and Air Quality (CMAQ) improvement and transportation enhancements programs, extension of programs for the construction of National Scenic Byways, pedestrian and bicycle paths, and recreational trails, as well as incentives to increase transit ridership. Finally, as with virtually every other transportation authorization bill, TEA-21 helped expand access to jobs and through innovative programs as well as continued the effective Disadvantaged Business Enterprise program.

The Safe Accountable Flexible Efficient Transportation Equity Act: A Legacy for Users (SAFETEA-LU)[14] was a funding bill signed in 2005 by George W. Bush. This bill, which guaranteed $244.1 billion in funding for highways, highway safety, and public transportation, had the following focus areas: safety, equity, innovative finance, congestion relief, mobility and productivity, efficiency, environmental stewardship, and environmental streamlining. Unique aspects of the bill include the establishment of the highway safety improvement program (HSIP) and other programs targeting safe routes to school, work zone safety, bicycle and pedestrian safety, and the improvement of traffic control devices targeted to older drivers and pedestrians, toll facilities, and motorcycle safety. Congestion relief provisions gave states more options to use road pricing to manage congestion and enhanced and clarified the use and operations of high-occupancy vehicle (HOV) lanes to ensure degradation of operations does not occur.

In 2012, President Obama signed the act entitled Moving Ahead for Progress in the 21st Century (MAP-21).[15] This bill had as its key tenets to strengthen America's highways by expanding the NHS to incorporate arterials, to establish the National Highway Performance Program, and to establish a performance-based program for more efficient investment of federal transportation resources. The bill authorized $82 billion for road, bridge, bicycling, and walking improvements to help create jobs and support economic growth. It continued the HSIP by doubling funding for infrastructure safety projects to improve progress toward reducing highway fatalities and also focused on distracted driving, transit safety, and motor carrier safety. Furthermore, it emphasized the importance of improving timely delivery of projects and efficiency in the development process from planning to completion.

The most recent authorization bill, signed by President Obama in 2015, was the Fixing America's Surface Transportation Act (FAST Act).[16] This legislation authorized $305 billion for highway, highway and motor vehicle safety, public transportation, motor carrier safety, hazardous materials safety, rail, research, technology, and statistics programs. Included in its major provisions were programs to improve safety, maintain the condition of the transportation system, reduce congestion and improve efficiency and freight movement, protect the environment, and to further reduce delays in project delivery. All of the programs were intended to help create jobs, support economic growth, and improve mobility for all citizens.

As evidenced by the progression of federal funding bills, the transportation industry has moved from the initial construction of the interstate system to the wholesale operation and maintenance of a system that is safer, more efficient, and sustainable. Today, the overall national policy agenda with respect to transportation focuses on maintaining and expanding the national transportation system and fostering a sound financial base for that system to create jobs and ensure its long-term reliability. Additional tenets focus on ensuring that the system supports public safety and national security, protects the environment and quality of life, is sustainable into the future, and looks to incorporating rapidly advancing technologies that can enhance the government's ability to provide a safe and efficient method of transporting people, goods, and services across the country. Transportation professionals inherit this system.

1.4   The Transportation Profession

The transportation profession, which originated within the discipline of civil engineering, has evolved to include a broad range of professionals across a multitude of disciplines. Today, civil engineers make up only one segment of the transportation profession. These more traditional players in the transportation industry are now joined by professionals with expertise in such fields as economics, psychology, geography, public administration, city planning, political science, industrial engineering, electrical engineering, physics, mechanical engineering, mathematics, statistics, logistics, communications, archeology, geology, and environmental engineering. They all work together as a team to advance the improvement of transportation for all users.

The critical challenges that these transportation professionals face on an ongoing basis include managing congestion, improving safety, providing equal access, and protecting the environment. They also strive to incorporate and adapt new technologies to enhance the system, work to secure financial resources for the transportation network, and develop institutional arrangements that foster collaboration and work toward a seamless network for the user. Sample focus areas include daily urban operations (Fig. 1.8), interchange design (Fig. 1.9), international border crossing inspections and

Figure 1.8   Houston TranStar control room. (© *TxDOT*.)

Figure 1.9   Interchange design. (© *TTI*.)

wait times (Fig. 1.10), bridge design (Fig. 1.11), pavement design (Fig. 1.12), and the impact of vehicle emissions on the environment (Fig. 1.13), in addition to a multitude of other topics all working to provide a safe and efficient transportation network for the traveling public.

Figure 1.10 U.S.-Mexico border crossing. (© *TTI*.)

FIGURE **1.11** Bridge research and inspection. (© *TTI.*)

FIGURE **1.12** Asphaltic pavement design research. (© *TTI.*)

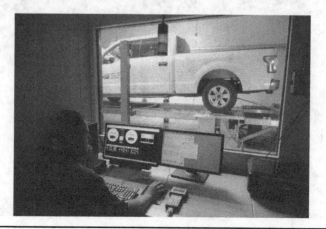

FIGURE **1.13** Environmental and emissions research. (© *TTI.*)

1.5 Summary

Transportation is a foundational component of society and contributes to the safety, security, and prosperity of global economies. Transportation professionals are responsible for ensuring that this complex network serves its primary purpose of moving people, goods, and services in a safe and efficient manner so that it is sustainable over the long term. This textbook will provide information on the critical design, analytical, and system operational elements and skills that transportation engineers need to undertake the challenge. With a focus on the technical aspects of the job and the recognition that collaboration with a broad range of professionals is essential, today's transportation engineers can ensure that future generations will enjoy the mobility needed to lead productive lives in society.

Glossary of Acronyms

CAA—Clean Air Act

CAAA—Clean Air Act Amendments

CMAQ—Congestion Mitigation and Air Quality

EA—Environmental assessment

EIS—Environmental impact statement

FAST Act—Fixing America's Surface Transportation Act

HOV—High-occupancy vehicle

ISTEA—Intermodal Surface Transportation Efficiency Act of 1991

MAP-21—The Moving Ahead for Progress in the 21st Century Act

NAAQS—National Ambient Air Quality Standards

NEPA—National Environmental Policy Act

NESHAP—National Emission Standards for Hazardous Air Pollutants

NPS—New Source Performance Standards

PSD—Prevention of Significant Deterioration

SAFTEA-LU—Safe Accountable Flexible Efficient Transportation Act: A Legacy for Users

SIP—State Implementation Plan

TEA-21—Transportation Equity Act for the 21st Century

U.S.DOT—United States Department of Transportation

Exercises

1.1 Write a paper (no more than 10 pages) on the critical link between transportation and economic prosperity at the federal, state, local, and individual level.

1.2 Write a paper (no more than 10 pages) providing a critical discussion on the national progression of federal transportation investments since 1916 and the positive and negative impacts it has had on communities and overall mobility for Americans.

1.3   Write a paper (no more than 10 pages) discussing how the advancement of technology has impacted the provision of transportation options to travelers over the past 30 years.

References

1. *Merriam-Webster's Online Dictionary*, https://www.merriam-webster.com/dictionary/engineering (accessed January 29, 2017).
2. Weingroff, Richard F., "Federal Aid Road Act of 1916: Building the Foundation," *Public Roads*, Vol. 60, No. 1, 1996, U.S. Department of Transportation, Federal Highway Administration Research and Technology, https://www.fhwa.dot.gov/publications/publicroads/96summer/p96su2.cfm (accessed January 29, 2017).
3. Full text, The Federal-Aid Road Act of 1916, https://archive.org/stream/federalaidroadac105unit/federalaidroadac105unit_djvu.txt (accessed January 29, 2017).
4. "National Interstate and Defense Highways Act (1956)," The National Archives and Records Administration, https://www.ourdocuments.gov/doc.php?doc=88&page=transcript (accessed January 29, 2017).
5. "Interstate Highway System—The Myths," Federal Highway Administration, U.S. Department of Transportation, https://www.fhwa.dot.gov/interstate/interstate-myths.cfm (accessed May 2018).
6. Shelton, T., and A. Gann, *Urban Interstate Rights-of-Way as Sites of Intervention*, https://utk.academia.edu/AmandaGann (accessed May 2018).
7. "Summary of the National Environmental Policy Act, 42 U.S.C. §4321 et seq. (1969)," United State Environmental Protection Agency, https://www.epa.gov/laws-regulations/summary-national-environmental-policy-act (accessed January 28, 2017).
8. "Summary of the Clean Air Act, 42 U.S.C. §7401 et seq. (1970)," United States Environmental Protection Agency, https://www.epa.gov/laws-regulations/summary-clean-air-act (accessed January 28, 2017).
9. "The Clean Air Act—Highlights of the 1990 Amendments," United States Environmental Protection Agency, https://www.epa.gov/clean-air-act-overview/clean-air-act-highlights-1990-amendments (accessed January 28, 2017).
10. "Information and Technical Assistance on the Americans with Disabilities Act," United States Department of Justice, Civil Rights Division, https://www.ada.gov/ada_intro.htm (accessed January 28, 2017).
11. "A Guide to Disability Rights Laws," U.S. Department of Justice, Civil Rights Division, Disability Rights Section, https://www.ada.gov/cguide.htm (accessed January 31, 2017).
12. "Legislation, Regulations, and Guidance: Intermodal Surface Transportation Efficiency Act of 1991 Information," U.S. Department of Transportation, Federal Highway Administration, https://www.fhwa.dot.gov/planning/public_involvement/archive/legislation/istea.cfm (accessed January 28, 2017).
13. "TEA-21: Moving Americans into the 21st Century," U.S. Department of Transportation, Federal Highway Administration, https://www.fhwa.dot.gov/tea21/index.htm (accessed January 28, 2017).

14. "SAFETEA-LU, Safe Accountable Flexible Efficient Transportation Equity Act: A Legacy for Users," U.S. Department of Transportation, Federal Highway Administration, https://www.fhwa.dot.gov/safetealu/ (accessed January 28, 2017).

15. "MAP-21: Moving Ahead for Progress in the 21st Century," U.S. Department of Transportation, Federal Highway Administration, https://www.fhwa.dot.gov/map21/ (accessed January 28, 2017).

16. "Fixing America's Surface Transportation (FAST) Act," U.S. Department of Transportation, Federal Highway Administration, https://www.fhwa.dot.gov/fastact/ (accessed January 28, 2017).

CHAPTER 2

Human Factors and Geometric Design

2.1 Introduction

The geometric design of transportation facilities involves the consideration of user characteristics and human factors in the design process. These limitations govern elements such as vertical and horizontal alignment, and influence how transportation engineers design facilities that meet the needs of system users for safe and efficient mobility. This chapter provides a discussion on user characteristics and human factors that impact geometric design; the concept of geometric design of transportation facilities; design standards, design speed, and sight distance; the fundamentals and elements of designing vertical alignments and horizontal alignments of roadways; and the project development process.

2.2 User Characteristics and Human Factors

The transportation professional is responsible for designing and operating the surface roadway network to ensure safe mobility by its users. In order to accomplish this challenge, the professional must first understand the primary elements of the highway system. As illustrated in Fig. 2.1, those interrelated elements are the system user, the vehicle, and the roadway itself. The transportation professional must ensure that these three elements are coordinated to provide a transportation system that is efficient and safe for system users. A high degree of control is exercised over the design of the vehicle and its safety components, including regulations that are established by the National Highway Traffic Safety Administration (NHTSA) that govern motor vehicle safety. The user of the transportation system—the driver in the case of the roadway network—must be accepted as is. The user is the one component of the driving scenario (road, vehicle, driver) that cannot be controlled. Thus, the transportation professional should be aware of the characteristics of the drivers on the road. These characteristics and the related human factors have a direct impact on their ability to navigate the roadway environment. Essentially, the transportation professional must accept the driver "as is." If transportation professionals understand the characteristics of drivers, then they can better design the roadway facility to help drivers navigate the network in a safe and efficient manner.

The following sections discuss various aspects of the system user, including human factors, driver characteristics and limitations, decision making, and accommodating the driver in the design process.

17

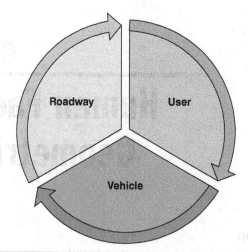

FIGURE 2.1   Elements of the roadway system.

2.2.1 Human Factors

The phrase "human factors" refers to measurable characteristics of human beings. Human factors engineering is the application of knowledge about these characteristics, including limitations, to the design of equipment, tasks, and jobs.[1] Within the context of transportation, the concept of human factors represents those human characteristics that have the potential to impact the design and operation of transportation facilities. In addition to learning the driving laws, regulations, and rules, a driver must learn the overall driving task.

The driving task consists of three components: control, guidance, and navigation, as shown in Fig. 2.2. Control with respect to a motor vehicle is the driver's ability to keep the vehicle under control by steering, accelerating, and braking, without crashing. Guidance refers to a driver keeping the vehicle along its path of travel on a roadway without veering into other lanes, onto shoulders, or elsewhere that is unintended. Finally, navigation is the driver's ability to move from one facility to another, along a network, from an origin to a desired destination. What is important about this pyramid of elements is that they are in priority order. A new driver learns to control the vehicle properly before learning the guidance task and navigation in that order. Hence, the most important element of the driving task serves as the foundation for the rest.

The driving task can be very complex, though it becomes easier over time as driver gains experience. Eventually, the act of controlling the vehicle becomes almost automatic in nature, with less effort needed to guide the vehicle as well. The driving task includes the ongoing act of collecting information by observing and monitoring events related to the roadway itself and to the traffic along that facility, including other vehicles, pedestrians, cyclists, and any other system users or elements that may impact their driving task. The driver must process this information and make appropriate decisions related to the three elements of the driving task, often at a very rapid rate. Typical events related to driving can take place at a rate of about 10 or more per second.

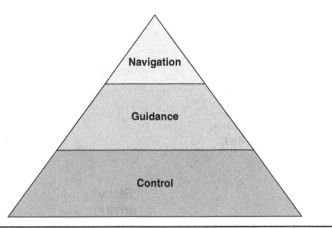

FIGURE 2.2   Elements of the driving task. (*Ref. 2.*)

In general, a driver can expect the following when driving based on experience, exposure, location of driving, and risk:

- To perceive two or more information elements per second
- To make one to three decisions per second
- To take 30 to 120 actions per minute, depending on the complexity of the driving environment
- To commit at least one error every 2 minutes
- To be involved in a hazardous situation every 1 to 2 hours
- To have one or two near collisions per month
- To be involved in a crash every 6 years
- To be involved in a crash resulting in an injury every 40 years
- To be involved in a fatal accident every 160 years

Obviously, many individuals will go their entire lives without being involved in a crash, but this list represents the typical risks associated with the driving task. It is the responsibility of the transportation professional to minimize these risks for the driver through facility design, operation, maintenance, and the related information system.

Drivers continually make errors when behind the wheel, and make adjustments to compensate for them. Most of these errors are minor and end up going unnoticed by the driver. They may include changing the position of the steering wheel, increasing or decreasing speed, or using brake pedals to slow down. Few errors committed by a driver cannot be corrected and result in failures. When a failure does occur, they can range from minor inconveniences to catastrophic crashes. Minor failures include being delayed, lost, or stranded. More serious failures might include erratic maneuvers or near misses. The most severe failures end in crashes that can damage property, cause personal injury, or result in a fatality.

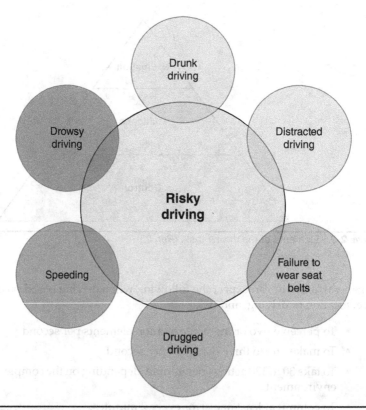

FIGURE 2.3 Risky driving behavior that contributes to crashes. (*Ref. 3.*)

Driver errors can occur for a variety of reasons, many of which may be a result of risky driving behavior. As illustrated in Fig. 2.3, this risky behavior includes drunk driving, distracted driving, drowsy driving, drugged driving, failure to use seat belts, and speeding.[3] The transportation professional can help eliminate this behavior through such efforts as research, public awareness campaigns, and by working with policy makers to implement laws that help reduce the likelihood of deaths resulting from risky behavior.

Driver errors can also result from factors associated with the roadway, for which transportation professionals are responsible. Examples might include the use of an improper traffic control device, the improper placement of a traffic control device along the roadway, or insufficient warning time provided to the driver. In such cases, drivers make errors if they are confused or do not have adequate information to make appropriate decisions and take action to avoid a crash in a timely manner. Highway and traffic engineers, contractors and maintenance supervisors, or any transportation professional responsible for elements of the roadway environment need to consider potential driver errors when performing their jobs. They need to consider errors in the design and operation of roadways, especially at construction and maintenance sites as they often present unexpected and unusual situations with increased hazards. Over time and with experience, the number of errors committed by a driver occurs with decreasing frequency. Drivers acquire a storehouse of knowledge through experience that they rely upon on a regular basis. The more consistent the information provided to the driver, the less likely they are to come upon unfamiliar situations that pose a risk.

2.2.2 Driver Characteristics and Limitations

Numerous human characteristics exist which affect driver behavior. These characteristics and capabilities of individual drivers illustrate the fact that there is no true "design driver." Driver characteristics and capabilities vary widely across the population, and may also vary widely for an individual across different time scales. As illustrated in Table 2.1, various characteristics can play a role in how an individual performs the driving task. In some cases, drivers perform at a level below their capability. To that end, the transportation professional needs to ensure that traffic control devices and features are designed for the below-average driver who may be tired, ill, or under the influence of drugs or alcohol.

As discussed previously, driving is a complex task that requires a considerable amount of time and practice to learn. The more exposure an individual has to a variety of conditions and roadway environments, the more skills they gain to confidently and safely complete the driving task. Errors occur with decreasing frequency as drivers gain that experience. Drivers build up a storehouse of knowledge over time upon which they can draw during a potentially difficult roadway situation. There is no substitution for experience that facilitates the ability to rapidly recognize detected conditions and events to which a driver must respond appropriately.

Drivers acquire information about the roadway environment through perception, or their ability to see the elements on the roadway. As noted in Fig. 2.4, human vision is described as a series of narrowing cones or fields that offer increased visual clarity the smaller the cone. The cone of best vision is approximately 3° wide. A driver's vision is most clear within this cone, which is determined when a person fixes and focuses their vision upon a particular object. The cone of clear vision extends to approximately 10°, and is one in which objects are in focus and can be readily interpreted. Traffic signals and signs should be placed within this cone so that drivers can easily read and interpret them while navigating a facility. The cone of satisfactory vision is approximately 20° wide, where visual acuity and color detection start to deteriorate. Peripheral vision is the outer cone of vision that covers an angle of approximately 120° to 160°. Within the peripheral vision, a driver is only generally aware of movement in the outer areas of

Variability Time Frame	Driver Characteristics
Minutes	Anger
	Attention/distraction
Hours/days	Fatigue
	Alcohol/drug influence
	Emotional state
Years	Physical capabilities
	Driver experience
	Driving skills
	Maturity

Table 2.1 Representative Driver Characteristic Variability over Time

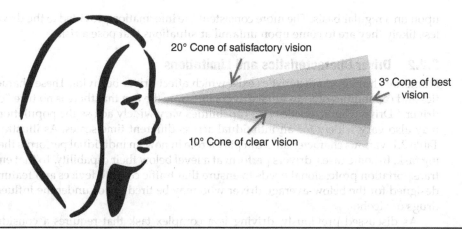

20° Cone of satisfactory vision

3° Cone of best vision

10° Cone of clear vision

Figure 2.4 Typical visual acuity of drivers.

this range, but color and clarity are significantly degraded. These cones of vision extend on both the horizontal and vertical planes.

It is important that the transportation professional responsible for developing information sources for drivers understand how drivers acquire information from the roadway environment. In western countries, people read text from left to right and from the top of a sign or page down to the bottom. Additionally, drivers can only read a few words on a sign from a fast-moving vehicle. Thus, the design of traffic control devices—and traffic signs in particular—should consider these factors. For example, a symbol or a single word message on a traffic sign is best to convey information quickly to the driver. A maximum of three words is ideal, with the key word being located on top or on the left of the sign. If multiple messages need to be provided, spacing those messages over time and/or space is important so that they are clearly recognized and understood. For example, guide signs that provide information about upcoming exits can be spaced in advance of the exit and provide more information the closer they are to the exit. If a complex message needs to be provided on a dynamic message sign, two separate panels of words can be alternated to provide that information so that drivers can process it easily. In a complex roadway environment—such as a congested urban street with a lot of vehicles, signage, or other visual clutter—even a simple graphic sign may need additional features to capture the driver's attention (see Fig. 2.5). These principles and more are taken into account in the design and locations of standard signs contained in the Manual on Uniform Traffic Control Devices (MUTCD).[4]

Drivers have a wide range of information they must remember throughout the driving task. It is the key to information storage, and directly related to traffic control methods. Human memory is divided into three broad categories: short-term, intermediate-term, and long-term. Short-term memory lasts approximately 1 to 5 seconds and is the equivalent of a driver looking in the rear-view mirror. Intermediate-term memory lasts approximately 1 to 2 minutes, while long-term memory extends to months or years. Understanding how information is retained in the driver's memory is important to roadway design for traffic engineers. If a message is conveyed to a driver too soon, then it may be forgotten by the time they need to act on it. If a conveyed message is too complex, a driver may not remember it correctly. Additionally, if a message is incorrect or misleading, a driver may disregard the message the next time it appears. Thus, traffic engineers responsible for designing traffic control devices need to ensure that messages

FIGURE 2.5   Research on flashing lights on traffic control devices. (© *Texas A&M Transportation Institute [TTI].*)

are clear, concise, unambiguous, and appropriate for conditions. This approach will help improve the likelihood that the message is processed, received, understood, and acted upon appropriately by drivers.

2.2.3   Decision Making

As discussed through this section, the driver must make numerous decisions throughout the driving task. A fundamental aspect of the decision-making task is the time required for a driver to recognize a situation that requires action and to perform that action. This time is called perception-reaction time. As noted in Fig. 2.6, the perception-reaction process consists of four steps: perception, intellection, decision, and reaction. Perception is the time a driver takes to become aware of a particular situation on the roadway. Intellection is the time the driver takes to understand the situation and begin to filter through the possible reactions to a situation. Decision is the amount of time a driver takes to decide which action to undertake, and reaction is the time a driver takes to initiate the action.

While this process seems lengthy, the perception-reaction process for drivers can be less than a second, especially for routine maneuvers such as decreasing speed, changing lanes, or reading traffic signs. However, drivers may require more time to go

Figure 2.6 Perception-reaction process for drivers.

through this process if a situation is unfamiliar, if they have several possible choices from which to choose, if the problem posed is complex, or if they are not performing at their best, either physically or mentally. Thus, the traffic engineer needs to consider the perception-reaction time in various aspects of design to ensure that drivers have ample time to make safe and appropriate decisions under less than ideal conditions. The perception-reaction process also seems very complex, but drivers actually develop habits as they encounter the same situation and make the same response repeatedly. These conditioned responses develop over time with exposure to a variety of situations and conditions, and consistent signage and messages help reinforce appropriate responses. Drivers require extra effort in situations where they must change from normal habits, such as in work zones or in inclement weather, as illustrated in Fig. 2.7. Conditions such as heavy rain or fog, temporary signs, detour routes, the presence of

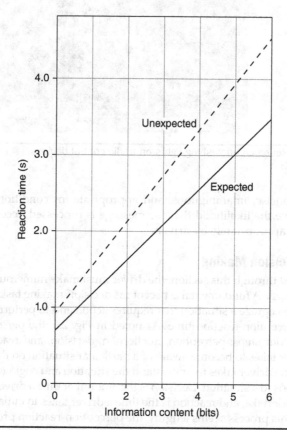

Figure 2.7 Median driver reaction time to expected and unexpected information. (*Ref. 6.*)

workers and equipment, or unexplained speed limits can create challenges for drivers and increase the time needed to complete the perception-reaction process. Consistency in these scenarios will help reinforce the expectancies of the driver. When expectancies are met, they aid the driving task and driver performance tends to be good. When expectancies are violated, drivers need more time to respond, performance is poorer, and they may commit errors that could lead to a crash.

2.3   Design Considerations

Once transportation professionals have a grasp of the user characteristics and human factors that influence the design of the transportation network, they need to understand the direct relationship of those characteristics to specific roadway design features. Overall concepts that professionals should consider include driver expectancy, consistency, and positive guidance. The limitations of the driver and the way in which they acquire information about the roadway environment are the driving force behind these concepts. Additionally, transportation professionals need to be aware of design standards, the concepts of design speed and sight distance, as well as the overall design process for transportation projects. All of these considerations help ensure that the transportation network presents an environment that is the most safe and efficient for all users.

2.3.1   Driver Expectancy, Consistency, and Positive Guidance

When considering the design of transportation facilities, transportation professionals need to remember that once the facility is complete, drivers will use the facility under all manner of conditions. Many of these conditions will not be ideal—whether they be those of the system user or the environment—and the objective is for the operation of the facility to be as safe as possible given those conditions. To that end, three principles of human factors relate to safe operations of the network: driver expectancy, consistency, and positive guidance.[5]

The concept of driver expectancy lies in the notion that drivers have certain expectancies about how a roadway will look and operate, be it a local road in their community or a freeway across the country. These expectancies may be associated with such features as the width of a lane, the presence of a shoulder, sign placement and color, or other elements of the roadway that impact operations. Drivers develop these expectancies over time by training, driving experience, and reinforcement from the roadway network.[6] Drivers also have expectancies associated with situations, such as coming upon freeway exits, curves in the roadway, interchanges, or lane drops. The more exposure a driver has to different types of facilities and situations, the more familiar they become of conditions they might encounter on a roadway. These conditions directly contribute to the development of expectancies and the ability for a driver to successfully operate their vehicle safely within the roadway environment.

Drivers experience difficulties when their expectations are violated and the roadway environment is not consistent from one section to another. Thus, transportation professionals work to design both information system of the roadway—both the roadway environment and traffic control devices—to be as consistent as possible across the entire network.[6] The more information that is provided to the driver, the faster they can develop experience, an awareness of the various elements of a facility, and be prepared for any situation they may encounter while driving along a facility. Consistency plays a role in the physical development of the facility itself, such as with lane widths, alignment, grades, roadside obstacles, bridge piers, and other physical elements of the roadway. Consistency in traffic control devices includes the size, shape, color, and operation of devices, and their placement along the roadway and in advance of specific geometric features.[6] As discussed previously, the more consistent a roadway, the less time a driver needs to process information about the environment or situation and successfully maneuver along the roadway.

The concept of positive guidance centers on the idea that a driver can successfully maneuver through a segment of roadway or a specific situation if provided the appropriate amount of information when it is needed and in a form best designed for quick consumption.[2] This information can come from either the roadway environment itself or the traffic control devices installed along a facility. Their consistency contributes to the positive guidance concept and they help reinforce driver expectancies if designed appropriately. Drivers are able to undertake the driving tasks of control, guidance, and navigation with limited errors. Transportation professionals need to consider positive guidance when designing a facility and its specific elements to ensure that drivers have the information necessary at the appropriate time.

2.3.2   Design Policies and Standards

Transportation engineers should adhere to various design standards or policies whenever possible when designing roadways. In the United States, the American Association of State Highway and Transportation Officials (AASHTO) develops standards for roadway design through various committees and task forces. Representatives from state departments of transportation across the country serve on these groups and work with their peers to develop standards with input from the Federal Highway Administration (FHWA), research efforts, and other activities that provide resources for consideration in the standards.

The foundational standards that govern the design of The Interstate System—also known as the Dwight D. Eisenhower National System of Interstate and Defense Highways—are established by FHWA in the Code of Federal Regulations.[7,8] This regulation adopts the revised design standards developed by AASHTO as the design standards for construction and reconstruction projects on the Interstate System.[9] This document, *A Policy on Design Standards—Interstate System*, includes minimum design standards that apply to either newly constructed or reconstructed segments of the Interstate System. Topics included in this standard are design vehicles, right of way (ROW), geometric controls and criteria, cross-section elements, interchanges, bridges, and other structures. Transportation engineers and roadway designers use this standard in concert with the AASHTO *A Policy on Geometric Design of Highways and Streets, 6th Edition Second Printing*[6] to design roadways that meet the federal minimum requirements. This second document, known as the "Green Book" for its green cover, provides detailed information on highway functions, design controls and criteria, elements of design, and cross-section elements. It also provides design policy by roadway type, including local roads and streets, collector roads and streets, rural and urban arterials, freeway, intersections, grade separations, and interchanges. States typically develop their own design guides or manuals that provide recommendations for geometric design and represent current operating practices. These documents serve as additional resources for transportation engineers designing roadways for public use.

A broader network of roadways in the United States that is governed by FHWA is the National Highway System (NHS). This system was established in 1995 and includes both the Interstate System along with other roadways that are considered important to the economic, defense, and mobility benefit of the country.[10] FHWA established requirements related to the design standards for projects on the NHS in the United States Code, ruling that standards used by State DOTs on NHS projects must be approved by the Secretary of the U.S. Department of Transportation.[11] Recent amendments to this section of the United States Code emphasize the importance of flexibility in design and the ability for designers to meet the functional and operational characteristics of all system users, not just drivers. The amendment related to the FAST Act (Fixing America's Surface Transportation Act[12]) recognizes the connection between communities and their citizens and the need to accommodate drivers, bicyclists, pedestrians, as well as transit within the local context of a community.[13] In all cases, transportation engineers should follow federal, state, and local standards and policies to design the most appropriate facility that meets the guidance as well as the needs of the local community.

Occasionally, a transportation agency may need or want to deviate from adopted design standards or policies for one of any number of reasons, including cost. Context-sensitive solutions that strive to meet the regional goals and objectives and provide safe, efficient mobility for all users can sometimes conflict with specific design criteria. Any highway element design that does not meet minimum values or ranges established for a particular facility or project is considered a design exception.[14] Design exceptions should not be arbitrary or sacrifice the safety of the traveling public. Rather, the transportation engineer should carefully consider any design exception and arrive at a balanced solution that reduces the risk of negative outcomes. The FHWA design criteria that control design exceptions include:

- Design speed
- Lane width
- Shoulder width
- Bridge width
- Horizontal alignment
- Superelevation
- Vertical alignment
- Grade
- Stopping sight distance
- Cross slope
- Vertical clearance
- Lateral offset to obstruction
- Structural capacity[14]

If a state wants to design a facility that does not meet the minimum requirements for these design elements, they must submit a formal written design exception to FHWA for approval. Additionally, they should follow their established design exception process, an example of which is shown in Fig. 2.8.

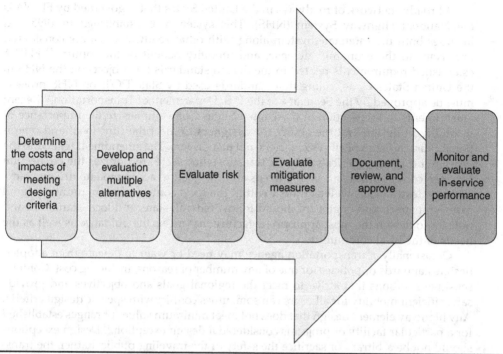

| Determine the costs and impacts of meeting design criteria | Develop and evaluation multiple alternatives | Evaluate risk | Evaluate mitigation measures | Document, review, and approve | Monitor and evaluate in-service performance |

FIGURE 2.8   Design exception process. *(Ref. 14.)*

2.3.3 Speed

When designing a roadway facility, the transportation engineer needs to consider the critical design element of speed. From the traveler's perspective, travel speed on a facility may impact their route choice for a particular trip. They are primarily concerned with reaching their destination in the most efficient manner possible without undue delays. From the transportation professional's perspective, speed is interrelated with the design of the facility itself. Their primary objective is to design a facility that balances the demands of the traveling public for efficient trips with a design that minimizes crashes and crash severity.[6] For example, a transportation engineer could design a facility for extremely low speeds, so much so that no crashes ever occur on the facility at any time and under any condition. While this design approach is economical for the operating agency, such a slow speed is not practical for the traveling public as travel times would be extremely long. Conversely, a transportation engineer could design a facility for extremely high speeds for those few drivers who prefer those speeds. Likewise, this design approach is impractical as the costs to design and build such facilities are astronomical simply to accommodate such a small percentage of system users. Thus, the transportation engineers need to balance these two extremes to design an efficient system that meets nearly all designs with a reasonable level of accuracy during even extreme roadway or traffic conditions.[6] Three variations of speed are part of the vernacular of the transportation engineers that drive this design approach: operating speed, running speed, and design speed.

Operating speed is the speed that is selected by drivers to operate their vehicles during free-flow conditions. Operating speed is typically the 85th percentile of the distribution of observed speeds at a particular location or geometric feature of a roadway facility.[6]

Running speed, which is the speed at which a vehicle travels over a section of highway, is typically used to assess level of service for a facility as well as road user costs. It is calculated by measuring the length of a highway section and dividing it by the running time for a vehicle to travel through that section.[6] The average running speed represents the average of all running speeds for all vehicles traveling through a section of roadway. Running speed can vary throughout the day, and may be different at individual locations along a section of roadway. To that end, when referencing running speed, the transportation professional should indicate if the speed represents peak or off-peak hours or some other measure such as the average running speed for the entire day.[6]

Transportation engineers select a design speed for a roadway facility, which in turn is used to determine the various geometric design features along that facility. As noted previously, the professional needs to select a design speed that balances the safety, mobility, and efficiency of the traveling public with a variety of constraints that include environmental quality, economic impact, aesthetic appeal, and any political or social impacts of the roadway.[6] The design speed can govern all manner of design features, including sight distance, cross-section elements, horizontal and vertical curvature, and superelevation, all of which are discussed later in this chapter. Designers should consider a broad range of factors and scenarios when selecting a design speed for a facility. These factors include, but are not limited to:

- Functional classification of the roadway
- Anticipated operating speed
- Terrain and topography of the area
- Adjacent land use
- Speeds drivers are likely to expect
- Travel habits and desires of most drivers expected to use the facility[6]

Posted speed limits, as a policy, are typically set to represent the 85th percentile speed rather than the highest speeds that drivers might travel along a facility. By measuring the speeds of a large sample of vehicles, the transportation professional can determine the 85th percentile speed.[6] It is important to note that practices and methodologies associated with setting speed limits vary across the world, with the profession lacking a clear consensus on the best approach. FHWA has published an informational report on the methods and practices for setting speed limits that presents the four primary practices associated with establishing speed limits: engineering approach, expert system, optimization, and injury minimization.[15] Serving as a guidance document, the report presents the procedures agencies undertake to set speed limits without making a specific recommendation on the best approach. Additionally, this document covers special situations related to speed limits including advisory speed limits, school zones, and work zone speeds.

2.3.4 Sight Distance

When designing a roadway to be used by the traveling public, one essential factor to accommodate is the ability for a driver to see the roadway ahead. The design feature that accounts for this factor is sight distance. The formal definition of sight distance is that distance along a roadway where a driver can continuously see an object of a particular height.[6] The transportation engineer should design a facility to provide enough sight distance to the driver so that they can safely and efficiently operate their vehicle without striking any unexpected objective in their path.[6] Sight distance typically falls into one of four categories: stopping sight distance (SSD), passing sight distance (PSD), decision sight distance (DSD), and intersection sight distance. Each of these sight distances is calculated based on several factors that are related to the action required of the driver.

Stopping Sight Distance

Stopping sight distance (SSD) is related to the driver and the vehicle. The following is a general equation for SSD as a combination of the distance traveled during the perception-reaction time of the driver and the distance required for the driver to stop the vehicle once they begin braking. Stopping sight distance is:

$$SSD = d_R + d_B$$

where SSD = stopping sight distance (ft/m)

  d_R = the distance traveled by vehicle during perception-reaction time (ft/m)
  d_B = the distance required to bring vehicle to stop at travel speed (ft/m)

The first element of the SSD equation is the brake reaction distance, which varies according to reaction time of the driver, such as individual driver characteristics and alertness. For the purposes of design, a brake reaction time of 2.5 s accounts for the characteristics of most drivers—including older drivers—and accommodates most locations and situations.[6] The formulas for brake reaction distance are:

$$d_R = 1.47Vt \text{ (U.S. Customary)} \qquad d_R = 0.278\ Vt \text{ (Metric)}$$

where d_R = distance traveled by a vehicle during perception/reaction time (ft/m)
  V = design speed, mph (U.S. Customary), km/h (Metric)
  t = brake reaction time, 2.5 s[6]

The second element of the SSD equation is braking distance: the distance traveled once the driver applies the brakes and the vehicle comes to a complete stop. As with the brake reaction distance, the braking distance varies according to various factors, such as the vehicle, the driver, and the roadway itself. The formulas for braking distance are:

$$d_B = 1.075\frac{V^2}{a} \text{ (U.S. Customary)} \qquad d_B = 0.039\frac{V^2}{a} \text{ (Metric)}$$

where d_B = distance required to bring vehicle to stop at travel speed, ft (U.S. Customary), m (Metric)
  V = design speed, mph (U.S. Customary), km/h (Metric)
  a = deceleration rate, ft/s² (U.S. Customary), m/s² (Metric)[6]

These formulas assume that the vehicle is traveling at the design speed on a level roadway. The deceleration rate, typically assumed to be 11.2 ft/s² (3.4 m/s²), assumes that the vehicle braking systems and the tire-pavement friction levels on wet pavement can typically provide this deceleration rate and also reflects a deceleration that is comfortable for most drivers.[6]

By substituting the formulas for brake reaction distance and braking distance, the complete formulas for SSD[6] are as follows:

$$SSD = 1.47Vt + 1.075\frac{V^2}{a} \text{ (U.S. Customary)} \qquad SSD = 0.278Vt + 0.039\frac{V^2}{a} \text{ (Metric)}$$

Design Speed (mph)	Brake Reaction Distance (ft)	Braking Distance on Level Roadway (ft)	Stopping Sight Distance (ft)	
			Calculated (ft)	Design (ft)
15	55.1	21.6	76.7	80
20	73.5	38.4	111.9	115
25	91.9	60.0	151.9	155
30	110.3	86.4	196.7	200
35	128.6	117.6	246.2	250
40	147.0	153.6	300.6	305
45	165.4	194.4	359.8	36
50	183.8	240.0	423.8	425
55	202.1	290.3	492.4	495
60	220.5	345.5	566.0	570
65	238.9	405.5	644.4	645
70	257.3	470.3	727.6	730
75	275.6	539.9	815.5	820
80	294.0	614.3	908.3	910

TABLE 2.2   Stopping Sight Distance on Level Roadways, U.S. Customary (*Ref. 6.*)

where SSD = stopping sight distance, ft (U.S. Customary), m (Metric)
    V = design speed, mph (U.S. Customary), km/h (Metric)
    t = brake reaction time (2.5 s)
    a = deceleration rate, 11.2 ft/s² (U.S. Customary), 3.4 m/s² (Metric)

Table 2.2 (U.S. Customary) and Table 2.3 (Metric) provide the SSDs typically used by transportation engineers in the design process. The design values are rounded up from the calculated numbers and they are result of the aforementioned assumptions for brake reaction time and deceleration rate.

The SSD values in Tables 2.2 and 2.3 assume the vehicle is traveling on a level roadway. It is important to note that the roadway grade has an impact on braking distance, thereby requiring a modification to the formula to account for whether a vehicle is traveling uphill or downhill while stopping. The formulas for braking distance when a highway has a grade are as follows:

$$d_B = \frac{V^2}{30\left[\left(\dfrac{a}{32.2}\right) \pm G\right]} \text{ (U.S. Customary)} \qquad d_B = \frac{V^2}{254\left[\left(\dfrac{a}{9.81}\right) \pm G\right]} \text{ (Metric)}$$

where d_B = distance required to bring vehicle to stop at travel speed on a grade
    ft (U.S. Customary), m (Metric)
    V = design speed, mph (U.S. Customary), km/h (Metric)
    a = deceleration rate, 11.2 ft/s² (U.S. Customary), 3.4 m/s² (Metric)
    G = grade, rise/run, ft/ft (U.S. Customary), m/m (Metric)[6]

When a vehicle is on an upgrade, the stopping distance needed is shorter than that on a level roadway because gravity aids in the stopping process. Conversely, the stopping

Design Speed (km/h)	Brake Reaction Distance (m)	Braking Distance on Level Roadway (m)	Stopping Sight Distance (m)	
			Calculated (m)	Design (m)
20	13.9	4.6	18.5	20
30	20.9	10.3	31.2	35
40	27.8	18.4	46.2	50
50	34.8	28.7	63.5	65
60	41.7	41.3	83.0	85
70	48.7	56.2	104.9	105
80	55.6	73.4	129.0	130
90	62.6	92.9	155.5	160
100	69.5	114.7	184.2	185
110	76.5	138.8	215.3	220
120	83.4	165.2	248.6	250
130	90.4	193.8	284.2	285

TABLE 2.3 Stopping Sight Distance on Level Roadways, Metric (*Ref. 6.*)

distance needed on a downgrade is longer than that on a level roadway. Table 2.4 (U.S. Customary) and Table 2.5 (Metric) show the SSD values for downgrades and upgrades computed for wet-pavement conditions.

When calculating SSD on grades, the designer should determine if it should be adjusted for a direction of travel. Since most roadways are traveled in both directions,

Design Speed (km/h)	Stopping Sight Distance (m)					
	Downgrades			Upgrades		
	3%	6%	9%	3%	6%	9%
15	80	82	85	75	74	73
20	116	120	126	109	107	104
25	158	165	173	147	143	140
30	205	215	227	200	184	179
35	257	271	287	237	229	222
40	315	333	354	289	278	269
45	378	400	427	344	331	320
50	446	474	507	405	388	375
55	520	553	593	469	450	433
60	598	638	686	538	515	495
65	682	728	785	612	584	561
70	771	825	891	690	658	631
75	866	927	1003	772	736	704
80	965	1035	1121	859	817	782

TABLE 2.4 Stopping Sight Distance on Grades, U.S. Customary (*Ref. 6.*)

Design Speed (km/h)	Stopping Sight Distance (m)					
	Downgrades			Upgrades		
	3%	6%	9%	3%	6%	9%
20	20	20	20	19	18	18
30	32	35	35	31	30	29
40	50	50	53	45	44	43
50	66	70	74	61	59	58
60	87	92	97	80	77	75
70	110	116	124	100	97	93
80	136	144	154	123	118	114
90	164	174	187	148	141	136
100	194	207	223	174	167	160
110	227	243	262	203	194	186
120	263	281	304	234	223	214
130	302	323	350	267	254	243

TABLE 2.5   Stopping Sight Distance on Grades, Metric (*Ref. 6.*)

calculating the SSD for the downgrade direction—which is typically longer than that for a level roadway or an upgrade—will likely accommodate the SSD for the upgrade direction.

The values typically used for SSD are those for passenger vehicle operations and not specifically for heavy trucks. While heavy trucks require greater SSDs on roadways, this added distance is typically accounted for by the fact that truck drivers can typically see further down the roadway because of their eye height, which is greater than that of a driver of a passenger vehicle. Thus, transportation engineers do not typically use separate SSDs for passenger vehicles and trucks. However, in situations where horizontal sight distance may be constrained, particularly on long downgrades, the truck driver's advantage of eye height is negligible. In those situations, a designer might consider an SSD longer than those in Tables 2.2 or 2.4.[6]

Example Problem 2.1.   Calculate the minimum stopping sight distance on +2.5% grade for a design speed of 65 mph.

Total required stopping sight distance:

$$SSD = d_R + d_B$$

Reaction distance:

$$d_R = 1.47Vt = 1.47(65 \text{ mph})(2.5 \text{ s}) = 238.9 \text{ ft}$$

Braking distance:

$$d_B = \frac{V^2}{30\left[\left(\dfrac{a}{32.2}\right) \pm G\right]} = \frac{65^2}{30\left[\left(\dfrac{11.2}{32.2}\right) + 0.025\right]} = 377.7 \text{ ft}$$

Total required stopping sight distance:

$$SSD = d_R + d_B = 238.9 \text{ ft} + 377.7 \text{ ft} = 616.6 \text{ ft}$$

Decision Sight Distance

The previous SSD discussion along with the values provided for SSD are reasonable values such that they can accommodate a typical driver who is alert, driving under typical conditions, and who needs to come to a stop in a hurry.[6] However, drivers often encounter unusual situations that push the boundaries of these SSDs or where they might prefer to perform an evasive maneuver (e.g., change lanes) rather than coming to an emergency stop. A typical example of such a situation might include a driver navigating through a visually complex driving environment with visual clutter. In this instance, a driver may find it difficult to perceive a potentially hazardous situation in sufficient time to respond accordingly and come to a complete stop. In these cases, the driver needs might require additional perception time or maneuver time to take an appropriate action. The resulting design element is DSD. Decision sight distance is defined as the distance needed for a driver to: (1) execute the perception reaction process discussed previously (detection, perception, intellection, reaction) under less-than-ideal conditions (e.g., complex interchange or intersection locations, visually cluttered segments, cross-section changes); (2) select an appropriate speed and path for the vehicle; and (3) execute complex driving maneuvers.[6] Decision sight distance, which is longer than SSD, provides a margin of error for the driver in these situations and provide sufficient distance for them to maneuver their vehicle at the same or reduced speed without being forced to come to a complete stop.

The formulas for DSD are based on the type of avoidance maneuver a driver is expected or likely to perform on the roadway segment. These maneuvers, which are a function of the driver's maneuver (stop vs. change speed, path, or direction), roadway location (rural, suburban, and rural), and pre-maneuver time, are provided in Table 2.6.

The formulas for DSD for avoidance maneuvers A and B are as follows:

$$DSD = 1.47Vt + 1.075\frac{V^2}{a} \text{ (U.S. Customary)} \qquad DSD = 0.278Vt + 0.039\frac{V^2}{a} \text{ (Metric)}$$

where DSD = decision sight distance, ft (U.S. Customary), m (Metric)
t = pre-maneuver time (s)
V = design speed, mph (U.S. Customary), km/h (Metric)
a = driver deceleration, 11.2 ft/s² (U.S. Customary), 3.4 m/s² (Metric)

Avoidance Maneuver	Description	Pre-Maneuver Time (s)
A	Stop on rural road	3.0
B	Stop on urban road	9.1
C	Speed/path/direction change on rural road	10.2–11.2
D	Speed/path/direction change on suburban road	12.1–12.9
E	Speed/path/direction change on urban road	14.0–14.5

TABLE 2.6 Decision Sight Distance Avoidance Maneuvers (*Ref. 6.*)

Design Speed (mph)	Decision Sight Distance (ft) Avoidance Maneuver				
	A	B	C	D	E
30	220	490	450	535	620
35	275	590	525	625	720
40	330	690	600	715	825
45	395	800	675	800	930
50	465	910	750	890	1030
55	535	1030	865	980	1135
60	610	1150	990	1125	1280
65	695	1275	1050	1220	1365
70	780	1410	1105	1275	1445
75	875	1545	1180	1365	1545
80	970	1685	1260	1455	1650

TABLE 2.7 Decision Sight Distance, U.S. Customary (*Ref. 6.*)

In this formula, the pre-maneuver distance is added to the braking distance to provide the DSD. The formulas for DSD for avoidance maneuvers C, D, and E are as follows:

$$DSD = 1.47\ Vt\ \text{(U.S. Customary)} \qquad DSD = 0.2078\ Vt\ \text{(Metric)}$$

where DSD = decision sight distance, ft (U.S. Customary), m (Metric)
   t = total pre-maneuver and maneuver time (s)
   V = design speed, mph (U.S. Customary), km/h (Metric)

In this formula, the braking distance is replaced with a maneuver distance that includes both the pre-maneuver time and time a driver takes to complete their chosen avoidance maneuver. Table 2.7 (U.S. Customary) and Table 2.8 (Metric) provide the appropriate DSDs based on the aforementioned factors.

Design Speed (mph)	Decision Sight Distance (ft) Avoidance Maneuver				
	A	B	C	D	E
50	70	155	145	170	195
60	95	195	170	205	235
70	115	235	200	235	275
80	140	280	230	270	315
90	170	325	270	315	360
100	200	370	315	355	400
110	235	420	330	380	430
120	265	470	360	415	470
130	305	525	390	450	510

TABLE 2.8 Decision Sight Distance, Metric (*Ref. 6.*)

The transportation engineer can use these rounded distances in two ways: (1) to determine the needed DSD for a particular location; or (2) to assess whether available sight distances are suitable for a location. Traffic control devices that provide advance warning of upcoming roadway conditions (e.g., horizontal curve, intersection, ramp, driveway, etc.) should be utilized at a location if the geometric features of a roadway make the provision of an adequate DSD impractical.

Example Problem 2.2. Calculate the decision sight distance needed for a driver to stop on a rural road with a design speed of 70 mph.

$$DSD = 1.47\ Vt + 1.075 \frac{V^2}{a} = 1.47(70 \text{ mph})(3.0 \text{ s}) + 1.075 \frac{70^2}{11.2} = 779.0 \text{ ft}$$

Example Problem 2.3. Calculate the decision sight distance needed for a driver making a speed/path/direction change on a rural roadway with a design speed of 60 mph and assuming a total maneuver time of 11 s.

$$DSD = 1.47\ Vt = 1.47(60 \text{ mph})(11.0 \text{ s}) = 1058.4 \text{ ft}$$

Passing Sight Distance

Passing sight distance (PSD) is another geometric element that transportation engineers need to consider when designing a facility. When traveling on a two-lane, two-way high-way, drivers often want to pass a slower moving vehicle. However, on these facilities, the driver must move into the opposing lane of traffic to pass a vehicle. It is essential that a driver have sufficient distance to make that passing maneuver before encountering an oncoming vehicle. PSD helps a prudent driver see far enough down the roadway to determine whether vehicles are in the opposing lane, and if not, whether there is enough distance to move into the opposing lane, accelerate past the slower vehicle, and return to their lane of travel safely.

PSDs work in concert with traffic control devices designating passing and no-passing zones to minimize conflicts on two-lane roadways. Current PSD design values are based on minimum sight distances used in the MUTCD[4] and are based on the design speed of the facility and the assumed speeds of the passing vehicle and the passed vehicle. The design values for PSD on two-lane highways are shown in Table 2.9 (U.S. Customary) and Table 2.10 (Metric). They are based on the minimum PSDs for horizontal or vertical curves that dictate the need for no-passing zone signs and markings.[4] A comparison of PSD with SSD design values is illustrated in Fig. 2.9 (U.S. Customary) and Fig. 2.10 (Metric), demonstrating that more distance is needed for a passing maneuver than for a stopping maneuver.

The transportation engineer needs to understand the various assumptions made regarding driver behavior in the mathematical models that yield these PSD design values. Specifically, these assumptions include:

- Speeds of the passing and opposing vehicles are the same and are equal to the roadway design speed.
- The passing vehicle travels at a uniform speed that is 12 mph (19 km/h) faster (speed differential) than the vehicle being passed.
- The acceleration capabilities of the passing vehicle are such that it can reach the passing speed differential by the time it reaches the critical point in the passing maneuver.

Design Speed (mph)	Assumed Speeds (mph)		Passing Sight Distance (ft)
	Passed Vehicle	Passing Vehicle	
20	8	20	400
25	13	25	450
30	18	30	500
35	23	35	550
40	28	40	600
45	33	45	700
50	38	50	800
55	43	55	900
60	48	60	1000
65	53	65	1100
70	58	70	1200
75	63	75	1300
80	68	80	1400

TABLE 2.9   Passing Sight Distance for Design of Two-Lane Highways, U.S. Customary (*Ref. 6.*)

Design Speed (km/h)	Assumed Speeds (km/h)		Passing Sight Distance (m)
	Passed Vehicle	Passing Vehicle	
30	11	30	120
40	21	40	140
50	31	50	160
60	41	60	180
70	51	70	210
80	61	80	245
90	71	90	280
100	81	100	320
110	91	110	355
120	101	120	395
130	111	130	440

TABLE 2.10   Passing Sight Distance for Design of Two-Lane Highways, Metric (*Ref. 6.*)

- Both the passing and passed vehicles are passenger vehicles and are assumed to be 19 ft (5.8 m) in length.
- The perception-reaction time of the passing driver when deciding whether to abort is 1 s.
- The passing vehicle will use a deceleration rate of 11.2 ft/s² (3.4 m/s²) when aborting a passing maneuver.

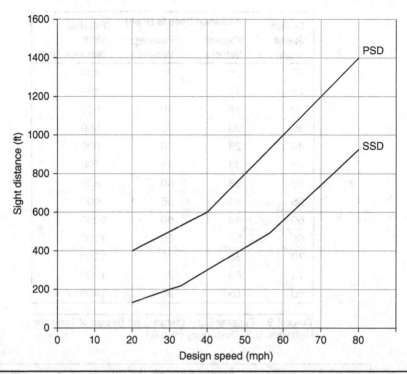

FIGURE 2.9 Comparison of stopping sight distance and passing sight distance, U.S. Customary. (*Ref. 6.*)

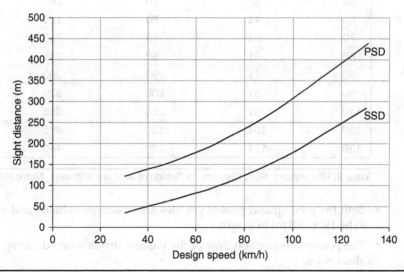

FIGURE 2.10 Comparison of stopping sight distance and passing sight distance, Metric. (*Ref. 6.*)

Design Criteria	Description/Value	Relevant Sight Distance
Driver's eye height	3.50 ft (1.08 m) above the road surface (passenger vehicle)	All
	7.60 ft (2.33 m) above the road surface (large truck)	All
Height of object	2.00 ft (0.60 m)	Stopping sight distance
	2.00 ft (0.60 m)	Decision sight distance
	3.50 ft (1.08 m)	Passing sight distance
	3.50 ft (1.08 m)	Intersection sight distance
Sight obstructions (tangent, horizontal, vertical curves)	Road surface, physical feature (e.g., longitudinal barrier, tree, foliage, backslope of cut section, fill slope)	All

TABLE 2.11   Criteria for Measuring Sight Distance, U.S. Customary/Metric (*Ref. 6.*)

- The space headway between the passing and passed vehicle, whether in a completed or aborted passing maneuver, is 1 s.
- The minimum clearance between the passing vehicle and an opposing vehicle in the case of a completed passing maneuver when it returns to the normal lane is 1 s.[6,16]

The PSD design values are specifically for two-lane two-way roadways. On multilane roadways, it is expected that drivers will complete passing maneuvers within one direction of travel and that SSD will be adequate.

Sight Distance Measurement Criteria

All of the sight distance design values are measured based on specific criteria that ensure that an object of a specific height is always visible to the driver.[6] These criteria include the height of the driver's eye above the roadway surface, the height of the object itself, and the presence of sight obstructions. The specific values for these criteria are provided in Table 2.11. Throughout the design process, the transportation engineer needs to ensure that sight distances are provided as appropriate.

2.4   Cross Section

The cross section of a roadway is a view of a roadway if one were to take a "slice" of it. AASHTO defines it as the vertical section of both the roadway and the ground at right angles to the centerline of the roadway.[6] Measuring from one ROW line to the other, the cross section includes the elements of the traveled way, shoulders, and the roadside.

The traveled way is that portion of the cross section that is reserved for vehicular travel as illustrated in Fig. 2.11 and includes all lanes designed for travel. The centerline on an undivided roadway is located at the center of the pavement. For a divided facility that has a median of some type, the centerline is located at the center of

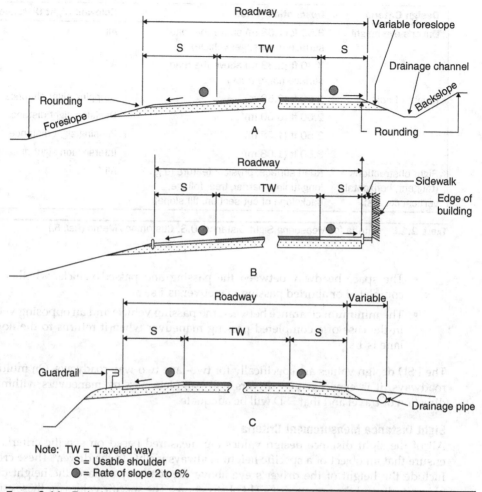

FIGURE 2.11 Typical roadway cross section, normal crown. (*Ref. 6.*)

Note: TW = Traveled way
S = Usable shoulder
● = Rate of slope 2 to 6%

the median. Lane widths are typically 12 ft (3.6 m), and require a minimum of at least 9 ft (2.7 m) to accommodate most vehicles of any design. The crown or cross slope of the roadway represents the slope of the travel lanes and helps facilitate drainage of the pavement. For an undivided roadway with a normal crown, the cross slope begins at the centerline and slopes down toward the shoulder. On paved roadways, the range in cross slope for a single lane is typically 1.5% to 2%, with that for an unpaved roadway being 2% to 6%.[6] Shoulders are designed to serve as a refuge or safety area next to the traveled way. They accommodate stopped vehicles and also provide support for the pavement layers. Shoulders also serve other purposes, including allowing vehicles to perform evasive maneuvers to avoid crashes, improving sight distance through cut segments, providing lateral clearance for signs and guardrails, and accommodating use by pedestrians and bicycles.[6] Shoulders can be paved or unpaved and typically have a usable width ranging from 2 to 10 ft depending on the type of roadway. The cross slope of the shoulder is typically greater than that for the travel way and may range from 2% to 6% since regular travel is not expected on the shoulder.

The roadside is a critical component of roadway design. When a driver loses control of their vehicle and leaves the roadway, the design of the roadside can impact the severity of a crash that may occur. A forgiving roadside incorporates the concept of a clear recovery area, also known as the clear zone.[6] The clear zone offers an unobstructed and traversable area beyond the edge of the traffic lane. To the extent possible, the transportation engineer should design a roadside that provides a full-width clear zone (typically 30 ft), and treat any roadside obstacles that are in that clear zone appropriately.[6] That treatment can include removal or redesign of the obstacle, relocation of the obstacle or the use of a breakaway device, shielding the obstacle with a barrier or crash cushion that will redirect a vehicle if struck, or delineating the obstacle.

The design of the roadside incorporates several elements: the hinge point, the foreslope, the toe of the slope, the ditch area, and the backslope. Each of these elements is displayed in Fig. 2.12, and they play an important role in the design and navigation of the roadway. The hinge point is designated as the top of the slope where the shoulder and roadside meet. The foreslope is the front edge of the roadside area, and the ditch area at the bottom of the foreslope is primarily designed for drainage. The backslope, which is the outermost portion of the roadside, is frequently designed as a function of the terrain and the roadside material.

The design of the roadside elements can help a driver maintain steering control if they leave the roadway surface. For example, the hinge point can contribute to a loss of steering control when crossed by a driver. A rounded hinge point that smoothly transitions to the foreslope can help reduce the likelihood of a vehicle becoming airborne as they cross to the foreslope. The foreslope offers the driver with an area to attempt a recover maneuver and to reduce their speed before an impact. The foreslope should be clear of any obstructions, and the slope—normally 1V:4H or flatter—should be as flat as possible to help prevent a rollover. Similarly, the designer should consider what may happen if a vehicle reaches the ditch area. In these circumstances, the ditch area should be as flat and "forgiving" as possible, with closed drainage structures if appropriate. Finally, the backslope can also help reduce the chances of vehicle rolling over, with a typical slope of 1V:3H to accommodate maintenance operations.[6] The flatter these segments, the higher the chances a driver can regain control of their vehicle along the roadside.

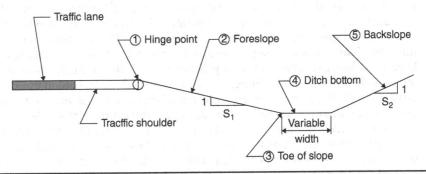

FIGURE 2.12 Designation of roadside regions. (*Ref. 6.*)

2.5   Horizontal Alignment

When designing a roadway facility, the transportation engineer can divide the design effort into two 2-dimensional components: the horizontal alignment and the vertical alignment. The horizontal alignment represents the plan view of the facility where one is looking down on the roadway from above. The design of a facility should be such that the vast majority of drivers can operate a vehicle along the roadway under normal conditions at the selected design speed. For straight, flat sections of roadway (i.e., tangents), the vehicle operating characteristics are fairly straightforward, as discussed previously when addressing SSD. However, when navigating a horizontal curve, the laws of mechanics govern how a vehicle operates on a curve. The specific elements that impact how a vehicle operates on a curve include the superelevation of the roadway, the side friction factor, speed, curve radius, and gravity. The following equations (i.e., the basic curve equations) illustrate the relationships between these factors:[6]

$$\frac{0.01e+f}{1-0.01ef} = \frac{v^2}{gR} = \frac{0.067V^2}{R} = \frac{V^2}{15R} \text{ (U.S. Customary)}$$

$$\frac{0.01e+f}{1-0.01ef} = \frac{v^2}{gR} = \frac{0.0079V^2}{R} = \frac{V^2}{127R} \text{ (Metric)}$$

where e = rate of roadway superelevation, percent
$\quad f$ = side friction (demand) factor
$\quad v$ = vehicle speed, ft/s (U.S. Customary), m/s (Metric)
$\quad g$ = gravitational constant, 32.2 ft/s^2 (U.S. Customary), 9.81 m/s^2 (Metric)
$\quad V$ = vehicle speed, mph (U.S. Customary), km/h (Metric)
$\quad R$ = radius of curve measures to a vehicle's center of gravity, ft (U.S. Customary), m (Metric)

The following sections provide a discussion on these elements and present the design values that are used by transportation engineers in horizontal alignment design.

2.5.1   Superelevation

When a vehicle travels around a horizontal curve at a constant speed, the vehicle accelerates toward the center of the curve. This centripetal acceleration is a function of the vehicle's speed and the radius of the curve.[17] The higher the speed and the sharper the curve, the greater will be the acceleration experienced by the vehicle. If the acceleration is too great, the vehicle leaves the roadway. Thus, external forces that are a function of the roadway design counteract the centripetal acceleration, also known as lateral acceleration. The relationship between the vehicle acceleration and external forces is shown in Fig. 2.13. Superelevation (e), which is the banking of the roadway, is the slope of the pavement along a horizontal curve and is represented as a percent.[17] The purpose of superelevation is to counteract the centripetal acceleration (F_c) produced as a vehicle rounds a curve. The surface friction (f) of the pavement also exerts force against the wheels as the vehicle travels along the curve, working to keep the wheels on the pavement. The weight of the vehicle (W) also helps counteract the centripetal acceleration.

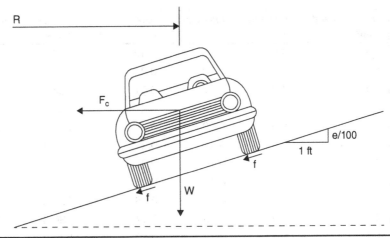

FIGURE 2.13 Cross section of vehicle on superelevated road. (*Ref. 17.*)

It is important to note that it is possible to provide too much superelevation on a roadway. If the design speed or operating speed is low for a roadway and the superelevation is steep, a vehicle can roll over if too much weight is carried on the down slope tires. For this reason, AASHTO provides guidance for maximum superelevation rates to minimize the likelihood of this occurring. These maximum rates are a function of the frequency of snow and ice on the facility, the type of terrain, whether the facility is in an urban or rural location, and the frequency that very slow-moving vehicles will travel the roadway. In these cases, a high superelevation rate can present safety issues. The maximum superelevation rates are provided in Table 2.12 (U.S. Customary) and Table 2.13 (Metric).

2.5.2 Side Friction Factor

Pavement friction is an important component of the forces acting on a vehicle as it navigates a curve. The friction between the tire and the pavement counteracts the side thrust developed as the vehicle travels around the curve. The coefficient of friction can be calculated by simplifying the basic curve equation discussed previously since the product of e and f is always small, making the $1 - 0.01\,ef$ almost equal to 1.[6] The formulas noted below yield slightly higher coefficients of friction, which are more conservative. They can confidently be used in roadway design because they inherently introduce a margin of safety.

$$f = \frac{V^2}{15R} - 0.01e \text{ (U.S. Customary)}$$

$$f = \frac{V^2}{127R} - 0.01e \text{ (Metric)}$$

It is important to note, however, that the coefficient of friction is only one factor in the design of a roadway. Other factors include the maximum lateral acceleration a driver is willing to tolerate driving around a horizontal curve as well as acceptable pavement surface conditions. The five methods of distributing e and f over a range of

Design Speed (mph)	Maximum e (%)	Maximum f	Total (e/100 + f)	Calculated Radius (ft)	Rounded Radius (ft)
10	4.0	0.38	0.42	15.9	16
15	4.0	0.32	0.36	41.7	42
20	4.0	0.27	0.31	86.0	86
25	4.0	0.23	0.27	154.3	154
30	4.0	0.20	0.24	250.0	250
35	4.0	0.18	0.22	371.2	371
40	4.0	0.16	0.20	533.3	533
45	4.0	0.15	0.19	710.5	711
50	4.0	0.14	0.18	925.9	926
55	4.0	0.13	0.17	1186.3	1190
60	4.0	0.12	0.16	1500.0	1500
10	6.0	0.38	0.44	15.2	15
15	6.0	0.32	0.38	39.5	39
20	6.0	0.27	0.33	80.8	81
25	6.0	0.23	0.29	143.7	144
30	6.0	0.20	0.26	230.8	231
35	6.0	0.18	0.24	340.3	340
40	6.0	0.16	0.22	484.8	485
45	6.0	0.15	0.21	642.9	643
50	6.0	0.14	0.20	833.3	833
55	6.0	0.13	0.19	1061.4	1060
60	6.0	0.12	0.18	1333.3	1330
65	6.0	0.11	0.17	1656.9	1660
70	6.0	0.10	0.16	2041.7	2040
75	6.0	0.09	0.15	2500.0	2500
80	6.0	0.08	0.14	3047.6	3050
10	8.0	0.38	0.46	14.5	14
15	8.0	0.32	0.40	37.5	38
20	8.0	0.27	0.35	76.2	76
25	8.0	0.23	0.31	134.4	134
30	8.0	0.20	0.28	214.3	214
35	8.0	0.18	0.26	314.1	314
40	8.0	0.16	0.24	444.4	444
45	8.0	0.15	0.23	587.0	587
50	8.0	0.14	0.22	757.6	758
55	8.0	0.13	0.21	960.3	960

TABLE 2.12   Minimum Radius Using Limiting Values of Superelevation and Side Friction Factor (U.S. Customary) (Ref. 6.)

Design Speed (mph)	Maximum e (%)	Maximum f	Total (e/100 + f)	Calculated Radius (ft)	Rounded Radius (ft)
60	8.0	0.12	0.20	1200.0	1200
65	8.0	0.11	0.19	1482.5	1480
70	8.0	0.10	0.18	1814.8	1810
75	8.0	0.09	0.17	2205.9	2210
80	8.0	0.08	0.16	2666.7	2670
10	10.0	0.38	0.48	13.9	14
15	10.0	0.32	0.42	35.7	36
20	10.0	0.27	0.37	72.1	72
25	10.0	0.23	0.33	126.3	126
30	10.0	0.20	0.30	200.0	200
35	10.0	0.18	0.28	291.7	292
40	10.0	0.16	0.26	410.3	410
45	10.0	0.15	0.25	540.0	540
50	10.0	0.14	0.24	694.4	694
55	10.0	0.13	0.23	876.8	877
60	10.0	0.12	0.22	1090.9	1090
65	10.0	0.11	0.21	1341.3	1340
70	10.0	0.10	0.20	1633.3	1630
75	10.0	0.09	0.19	1973.7	1970
80	10.0	0.08	0.18	2370.4	2370
10	12.0	0.38	0.50	13.3	13
15	12.0	0.32	0.44	34.1	34
20	12.0	0.27	0.39	68.4	68
25	12.0	0.23	0.35	119.0	119
30	12.0	0.20	0.32	187.5	188
35	12.0	0.18	0.30	272.2	272
40	12.0	0.16	0.28	381.0	381
45	12.0	0.15	0.27	500.0	500
50	12.0	0.14	0.26	641.0	641
55	12.0	0.13	0.25	806.7	807
60	12.0	0.12	0.24	1000.0	1000
65	12.0	0.11	0.23	1224.6	1220
70	12.0	0.10	0.22	1484.8	1480
75	12.0	0.09	0.21	1784.7	1790
80	12.0	0.08	0.20	2133.3	2130

table

TABLE 2.12   Minimum Radius Using Limiting Values of Superelevation and Side Friction Factor (U.S. Customary) (*Ref. 6.*) (*Continued*)

Design Speed (km/h)	Maximum e (%)	Maximum f	Total (e/100 + f)	Calculated Radius (m)	Rounded Radius (m)
15	4.0	0.40	0.44	4.0	4
20	4.0	0.35	0.39	8.1	8
30	4.0	0.28	0.32	22.1	22
40	4.0	0.23	0.27	46.7	47
50	4.0	0.19	0.23	85.6	86
60	4.0	0.17	0.21	135.0	135
70	4.0	0.15	0.19	203.1	203
80	4.0	0.14	0.18	280.0	280
90	4.0	0.13	0.17	275.2	375
100	4.0	0.12	0.16	492.1	492
15	6.0	0.40	0.46	3.9	4
20	6.0	0.35	0.41	7.7	8
30	6.0	0.28	0.34	20.8	21
40	6.0	0.23	0.29	43.4	43
50	6.0	0.19	0.25	78.7	79
60	6.0	0.17	0.23	123.2	123
70	6.0	0.15	0.21	183.7	184
80	6.0	0.14	0.20	252.0	252
90	6.0	0.13	0.19	335.7	336
100	6.0	0.12	0.18	437.4	437
110	6.0	0.11	0.17	560.4	560
120	6.0	0.09	0.15	755.9	756
130	6.0	0.08	0.14	950.5	951
15	8.0	0.40	0.48	3.7	4
20	8.0	0.35	0.43	7.3	7
30	8.0	0.28	0.36	19.7	20
40	8.0	0.23	0.31	40.6	41
50	8.0	0.19	0.27	72.9	73
60	8.0	0.17	0.25	113.4	113
70	8.0	0.15	0.23	167.8	168
80	8.0	0.14	0.22	223.1	229
90	8.0	0.13	0.21	303.7	304
100	8.0	0.12	0.20	393.7	394
110	8.0	0.11	0.19	501.5	501
120	8.0	0.09	0.17	667.0	667
130	8.0	0.08	0.16	831.7	832

TABLE 2.13   Minimum Radius Using Limiting Values of Superelevation and Side Friction Factor (Metric) (*Ref. 6.*)

Design Speed (km/h)	Maximum e (%)	Maximum f	Total (e/100 + f)	Calculated Radius (m)	Rounded Radius (m)
15	10.0	0.40	0.50	3.5	4
20	10.0	0.35	0.45	7.0	7
30	10.0	0.289	0.38	18.6	19
40	10.0	0.23	0.33	38.2	38
50	10.0	0.19	0.29	67.9	68
60	10.0	0.17	0.27	105.0	105
70	10.0	0.15	0.25	154.3	154
80	10.0	0.14	0.24	210.0	210
90	10.0	0.13	0.23	277.3	277
100	10.0	0.12	0.22	357.9	358
110	10.0	0.11	0.21	453.7	454
120	10.0	0.09	0.19	596.8	597
130	10.0	0.18	0.18	739.3	739
15	12.0	0.40	0.52	3.4	3
20	12.0	0.35	0.47	6.7	7
30	12.0	0.28	0.40	17.7	18
40	12.0	0.23	0.35	36.0	36
50	12.0	0.19	0.37	63.5	64
60	12.0	0.17	0.29	97.7	98
70	12.0	0.15	0.27	142.9	143
80	12.0	0.14	0.26	193.8	194
90	12.0	0.13	0.25	255.1	255
100	12.0	0.12	0.24	328.1	328
110	12.0	0.11	0.23	414.2	414
120	12.0	0.09	0.21	539.9	540
130	12.0	0.08	0.20	665.4	665

TABLE 2.13   Minimum Radius Using Limiting Values of Superelevation and Side Friction Factor (Metric) (*Ref. 6.*) (*Continued*)

curves are complex and related to both design speed and running speed. They are beyond the scope of this textbook, but address such issues as low-speed urban streets, overdriving, and asymmetry of curves.[6]

2.5.3   Minimum Radius

As with superelevation and side friction, the radius of a curve plays a role in physics associated with keeping a vehicle on the roadway as it navigates a curve. For a specific design speed, the maximum superelevation and maximum coefficient of friction govern the radius of curvature. This minimum radius is based on these factors as well as the comfort level of a driver while navigating the curve, while providing a measure of safety to minimize the likelihood of the vehicle skidding off the roadway or rolling over.[6]

By rearranging the simplified curve equations, the minimum radius can be determined based on these three values. As illustrated in Tables 2.12 and 2.13, the minimum radius is provided for a range of maximum superelevation rates, from 4% to 12%.

$$R_{min} = \frac{V^2}{15(0.01e_{max} + f_{max})} \text{ (U.S. Customary)}$$

$$R_{min} = \frac{V^2}{127(0.01e_{max} + f_{max})} \text{ (Metric)}$$

It is important to note that the radii in the equations are measured to the center of gravity of a vehicle, which is typically assumed to be at the center of the innermost travel lane of the roadway. In order to physically lay out a curve, the radius is typically measured to the horizontal control line, which is typically the centerline of the alignment.[6] Additionally, these equations do not account for the location of the horizontal control line or the width of the travel lanes. For general design purposes, the radius of a horizontal curve should be measured to the inside edge of the innermost travel lane to accommodate any motorist driving in the innermost travel lane on multilane facilities and to the centerline for two-lane roadways.[6]

Example Problem 2.4.   Calculate the coefficient of friction for a curve with a design speed of 60 mph, a radius of 1000 ft, and a maximum allowable superelevation rate of 4%? Based on Table 2.12, what can you state about this f? What would be the coefficient of friction if the curve had the minimum radius from the table?

$$f = \frac{V^2}{15R} - 0.01e = \frac{(60 \text{ mph})^2}{15(1000 \text{ ft})} - 0.01(4) = 0.20$$

The coefficient of friction of 0.24 is too high for a design speed of 60 mph and a superelevation of 4%. Using a minimum radius of 1500 ft, the coefficient of friction would be as follows:

$$f = \frac{V^2}{15R} - 0.01e = \frac{(60 \text{ mph})^2}{15(1500 \text{ ft})} - 0.01(4) = 0.12$$

Example Problem 2.5.   Calculate the minimum radius for a horizontal curve on a roadway with a design speed of 75 mph with a maximum superelevation of 8% and assuming a coefficient of friction of 0.08. How does this minimum radius compare to that recommended in Table 2.12? What would be the rounded radius a designer might use?

$$R_{min} = \frac{V^2}{15(0.01e_{max} + f_{max})} = \frac{75^2}{15(0.01 \times 8 + 0.08)} = 2344 \text{ ft}$$

The minimum curve radius of 2344 ft is larger than the minimum required curve radius in the table because the coefficient of friction assumed is less than the maximum provided in the table. A rounded radius would be 2350 ft.

2.5.4   Sight Distance on Horizontal Curves

Horizontal curves can provide sight distance limitations depending on the cross section and nearby obstructions. Roadside elements such as barriers, walls, slopes, trees, or buildings can obscure a driver's view around the curve, thereby limiting the SSD (see Fig. 2.14). As illustrated in Fig. 2.15, the sight distance on a horizontal curve is a function of the radius of the curve, the location of the obstruction, and the location of the centerline of the inside lane. It is important that the transportation engineer ensure that a facility provides adequate sight distance on both tangents and on horizontal curves.

FIGURE 2.14 Horizontal curve with sight distance obstruction. (© *Jim Lyle, TTI.*)

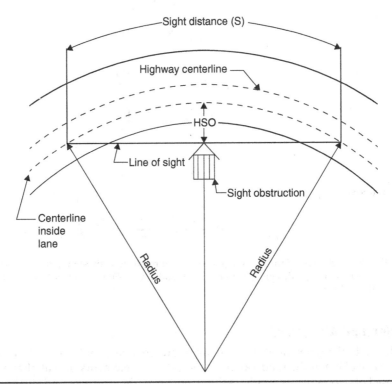

FIGURE 2.15 Components for determining sight distance on horizontal curves. (*Ref. 6.*)

The formula to calculate the needed horizontal sight offset necessary to provide sufficient SSD on a horizontal curve is as follows[6]:

$$HSO = R\left[1-\cos\left(\frac{28.65S}{R}\right)\right] \text{ (U.S. Customary/Metric)}$$

where HSO = horizontal sight line offset, ft (U.S. Customary)/m (Metric)
$\quad\quad S$ = stopping sight distance, ft (U.S. Customary)/m (Metric)
$\quad\quad R$ = radius of curve, ft (U.S. Customary)/m (Metric)

Example Problem 2.6.   A corner of a building is 30 ft from the centerline on a curved portion of a two-lane highway with 12 ft lanes. The radius of the curve is 700 ft. Is the radius of the horizontal curve sufficient to provide adequate stopping sight distance? Assume the design speed on the roadway is 60 mph.

The first step is to rearrange the equation to solve for S.

$$HSO = R\left[1-\cos\left(\frac{28.65S}{R}\right)\right]$$

$$R\left[1-\cos\left(\frac{28.65S}{R}\right)\right] = HSO$$

$$1-\cos\left(\frac{28.65S}{R}\right) = \frac{HSO}{R}$$

$$\cos\left(\frac{28.65S}{R}\right) = 1-\frac{HSO}{R}$$

$$\frac{28.65S}{R} = \cos^{-1}\left(1-\frac{HSO}{R}\right)$$

$$S = \frac{R}{28.65}\left[\cos^{-1}\left(1-\frac{HSO}{R}\right)\right]$$

The second step is to solve for S.

$$S = \frac{R}{28.65}\left[\cos^{-1}\left(1-\frac{HSO}{R}\right)\right] = \frac{700}{28.65}\left[\cos^{-1}\left(1-\frac{40}{700}\right)\right] = 476 \text{ ft}$$

Finally, check to see if the S is adequate for a flat roadway with 60 mph design speed. In Table 2.2, the SSD for 60 mph design speed on a level roadway is 570 ft. The S is NOT SUFFICIENT for the radius of 700 ft.

2.6   Vertical Alignment

The vertical alignment of the roadway represents the profile view of the facility where one is looking at the roadway from the side. The elements of that alignment are composed of two elements: grades—the steepness of the roadway, and vertical curves. Both of these elements impact how vehicles operate on roadway facilities. It is essential that the transportation engineer understand how to design these specific roadway elements to ensure proper roadway drainage and acceptable level of safety.

2.6.1 Grades

For all roadways, the transportation engineer needs to consider the terrain of the land in the design process. Typically, terrain is separated into three categories: level, rolling, and mountainous,[6] each of which has an impact on both the operation of a vehicle and the sight distances afforded drivers. Level terrain normally has little impact on operations and sight distances, which are naturally long or can be constructed easily and without major cost implications. Vehicles have little to no difficulty operating on level terrain since grades are nominal, presenting little strain on the acceleration capabilities of all vehicles. Rolling terrain has natural slopes that rise above or below what would be a level roadway alignment and feature steeper grades than level roadways. Rolling terrain can occasionally present sight distance limitations, which may require additional design changes and construction costs to mitigate them. Additionally, some vehicles—namely, heavy trucks and recreational vehicles—are forced to operate at slower speeds than passenger cars because of the steeper grades. Finally, mountainous terrain features abrupt changes in ground elevation, frequently requiring significant excavation and fill to level out the roadway to provide acceptable alignment.[6] Heavy vehicles have even more difficulty operating in mountainous terrain. The cost of road construction in mountainous terrain can be considerable because of the added expense of leveling out the roadway.

When designing a roadway facility, the transportation engineer should work to ensure that a vehicle operates at a fairly constant speed as much as possible. For passenger cars, grades up to 5% do not pose much of a strain on the capability to maintain speed when compared to a level roadway. However, the same cannot be said for trucks and recreational vehicles. The impact of steep grades on these vehicles is greater and is function of the length and rate of the roadway grade, the tractive effort of the vehicle, and the gross vehicle weight.[6] Various recommended maximum grades based on the functional classification of a roadway are presented in Table 2.14. Additionally, the critical length of those grades varies based on the design vehicle (e.g., typical heavy truck) operating on the facility, the percent grade, and the anticipated speed reduction of the vehicle along the facility. When grades are significant in length, the transportation engineer may choose to incorporate climbing lanes to offer opportunities for vehicles to pass other slow-moving vehicles to improve operations and safety. Climbing lanes are typically used on two-lane highways, most often in rural locations.

2.6.2 Crest Vertical Curves

Transportation engineers use vertical curves to transition between tangent grades along roadway. The types of grades used, as shown in Fig. 2.16, are crest vertical curves and sag vertical curves. For crest vertical curves, the primary design control is sight distance. Other factors to consider include the ability for a driver to maintain control of the vehicle, driver comfort, roadway drainage, and the overall appearance of the curve.

Typically, a crest vertical curve requires a minimum length based on sight distance criteria. These criteria also yield crest vertical curves that also meet overall preferences for safety, comfort, and appearance.[6] The formulas for calculating the length of a parabolic crest vertical curve based on grade and sight distance are shown below:

When S is less than L:

$$L = \frac{AS^2}{100\left(\sqrt{2h_1} + \sqrt{2h_2}\right)^2} \text{ (U.S. Customary/Metric)}$$

Terrain Type	Facility Type						
	Local Rural Roads [Speeds 15–60 mph (U.S. Customary)/20–100 km/h (Metric)]	Recreational Roads [Speeds 10–40 mph (U.S. Customary)/20–60 km/h (Metric)]	Rural Collectors [Speeds 20–60 mph (U.S. Customary)/30–100 km/h (Metric)]	Urban Collectors [Speeds 20–60 mph (U.S. Customary)/30–100 km/h (Metric)]	Rural Arterials [Speeds 40–80 mph (U.S. Customary)/60–130 km/h (Metric)]	Urban Arterials [Speeds 30–60 mph (U.S. Customary)/50–100 km/h (Metric)]	Rural and Urban Freeways [Speeds 50–85 mph (U.S. Customary)/80–130 km/h (Metric)]
Level	5–9%	7–8%	5–7%	6–9%	3–5%	5–8%	3–4%
Rolling	6–12%	9–12%	6–10%	6–12%	4–6%	6–9%	4–5%
Mountainous	10–17%	12–18%	8–12%	9–14%	5–8%	8–11%	5–6%

TABLE 2.14 Maximum Grades for Roadway Types (Ref. 6.)

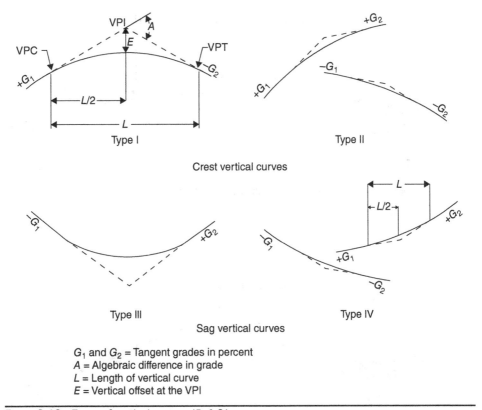

G₁ and G₂ = Tangent grades in percent
A = Algebraic difference in grade
L = Length of vertical curve
E = Vertical offset at the VPI

Figure 2.16 Types of vertical curves. (*Ref. 6.*)

When S is greater than L:

$$L = 2S - \frac{200\left(\sqrt{h_1} + \sqrt{h_2}\right)^2}{A} \text{(U.S. Customary/Metric)}$$

where L = length of vertical curve, ft (U.S. Customary)/m (Metric)
    A = algebraic difference in grades, percent
    S = sight distance, ft (U.S. Customary)/m (Metric)
    h_1 = height of eye above roadway surface, ft (U.S. Customary)/m (Metric)
    h_2 = height of objective above roadway surface, ft (U.S. Customary)/m (Metric)

Figure 2.17 illustrates these parameters used in determining both SSD and PSD along a crest vertical curve.

If one assumes that the height of the eye above the roadway is 3.50 ft (1.08 m) and the height of the object is 2.00 ft (0.60 m), then the formulas for minimum crest vertical curve length based on SSD can be simplified as follows:

When S is less than L:

$$L = \frac{AS^2}{2158} \text{ (U.S. Customary)} \qquad L = \frac{AS^2}{658} \text{ (Metric)}$$

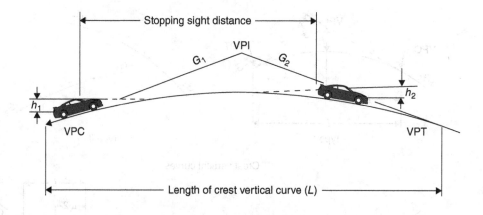

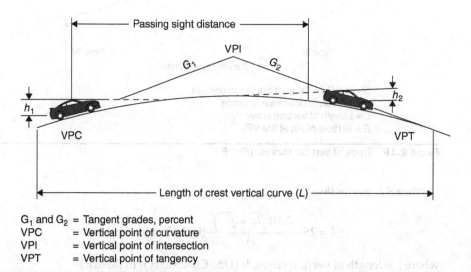

G₁ and G₂ = Tangent grades, percent
VPC   = Vertical point of curvature
VPI   = Vertical point of intersection
VPT   = Vertical point of tangency

FIGURE 2.17   Parameters considered in determining the length of a crest vertical curve to provide sight distance. (*Ref. 6.*)

When S is greater than L:

$$L = 2S - \frac{2158}{A} \text{ (U.S. Customary)} \qquad L = 2S - \frac{658}{A} \text{ (Metric)}$$

The typical procedure for designing a crest vertical curve based on sight distance, either SSD or PSD, is as follows:

- STEP 1: compute algebraic difference in grade, *A*
- STEP 2: assume *S* < *L*
- STEP 3: compute L using the equation assuming *S* is less than *L*

- STEP 4: check assumption
  - If S is less than L, go to STEP 6
  - If S is greater than L, go to STEP 5
- STEP 5: compute L using the equation assuming S is greater than L
- STEP 6: round up to the next highest interval

Example Problem 2.7.   Determine the minimum length of a crest vertical curve between a +1.5% grade and a −2.5 grade for a roadway with a 70 mph design speed. The vertical curve must provide at least 730 ft of stopping sight distance. Round up to the nearest 50-ft interval.

STEP 1: algebraic difference in grade = 1.5 −(−2.5) = 4%

STEP 2: assume $S < L$

STEP 3: calculate L using the correct formula

$$L = \frac{AS^2}{2158} = \frac{(4)(730)^2}{2158} = 987.77 \text{ ft}$$

STEP 4: check assumption

Is $S < L$? 730 ft < 987.77 ft   YES   (go to STEP 6)

STEP 6: round up to the nearest 50-ft interval

$$L = 1000 \text{ ft}$$

Frequently, the design control is PSD rather than SSD. This assumption changes the formula by assuming that the height of the eye above the roadway is 3.50 ft (1.08 m) and the height of the object is 3.50 ft (1.08 m) as well. Thus, the formulas for minimum crest vertical curve length based on PSD can be simplified as follows:

When S is less than L:

$$L = \frac{AS^2}{2800} \text{ (U.S. Customary)} \qquad L = \frac{AS^2}{864} \text{ (Metric)}$$

When S is greater than L:

$$L = 2S - \frac{2800}{A} \text{ (U.S. Customary)} \qquad L = 2S - \frac{864}{A} \text{ (Metric)}$$

Example Problem 2.8.   Determine the minimum length of a crest vertical curve between a +2.5% grade and a −1.0 grade for a roadway with a 65 mph design speed. The vertical curve must provide at least 1100 ft of passing sight distance. Round up to the nearest 50-ft interval.

STEP 1: algebraic difference in grade = 2.5 −(−1.0) = 3.5%

STEP 2: assume $S < L$

STEP 3: calculate L using the correct formula

$$L = \frac{AS^2}{2800} = \frac{(3.5)(1100)^2}{2800} = 1512.50 \text{ ft}$$

STEP 4: check assumption

Is $S < L$? 1100 ft < 1512.50 ft   YES   (go to STEP 6)

STEP 6: round up to the nearest 50-ft interval

$$L = 1550 \text{ ft}$$

2.6.3   Sag Vertical Curves

Sag vertical curves have four design criteria that establish the appropriate length of the curve: headlight sight distance, the comfort of the passenger, drainage, and general appearance.[6] Obviously, sight distance is not limited on a sag vertical curve during the day. Thus, the sight distance afforded by a vehicle's headlights at night becomes the critical design factor. The position of the headlights is typically assumed to be 2 ft (0.60 m) above the roadway with a 1° upward divergence of the light beam from the longitudinal axle of the vehicle.[6] Given this assumption, the formulas to calculate the sight distance for a sag vertical curve based on headlight distance are below. These formulas assume that the headlight beam distance is approximately the same as the SSD needed for a particular design speed.

When S is less than L:

$$L = \frac{AS^2}{200[2.0 + S(\tan 1°)]} \text{ (U.S. Customary)} \qquad L = \frac{AS^2}{200[0.6 + S(\tan 1°)]} \text{ (Metric)}$$

or

$$L = \frac{AS^2}{400 + 3.5S} \text{ (U.S. Customary)} \qquad L = \frac{AS^2}{120 + 3.5S} \text{ (Metric)}$$

When S is greater than L:

$$L = 2S - \frac{200[2.0 + S(\tan 1°)]}{A} \text{ (U.S. Customary)}$$

$$L = 2S - \frac{200[0.6 + S(\tan 1°)]}{A} \text{ (Metric)}$$

or

$$L = 2S - \frac{200 + 3.5S}{A} \text{ (U.S. Customary)} \qquad L = 2S - \frac{120 + 3.5S}{A} \text{ (Metric)}$$

where L = length of sag vertical curve, ft (U.S. Customary)/m (Metric)
   A = algebraic different in grades, percent
   S = light beam distance (i.e., sight distance), ft (U.S. Customary)/m (Metric)

Sag vertical curves are also designed to accommodate the comfort of the passenger. The formulas that account for passenger comfort are noted below:

$$L = \frac{AV^2}{46.5} \text{ (U.S. Customary)} \qquad L = \frac{AV^2}{395} \text{ (Metric)}$$

where L = length of sag vertical curve, ft (U.S. Customary)/m (Metric)
   A = algebraic difference in grades, percent
   V = design speed, mph (U.S. Customary)/km/h (Metric)

Drainage and appearance are also factors that an engineer can consider when designing a sag vertical curve. In general, a nominal amount of grade is needed to accommodate drainage of the roadway. Additionally, some sag vertical curves may have an improved appearance with longer lengths when compared to that based on sight distance. The details associated with these factors are beyond the scope of this textbook, but they are factored into guidance provided by AASHTO.

The typical procedure for designing a sag vertical curve (omitting the check for drainage and appearance) is as follows:

- STEP 1: compute algebraic difference in grade, A
- STEP 2: compute L curve to satisfy headlights
  - Assume $S < L$
  - Compute L using first equation
  - Check assumption
  - If assumption is not satisfied, compute L using second equation
- STEP 3: check comfort criteria
- STEP 4: select largest L
- STEP 5: round up to the next highest interval

Example Problem 2.9. Determine the minimum length of a sag vertical curve between a –3.4% grade and a –0.7 grade for a roadway with a 60 mph design speed. The vertical curve must provide at least 900 ft of sight distance. Round up to the nearest 50-ft interval.

STEP 1: algebraic difference in grade = $|-3.4 - (-0.7)| = 2.7\%$

STEP 2: assume $S < L$
  calculate L using the correct formula

$$L = \frac{2.7(900)^2}{400 + 3.5(900)} = 616.06 \text{ ft}$$

check assumption

Is $S < L$? 900 ft < 616.06 ft   NO (recalculate)

$$L = 2(900) - \frac{200 + 3.5(900)}{2.7} = 559.26 \text{ ft}$$

Is $S > L$? 900 ft > 559.26 ft   YES

STEP 3: check for comfort

$$L = \frac{2.7(60)^2}{46.5} = 209.03 \text{ ft}$$

STEP 4: select larger L

$$L = 559.26 \text{ ft}$$

STEP 5: round to the next highest interval

$$L = 560 \text{ ft}$$

2.7   The Project Development and Design Process

The content of this chapter focuses on the geometric design of the roadway facility. However, it is important to note that the design of a facility is only one step in the overall development of a roadway project. The development of any transportation infrastructure project starts with the planning and programming effort that identifies both the need for a project, specific requirements, and the identification of funding. At that point, the transportation agency moves forward with the longer project development process, which can take a number of years depending on the complexities of the project and any challenges that may arise in any of the project phases.

A typical project development and design process is illustrated in Fig. 2.18; this is what is used by the Texas Department of Transportation (TxDOT).[18] Most state DOTs have similar manuals that govern the development of transportation projects on the state roadway system. Likewise, FHWA has a similar document that provides policies and guidance for the development of transportation on federal lands, many of which are interdisciplinary in nature and require coordination both internal and external to the Department.[19] Overall, project development processes across the country are similar in nature and include the general steps that agencies should follow to implement a transportation project.

A description of the planning, policy, and design elements incorporated in the project development process is provided in Table 2.15. As illustrated in this process, the transportation engineer stays engaged throughout the entire project development process

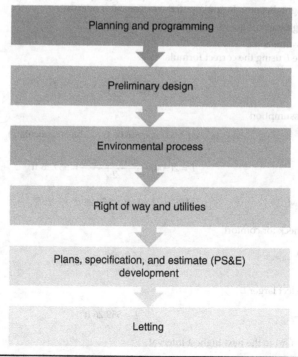

Figure 2.18   Project development process, (TxDOT) (*Ref. 18.*)

Project Phase	Phase Steps	Description
Planning and programming	Needs identification	Process of identifying and documenting the need for a project, including project need and scope.
	Project authorization	Process of securing the authorization to proceed with project development from the appropriate oversight entity.
	Compliance with planning requirements	Process to ensure the project complies with various local, regional, and statewide planning policies and processes.
	Study requirements determination	Process of determining the project's scope and addressing regional, state, and federal requirements and policies that impact project development.
	Construction funding identification	Activities to identify potential local, regional, state, federal, and outside funding sources for construction.
Preliminary design	Preliminary design concept conference	Define the general project location, design concepts, and establish parameters for final design.
	Data collection/ preliminary design preparation	Collection of data needed to make engineering and environmental decisions related to project design.
	Public meeting(s)	Process for obtaining public input and incorporation of that input into project design.
	Preliminary schematic	Development of preliminary schematic of the project to communication design concepts to stakeholders.
	Geometric schematic	Refining of alignments and geometrics, analyses, and preparation of preliminary plans and layouts.
	Value engineering	Process to evaluate a project concept and design to identify ways to improve the value and quality of the project.
	Geometric schematic approval	Internal approval of geometric schematic, review with stakeholders, securing of design exceptions and waivers, incorporation of public input, and final approval.
Environmental process	Preliminary environmental issues	Identification of project's environmental variables and the planning of public involvement.
	Interagency coordination/permits	Coordination of efforts with regulatory and resource agencies and determination of environmental permit requirements.
	Environmental documentation	Documentation of social, economic, and environmental impacts of project to decision makers and stakeholders.
	Public hearing	Identification and hosting of public hearing and response to comments.
	Environmental clearance	Process to finalize environmental documentation and public involvement and to obtain environmental clearance for project.

TABLE 2.15 Typical Roadway Project Development Process (*Ref. 18.*)

Project Phase	Phase Steps	Description
Right of way (ROW) and utilities	ROW and utility data collection	Collection of preliminary ROW information and location of existing utilities in the existing ROW.
	ROW map and property descriptions	Preparation and submission of ROW maps and property descriptions prior to acquiring property for a project.
	ROW appraisals and acquisition	Process for preparing property appraisals of ROW and acquiring property for project, including relocation assistance and removal of improvements on the ROW.
	Utility adjustments	Process of notifying and coordinating with utility owners adjusting facilities to prepare clearance certifications prior to construction.
Plan, specification, and estimate (PS&E) development	Design conference	The process of providing the opportunity for key individuals and stakeholders to review, accept, or change basic design criteria and endorse for full design work process.
	Begin detailed design	Initiation of detailed design effort, including traffic control, permits and agreements, design data collection, and stream crossing hydraulics.
	Final alignments/ profiles	Finalization of alignments and profiles prior to detailed design and plan development.
	Roadway design	Design of final plan/profile and cross sections of the proposed facility and other related design details for approval.
	Operational design	Design of final operational design elements of the proposed facility, including illumination, intelligent transportation system (ITS), signalization, signing, and pavement markings for approval.
	Bridge design	Design of final bridge layouts, details, plans, and designs for approval.
	Drainage design	Design of final drainage elements, including crossing hydraulics, culverts, storm drains, pump stations, and storm water pollution prevention plan for approval.
	Retaining/noise walls and miscellaneous structures	Design of final project elements related to retaining walls, noise walls, and other miscellaneous structures for approval.
	Traffic control plan	Design of final traffic control plans for construction staging and phasing, detours, temporary signing, striping, and pavement markings for approval.
	PS&E assembly/ design review	Preparation of plans, specifications, and estimate package and supporting documents for design review.
Letting	Final processing and letting	Completion of the PS&E package, supporting documents, and proposal for release to contractors for bidding.

TABLE 2.15 Typical Roadway Project Development Process (*Ref. 18.*) (*Continued*)

and does not function in a vacuum. Opportunities for stakeholder and public input occur throughout the various phases, presenting the designer with elements that may need to be revised to ensure the overall project meets the needs of the region and the system user without increasing the negative social, economic, and environmental impacts.

Recent trends associated with the project development process look to address the impacts of projects during construction. Throughout the design process, the transportation agencies focus on ensuring that, upon completion, the project meets the regional goals and objectives while minimizing any negative impacts. However, it is also important to minimize the negative impacts on the project throughout the entire construction process, which can be very lengthy for some major reconstruction and expansion projects. FHWA has worked to develop guidance for agencies on best practices that can help improve work zone mobility and safety. These practices fall into a broad range of categories, all of which influence the project development process and work to minimize the negative impacts of a major construction prior to completion. These categories include:

- Policy and procedures
- Public relations, education and outreach (program level)
- Modeling and impact analysis
- Planning and programming
- Project development and design
- Contracting and bidding procedures
- Construction/maintenance materials, methods, practices, and specifications
- Traveler and traffic information (project related)
- Enforcement
- ITS and innovative technology
- Evaluation and feedback[20]

State and local agencies have had success in implementing a variety of strategies across these themes, in cooperation with regional stakeholders, to help mitigate the impacts of major construction projects. This approach to design and project development reinforce the notion that transportation does not operate in a vacuum. The incorporation of all stakeholders in the entire process helps ensure that the needs and objectives of the community with respect to safety and mobility are met through cooperation and collaboration, all in an effort to minimize the negative impacts throughout the planning, construction, and operation phases of a project.

2.8   Case Studies

2.8.1   Design for Safety Partnership—California Department of Transportation (Caltrans)

Caltrans formed a cross-functional task force to address the safety needs of workers during construction.[20] The task force, comprising representatives from design, construction, and maintenance groups, identified a number of safety-related issues that could be addressed to develop worker safety practices for designers. Topics such as how maintenance workers safely access the facility both during construction and after completion were identified as issues that can influence the project development process. In this particular case, practical considerations to address this access included the purchase of additional ROW or modifying the design of the roadside slope to facilitate access by workers. These and other safety improvements are being incorporated into the Caltrans Project Engineer Academy to ensure designers have these considerations at their disposal when designing projects.

2.8.2 Construction Traffic Management Strategies—Ohio Department of Transportation (ODOT)

While the end goal of a transportation construction project is typically to improve safety and mobility of the system users, the construction process itself has the potential to have negative impacts in these areas along the way. To address these impacts of construction, ODOT developed a list of strategies and options that transportation should consider to maximize capacity while maintaining traffic flow through major work zones.[20] Specific strategies fell into six topic areas:

- Construction/traffic maintenance strategies
- Options outside the work zone
- Options inside the work zone
- Time limitations with liquidated damages
- Contracting procedures
- Administrative options

All of these strategies address specific stages in the project development process, ensuring that the overall impact of the project during construction is minimized to the extent possible. ODOT branded these strategies as the "Compendium of Options," and they have been in use for over 20 years in the districts throughout the state. This compendium helps ODOT move toward its goal of reducing delay and improving safety of work zones for both workers and the traveling public.

2.8.3 Construction Practices—Illinois Department of Transportation (IDOT)

State transportation agencies utilize various techniques to minimize the delay encountered by motorists as a result of a major work zone. During a major reconstruction project involving a seismic retrofit and resurfacing effort along I-47 in Illinois, IDOT incorporated several innovative techniques to help minimize delays and the resulting inconvenience to travelers. These strategies included, but were not limited to:

- The consolidation of several projects into a single combined project
- Utilization of fast setting mixes for bridge work and pavement patching
- Completion of multiple tasks by the contractor during a lane closure
- Utilizing lane rental strategies and incentive/disincentive contracting[20]

These and other techniques work to expedite the construction process and reduce the overall impact on the traveling public.

2.9   Summary

The design of transportation facilities is complex. The designer needs to have an understanding of the system users and how they interact with the system to assess the potential limitations that might impact design. These human factors are interrelated with such design features as design speed, sight distance, and alignment. Knowledge of human factors and the overall needs of the traveling public and other stakeholders also impact the project development process. Transportation professionals are the caretakers of the mobility network, and this knowledge is essential to ensuring that the network meets the needs of the public while minimizing the negative impact it may have on safety and mobility for all users.

Glossary of Acronyms

AASHTO—American Association of State Highway and Transportation Officials

Caltrans—California Department of Transportation

DSD—decision sight distance

FDOT—Florida Department of Transportation

FHWA—Federal Highway Administration

IDOT—Illinois Department of Transportation

ITS—intelligent transportation system

NHTSA—National Highway Traffic Safety Administration

MUTCD—Manual on Uniform Traffic Control Devices

ODOT—Ohio Department of Transportation

PSD—passing sight distance

PS&E—plan, specification, and estimate

ROW—right of way

SSD—stopping sight distance

TxDOT—Texas Department of Transportation

Exercises

2.1 Write a paper (no more than 10 pages) providing an overview of the most recent crash statistics, trends, and three countermeasures agencies that can undertake to reduce roadway fatalities.

2.2 Write a paper (no more than 10 pages) providing a critical discussion on how human factors and human characteristics influence the design of the roadway environment.

2.3 Write a paper (no more than 10 pages) discussing circumstances under which a transportation agency might request a design exception and how they would mitigate that exception to minimize the impact on safety.

2.4 Calculate the minimum stopping sight distance on a +4.5% grade for a design speed of 70 mph.

2.5 Calculate the minimum stopping sight distance on a –2.5 grade for a design speed of 55 mph.

2.6 Determine if the available stopping sight distance of 825 ft is adequate for a –2.0% grade and a design speed of 80 mph. Justify your answer.

2.7 Calculate the decision sight distance needed for a driver to make a speed/path/direction change on a suburban road with a design speed of 50 mph and a total pre-maneuver and maneuver time of 12.5 s.

2.8 Determine if the decision sight distance of 1300 ft is adequate for a driver to make a speed/path/direction change on an urban roadway with a design speed of 70 mph. Justify your answer.

2.9 Calculate the coefficient of friction for a curve with a design speed of 65 mph, a radius of 1200 ft, and a maximum allowable superelevation rate of 6%? Based on Table 2.12, what can you state about this f? What would be the maximum allowable coefficient of friction if the curve had the minimum radius from the table? Using a superelevation of 6% and a coefficient of friction of 0.08, what would be the minimum radius required for the curve?

2.10 Calculate the superelevation for a horizontal curve of a design speed of 80 mph with a coefficient of friction of 0.065 and a radius of 3200 ft? Based on Table 2.12, what can you state about this e? What would be the superelevation if the curve had the minimum radius from the table for the design speed? Is this practical? Why or why not?

2.11 Calculate the minimum radius for a horizontal curve on a roadway with a design speed of 70 mph with a maximum superelevation of 10% and assuming a coefficient of friction of 0.08. How does this minimum radius compare to that recommended in Table 2.12. What would be the rounded radius a designer might use?

2.12 A cluster of trees is 25 ft from the centerline on a curved portion of a two-lane highway with 12 ft lanes. The radius of the curve is 800 ft. Is the radius of the horizontal curve sufficient to provide adequate stopping sight distance? Assume the design speed on the roadway is 55 mph. What HSO would be needed to provide adequate stopping sight distance?

2.13 Compute the minimum length of vertical curve to provide the maximum stopping sight distance for a design speed of 60 mph at the intersection of a +2.5% grade with a –1.3% grade. Round to the greatest 50-ft interval.

2.14 Compute the minimum length of vertical curve to provide passing sight distance for a design speed of 70 mph at the intersection of a +1.4% grade with a –0.7% grade. Round to the greatest 20-ft interval.

2.15 Compute the minimum length of a vertical curve to provide stopping sight distance for a design speed of 55 mph at the intersection of a +3.2% grade with a +0.5% grade. Round to the greatest 50-ft interval.

2.16 Design a sag vertical curve between a –3.4% grade and a +1.8% grade for a road with a design speed of 65 mph. Make sure to check for stopping sight distance and comfort. Round to the greatest 50-ft interval.

2.17 Design a sag vertical curve between a –2.5% grade and a –0.7% grade for a road with a design speed of 80 mph. Make sure to check for stopping sight distance and comfort. Round to the greatest 20-ft interval.

References

1. "Human Factors," U.S. Department of Transportation, NHTSA, https://www.nhtsa
   .gov/research-data/human-factors (accessed November 2017).
2. Alexander, G. H., and H. Lunenfeld, *Driver Expectancy in Highway Design and Operations*, FWHA-TO-86-1. Federal Highway Administration, U.S. Department of Transportation, Washington, D.C., 1986.
3. "Risky Driving," U.S. Department of Transportation, NHTSA, https://www.nhtsa
   .gov/risky-driving (accessed October 2017).
4. *Manual on Uniform Traffic Control Devices, 9th Edition*. Federal Highway Administration, U.S. Department of Transportation, Washington, D.C., 2012.
5. Russell, E. R., "Using Concepts of Driver Expectancy, Positive Guidance and Consistency for Improved Operation and Safety," in *1998 Transportation Conference Proceedings*, pp. 155–158.
6. *A Policy on Geometric Design of Highways and Streets, 6th Edition*. American Association of Highway and State Transportation Officials, Washington, D.C., 2011.
7. "Interstate System," U.S. Department of Transportation, Federal Highway Administration, https://www.fhwa.dot.gov/programadmin/interstate.cfm (accessed December 2017).
8. "23 CFR Part 625," Design Standards for Highways; Interstate System, http://www
   .gpo.gov/fdsys/pkg/FR-2006-05-05/pdf/06-4228.pdf (accessed December 2017).
9. *A Policy on Design Standards—Interstate System, 6th Edition*. American Association of Highway and State Transportation Officials, Washington, D.C., 2016.
10. "The National Highway System Designation Act of 1995." 23 USC, https://www
    .fhwa.dot.gov/legsregs/nhsdatoc.html (accessed December 2017).
11. Title 23 U.S. Code §109, https://www.gpo.gov/fdsys/granule/USCODE-2011-title23/USCODE-2011-title23-chap1-sec109 (accessed December 2017).
12. "Fixing America's Surface Transportation Act," U.S. Government Publishing Office, Washington, D.C., https://www.gpo.gov/fdsys/pkg/PLAW-114publ94/html/PLAW-114publ94.htm (accessed December 2017).
13. "Design Standards and Section 1404 of the FAST Act," U.S. Department of Transportation, Federal Highway Administration, Washington, D.C., https://www.fhwa.dot.gov/design/standards/161006.cfm (accessed December 2017).
14. *Mitigation Strategies for Design Exceptions*. U.S. Department of Transportation, Federal Highway Administration, Washington, D.C., 2007, https://safety.fhwa.dot.gov/geometric/pubs/mitigationstrategies/(accessed December 2017).
15. Forbes, G., T. Gardner, H. McGee, and R. Srinivasan, *Methods and Practices for Setting Speed Limits: An Informational Report*. Institute of Transportation Engineers for Federal Highway Administration, U.S. Department of Transportation, Washington, D.C., https://safety.fhwa.dot.gov/speedmgt/ref_mats/fhwasa12004/fhwasa12004.pdf (accessed January 2018).
16. Harwood, D. W., D. K. Gilmore, K. R. Richard, J. M. Dunn, and C. Sun, *National Cooperative Highway Research Program Report 605: Passing Sight Distance Criteria*. National Cooperative Highway Research Program, Transportation Research Board, Washington, D.C., 2007.

17. Donnell, E. T., S. C. Hines, K. M. Mahoney, R. J. Porter, and H. McGee, *Speed Concepts: Informational Guide*. Report FHWA-SW-10-001. Thomas D. Larson Pennsylvania Transportation Institute and Vanesse Hangen Brustlin, Inc., for Federal Highway Administration, U.S. Department of Transportation, Washington, D.C., 2009.

18. *Project Development Process Manual*. Texas Department of Transportation, Austin, TX, April 2017.

19. *Federal Lands Highway Project Development and Design Manual*. Federal Highway Administration, U.S. Department of Transportation, Washington, D.C., 2018.

20. *Work Zone Operations Best Practices Guidebook (Third Edition)*. Report FHWA-HOP-13-012. Science Applications International Corporation (SAIC), for Federal Highway Administration, U.S. Department of Transportation, Washington, D.C., 2013.

CHAPTER 3

Traffic Flow
Theory and Capacity

3.1 Introduction

As discussed in Chap. 1, the primary purpose of a transportation system is to provide for the movement of people, goods, and services in a safe and efficient manner. An important aspect of this objective is for transportation professionals to be able to determine to what extent the system accomplishes that purpose. Understanding the appropriate performance measures to determine that effectiveness and collecting the appropriate data to use in that assessment is critical to traffic analysis. To that end, the transportation professional must be able to qualitatively and quantitatively determine the effectiveness of the system. The first step in understanding the network is to focus on the traffic stream—the collection of vehicles flowing through a facility. This chapter addresses the specific operating conditions exhibited by traffic on the network, which impacts the way in which the network might be analyzed. The chapter also discusses the concept of traffic flow theory and its related parameters, examining the fundamental way in which traffic behaves within a transportation network. It discusses the basic characteristics of traffic and how transportation professionals might consider them in an analysis, including the specific data transportation professionals used to measure and analyze traffic flow and the relationship between them. The chapter briefly presents the different types of simulation models that professionals can use to predict how traffic will behave in a specific environment. Finally, the related topic of highway capacity is introduced to illustrate the interrelationships between traffic flow, vehicle performance, and capacity on the network. It is important to note that while the principle focus of this textbook is on the surface roadway network, traffic flow characteristics are fundamental to all transportation systems, including air transport, water transport, and fixed guideway systems such as freight or passenger rail systems.

3.2 Traffic Operating Conditions

When analyzing the flow of traffic on the transportation network, the transportation professional needs to understand the types of flow experienced by the vehicles on the network. Traffic can be characterized by either the particular type of facility on which it is operating or by the specific type flow experienced on a facility. These facilities and flow types are as follows:

- Type of facility
  - Uninterrupted flow
  - Interrupted flow
- Type of flow on a facility
  - Undersaturated flow
  - Oversaturated flow
  - Queue discharge flow

The following sections provide a brief overview of these operating conditions and provide examples for context.

3.2.1 Uninterrupted Flow

The first type of facility with which transportation professionals are concerned is an uninterrupted flow facility. As the name implies, an uninterrupted flow facility is one in which no fixed cause of delay or interruption in the flow of vehicles occurs along the facility.[1] Figure 3.1 presents an urban freeway, which is a typical uninterrupted flow facility. These facilities include, but are not *limited* to, freeway facilities, basic freeway segments, freeway weaving segments, freeway merge and diverge segments, multilane highways, and two-lane highways. As the description implies, the traffic on these facilities can move along the facility without intentional or unintentional interruptions. Some facilities, such as multilane highways or two-lane highways, can have intentional interruptions such as traffic signals, though they can offer long sections of uninterrupted flow. For uninterrupted facilities, vehicles in the traffic stream typically interact only with each other and the geometric features of the facility. Depending on the amount of traffic on a facility, drivers can select their travel speed and navigate through a network of roadways without having to stop until they choose to exit the facility.

Figure 3.1   Uninterrupted flow facility. (© *Jim Lyle, Texas A&M Transportation Institute [TTI]*.)

This chapter provides information on how to determine the capacity of uninterrupted flow facilities as a function of specific geometric features. Unintentional interruptions on the traffic stream include recurring congestion as well as nonrecurring congestion conditions such as work zones, traffic incidents, road weather conditions, or planned special events. These topics along with how to manage the system in response to these conditions are discussed in Chap. 7.

3.2.2   Interrupted Flow

The second type of transportation facility that serves the traffic stream is an interrupted flow facility. In contrast to uninterrupted flow facilities, interrupted flow facilities have periodic delay or interruptions caused by a fixed feature on the facility.[1] Interrupted flow facilities include urban streets and urban street segments, signalized intersections, two-way stop-controlled intersections, all-way stop-controlled intersections, round-abouts, interchange ramp terminals, and off-street pedestrian and bicycle facilities. For interrupted flow facilities, like that depicted in Fig. 3.2, the flow of traffic is interrupted periodically by such treatments as a traffic signal, a STOP sign, a YIELD sign, or a roundabout. Traffic on these facilities must navigate through such interruptions but are also subject to the geometric design features of the roadway. The more complex the interruption and the more elements of the traffic stream that need to be accommodated (e.g., pedestrians, bicycles, turns, transit, emergency vehicles, etc.), the more impact that interruption has on the traffic flow. For example, when the vehicle mix is diverse at an intersection, the traffic signal timing plan needs to be able to accommodate all of the users at the intersection. As with uninterrupted flow facilities, recurring and nonrecurring congestion also occur on interrupted flow facilities. This congestion impacts their ability to provide efficient movement to all system users. This chapter provides information on how to determine the capacity of interrupted flow facilities as a function of specific geometric features as well as the mix of users at the intersection. Additionally, strategies for effectively managing the operations of all transportation facilities, including interrupted flow facilities, in response to all types of congestion are discussed in Chap. 7.

Figure 3.2 Interrupted flow facility. (© *Jim Lyle, TTI.*)

3.2.3 Undersaturated Flow

Uninterrupted and interrupted flow facilities are terms that describe the type of facility that provides movement for vehicles. However, they do not describe how the traffic actually flows on a facility and what the drivers experience as they navigate the system. Undersaturated flow is a term that describes the condition where the traffic flow is below that which the facility can handle. Undersaturated flow, which can be used to describe either uninterrupted or interrupted flow facilities, is characterized by one of the three conditions:

- The arrival flow rate of vehicles on an undersaturated facility is less than the capacity that is provided by the segment or point of measurement.

- No queues are present on the facility resulting from previous interruptions, whether intentional or unintentional.

- Downstream conditions do not impact the traffic flow along the facility.[1]

Figure 3.3 presents an interrupted flow facility (e.g., an intersection) that is experiencing undersaturated flow. Traffic on the facility is nominal, vehicles are allowed to travel through the intersection with little to no delay when the signal indication is green, and no queues exist at the intersection beyond a single cycle of the traffic signal. As a rule of thumb, a facility is considered undersaturated if all traffic demand during a 15-minute analysis period can be adequately serviced by the capacity of the facility, whether interrupted or uninterrupted in type.[1] In the case of an uninterrupted facility, travel speeds approximate free-flow speeds (FFSs) and queues do not form during the time period. In the case of an interrupted facility, any queues that form due to the intentional interruptions dissipate within the 15-minute analysis period. In short, transportation facilities are able to adequately serve the demand during undersaturated flow conditions and travelers do not experience delay on a typical trip.

Figure 3.3 Interrupted flow facility experiencing undersaturated flow. (© *Jim Lyle, TTI.*)

3.2.4 Oversaturated Flow

Oversaturated flow on a facility is as the name implies: the facility is oversaturated with vehicle demand and is unable to handle that demand sufficiently during the 15-minute analysis period. If the demand exceeds capacity on a regular basis, this phenomenon is known as recurring congestion. If the oversaturation is a result of some unique event, such as reduction in capacity from an incident or work zone, then the phenomenon is known as nonrecurring congestion. Additional information on these types of congestion is provided in Chap. 8. Specifically, oversaturated conditions are characterized by one of the three following conditions:

- The arrival flow rate of vehicles on an oversaturated facility is higher than the capacity that is provided by the segment or point of measurement.
- Queues occur resulting from previous interruptions or breakdowns and propagate back from the point of origin.
- Downstream conditions affect the traffic flow along the facility.[1]

For uninterrupted flow facilities, oversaturation typically occurs at a bottleneck where the facility is incapable of providing the capacity needed for the number of vehicles demanding service. Recurring bottlenecks include any condition that reduces roadway capacity, such as a lane drop or exclusive exit on a freeway, or a merge point along a facility where additional demand is placed on the facility. Figure 3.4 illustrates an uninterrupted flow facility experiencing oversaturated flow conditions during the peak period. For an interrupted flow facility, vehicles arrive at the intersection faster than they can be discharged during the analysis period. Queues build and extend backward from the intersection and last beyond the analysis period. Problems arise with both uninterrupted and interrupted flow facilities when queues' lengths grow. For example, significant queues at intersections or ramp meters can impact operations at intersections upstream of the oversaturated location. If the oversaturated intersection is near the termination of an exit ramp, the queue might even spill back onto a freeway, creating another bottleneck on the facility.

Figure 3.4 Uninterrupted flow facility experiencing oversaturated flow (© *Jim Lyle, TTI.*)

3.2.5   Queue Discharge Flow

The final type of flow that can describe a traffic stream is queue discharge flow. This flow type is particularly important on uninterrupted flow facilities with bottlenecks, especially if that bottleneck is a result of an incident. It describes the flow of traffic immediately past a bottleneck as the vehicles accelerate back to FFS.[1] As long as no additional bottleneck downstream impedes traffic, the vehicles exit the bottleneck at a discharge rate that typically results in FFS within a mile downstream.

3.3   Traffic Flow Characteristics

One of the most critical concepts the transportation professional needs to grasp is that of fundamental traffic flow theory. The three characteristics of flow, speed, and density form the foundation of traffic flow and all traffic analyses start from these three parameters. The following sections provide a discussion on these parameters and related concepts that derive from these characteristics, presenting the reader with a general understanding of how they are interrelated. It also illustrates how to calculate these parameters for basic traffic flow analysis.

3.3.1   Flow

The first of the three primary traffic flow theory parameters of which a practitioner needs to be familiar is flow. Flow rate and volume are terms that describe the vehicular loadings on a facility. They represent the number of vehicles that pass a designated point on a facility (e.g., surface street, freeway) in a given period of time, generally expressed in vehicles per unit of time. Volume and flow rate are similar and both reflect how many vehicles are using a facility. The difference between these two parameters lies in the way in which the terms are calculated. For example, volume is the total number of vehicles that pass a point over a given period of time interval. The practitioner can select any time period for which they want to calculate volume for a roadway, but they typically express volumes in terms of annual, daily, hourly, or subhourly time periods.[1] Flow rate differs from volume in that it reflects an equivalent hourly rate at which vehicles pass a point on a facility, typically measured for a time period less than 1 hour. In short, volumes can be said to be directly measured, while flow rates are typically calculated—though both are expressed in vehicles per unit time. Both of these parameters are used to reflect the demand being placed on a transportation network by system users.

The transportation practitioner collects or predicts volumes for transportation facilities for a variety of purposes. For example, daily volumes can be used for planning purposes and for observing general trends through a particular day. Expressed in terms of vehicles per day, daily volumes represent the total amount of traffic using an entire facility at a specific location. Daily volumes are typically not lane- or direction-specific, but they can paint a clear picture of how traffic ebbs and flows through the day on a facility. They can help the practitioner identify the peak periods of flow that are likely to present challenges to daily operations.

Practitioners also often calculate average annual daily traffic (AADT) and average daily traffic (ADT) for use in their responsibilities as system operators. AADT is the average 24-hour volume that moves through a facility. The practitioner calculates the AADT by taking the total number of vehicles that pass a point or through a short segment on a facility in a single year and dividing that total volume by 365 days. These volumes are typically collected at permanent count stations, many of which are maintained by regional metropolitan planning organizations (MPOs) or state departments of transportation (DOTs) for use in planning and analysis activities. AADT describes the amount of traffic using a facility on any typical day and accounts for seasonal, monthly, and daily variations in traffic flow. ADT represents the average 24-hour volume on a facility. The ADT is collected for some period less than a year (e.g., over a season, months, weeks, days) and is only valid for period over which it was measured. For example, an ADT gathered on a holiday that falls during the middle of a week would not be representative of a typical weekday volume.

Practitioners are also concerned with hourly volumes, peak hour volumes, and subhourly volumes, all of which are used in different ways to analyze the transportation network. Hourly volumes help illustrate how volumes can vary greatly by time of day. Every traveler knows that volumes are higher during the day than in the middle of the night. Hourly volumes measure demand over a 1-hour period by direction, and might be used in design or operations activities of a transportation agencies. The peak hour volume is that hourly volume that occurs during the peak hour or "rush hour." It is defined as the single hour of day that has the highest hourly volume. Ideally, if a facility can accommodate the peak hour traffic, it can accommodate traffic from other normal periods. However, it is important to note that within the reality of limited resources, designing for the peak hour is not always practical. Additional information related to management and operations of the transportation system, which can help address the design limitation, is included in Chap. 7. Finally, transportation professionals frequently look at subhourly volumes to determine traffic ebbs and flows throughout an hour. Based on counts less than 1 hour in length, subhourly volumes are expressed as equivalent hourly flow rates. For example, the conversion of a subhourly volume count to an hourly rate is shown below:

$$\frac{750 \text{ veh}}{15 \text{ min}}/\text{h} \times \frac{60 \text{ min}}{1 \text{ h}} = 3000 \text{ veh}$$

Figure 3.5 illustrates how traffic might behave along a facility during the peak hour between 7:00 am and 8:00 am. This information can be beneficial to a transportation practitioner in understanding how flow rates change throughout the peak hour and whether operational changes are needed to address the demand over time, such as modifying the traffic signal timing plan or implementing an active traffic management (ATM) strategy on a freeway to provide additional capacity temporarily to address the higher demand. More information on ATM strategies is provided in Chap. 7.

The basic equation for the flow rate on a transportation facility is provided below:

$$q = \frac{N}{t}$$

where q = flow rate or volume, vehicles per unit time
N = number of vehicles counted during time t
t = specified time interval

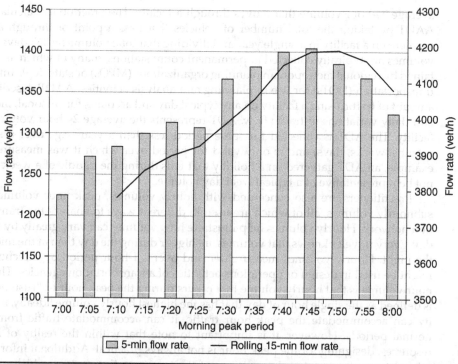

FIGURE 3.5 Illustration of subhourly flow rates.

Example Problem 3.1. If a transportation practitioner performs a vehicle count on a freeway over a 15-minute period, what is the hourly flow rate for the facility if the practitioner counts 923 vehicles during selected time period?

$$q = \frac{N}{t} = \frac{923 \text{ veh}}{15 \text{ min}} \times \frac{60 \text{ min}}{1 \text{ h}} = 3692 \text{ veh/h}$$

The transportation practitioner frequently uses the peak hour factor (PHF) as an input to *Highway Capacity Manual* (HCM) procedures to measure demand. The PHF is applicable to any analysis hour, whether peak or off-peak, and is a reflection of the demand during the hour. PHF is a ratio of the total hourly volume over the maximum 15-minute flow rate, as shown below:

$$\text{PHF} = \frac{\text{hourly volume}}{\text{peak flow rate (within the hour)}} = \frac{V}{4 \times V_{15}}$$

where PHF = the peak hour factor
    V = the hourly volume, vehicles/hour
    V_{15} = the volume measured during the peak 15 minutes of the analysis hour, veh/15 min[1]

Example 3.2. Calculate the PHF of a freeway facility if the hourly volume is 3245 veh/h and the peak 15-minute volume during that hour is 895 veh/15-min.

$$\text{PHF} = \frac{V}{4 \times V_{15}} = \frac{3245 \text{ veh/h}}{4 \times 895 \text{ veh/15 min}} = 0.91$$

Example 3.3. What is the hourly flow rate for a facility if the PHF is 0.96 and the peak 15-minute flow rate is 784 veh/15 min?

$$\text{PHF} = \frac{V}{4 \times V_{15}}$$

$$V = \text{PHF}(4 \times V_{15}) = 0.96(4 \times 784) = 3011 \text{ veh/h}$$

3.3.2 Speed

Speed is another parameter used to characterize traffic flow on a facility. Determined by taking the inverse of the time taken by a vehicle to travel a given distance, speed is reflected in distance per unit of time. Practitioners use several parameters associated with speed that are discussed herein. These include time mean speed (TMS), space mean speed (SMS), FFS, average running speed, and 85th percentile speed. Each of these parameters is measured differently and is used in different ways when analyzing traffic flow.

TMS, which is an arithmetic mean, is the average speed of all vehicles passing a point or short segment of freeway over some specified time interval. The general formula for TMS is shown below:

$$\bar{u}_t = \frac{\sum_{i=1}^{n} u_i}{n}$$

where $\bar{u}_t$ = time mean speed, unit distance per unit time

u_i = individual spot speed of the ith vehicle measured at a designated point on a roadway

n = the total number of vehicles for which spot speeds were measured

SMS is defined as the average speed of all vehicles occupying a given section of a roadway over some specified time interval. Also known as average travel speed, this measurement is a harmonic mean of speeds rather than an arithmetic mean. The formula for SMS is shown below:

$$\bar{u}_s = \frac{l}{\bar{t}}$$

with

$$\bar{t} = \frac{\sum_{i=1}^{n} t_i}{n}$$

where $\bar{u}_s$ = space mean speed, unit distance per time

t_i = individual travel time of the ith vehicle measured over a set length of roadway, assuming that all vehicles travel the same distance

n = the total number of vehicles for which travel times were measured

Example 3.4.   The speeds of five vehicles were measured as spot speeds at the midpoint of a 1.0-mile (1.609 km) section of roadway. Calculate the TMS and SMS for the vehicles assuming each vehicle traveled the entire length of roadway at a uniform speed. The speeds collected were as follows:

Vehicle	Speed (mph)	Speed (km/h)
1	57	91.7
2	62	99.8
3	55	88.5
4	59	95.0
5	58	93.3

For TMS:

$$\bar{u}_t = \frac{\sum_{i=1}^n u_i}{n} = \frac{(57 + 62 + 55 + 59 + 58)}{5} = 58.2 \text{ mph}$$

$$\bar{u}_t = \frac{\sum_{i=1}^n u_i}{n} = \frac{(91.7 + 99.9 + 88.5 + 95.0 + 93.3)}{5} = 93.7 \text{ km/h}$$

For SMS:

$$\bar{u}_s = \frac{l}{\left(\dfrac{\sum_{i=1}^n t_i}{n}\right)} = \frac{1 \text{ mi}}{\left(\dfrac{\dfrac{1}{57} + \dfrac{1}{62} + \dfrac{1}{55} + \dfrac{1}{59} + \dfrac{1}{58}}{5}\right)} = 58.1 \text{ mph}$$

$$\bar{u}_s = \frac{l}{\left(\dfrac{\sum_{i=1}^n t_i}{n}\right)} = \frac{1 \text{ mi}}{\left(\dfrac{\dfrac{1}{91.7} + \dfrac{1}{99.9} + \dfrac{1}{88.5} + \dfrac{1}{95.0} + \dfrac{1}{93.3}}{5}\right)} = 93.5 \text{ km/h}$$

FFS is another speed parameter that practitioners use to describe low-volume conditions. It is described as the average speed of vehicles on a specific segment of roadway when volumes are low and drivers are free to select their preferred speed without interference from other vehicles or traffic control devices.[1] Average running speed is based on similar SMS in that it is measured by observing the travel times of vehicles as they travel a portion of roadway with a known length. Average running speed is equal to average travel speed in an uninterrupted flow facility operating with undersaturated flow.[1]

The final speed that transportation practitioners frequently use is the 85th percentile speed. This is the speed which 85% of drivers travel at or below that speed. It is usually a good indicator of the prevailing or reasonable speed for a facility, meaning reasonable and prudent drivers feel comfortable traveling at that speed. The 85th percentile speed, which is also a TMS, is typically based on radar measurements. Practitioners often use the 85th percentile speed to set speed limits for roadway facilities.

3.3.3   Density

Density is defined as the number of vehicles occupying a given length of lane or roadway averaged over time. It is measured in vehicles per unit distance if the entire facility is of concern. It can also be represented in vehicles per unit distance per lane when considering one lane of a facility. It is a measure of how many vehicles are on a stretch of roadway at the same instant, or how dense the traffic is on the facility. The formula for density is as follows:

$$k = \frac{n}{l}$$

where k = density, veh/m (veh/km)
$\quad$ n = number of vehicles occupying the same length of roadway at a specific point of time
$\quad$ l = the length of roadway about which the density is measured, mi (km)

Traffic density can vary from a value of 0—implying a total absence of vehicles on the facility—to a value of 100 percent representing bumper-to-bumper traffic and vehicles at a standstill. Factors affecting density include the length of vehicles and the distance gap between vehicles. Density terms of note include jam density, which represents the upper limit of density on a facility, typically at breakdown. Optimum density is the density level that exists when traffic is flowing at full capacity.

3.3.4   Occupancy and Related Parameters

Occupancy is a traffic flow parameter that is related to density. Often called percent occupancy, occupancy is the percentage of time at a single point or short section of freeway is occupied by vehicles. It is not the vehicle occupancy, which is the number of occupants in a single vehicle but rather the fraction of time that vehicles are over a detector at the measurement point.[2] It is related to the average vehicle length in the traffic stream as well as the number of vehicles on the facility at the same time. The basic equation for occupancy, reflected as a percentage, is noted below:

$$OCC = \frac{\sum_{i=1}^{n} t_i}{T} \times 100$$

where t_i = the amount of time a point on the roadway is occupied by one vehicle
$\quad$ T = the total length of time in the measurement period

Occupancy can range from a value of 0 percent, which represents an absence of vehicles to 100 percent, which represents vehicles being completely stopped on a roadway. Occupancy is related to density, and is represented by the following equation:

$$k = \frac{10}{L_V = L_D} \%OCC$$

where k = density
$\quad$ L_V = average vehicle length (ft/m)
$\quad$ L_D = average zone length (ft/m)
$\quad$ %OCC = percent occupancy

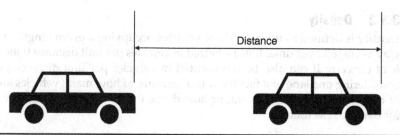

FIGURE 3.6   Vehicle spacing diagram.

Occupancy is related to the spacing of vehicles on the roadway. Vehicle spacing describes the distance between successive vehicles in a lane of traffic, measured from the same point on those vehicle (e.g., the front). As illustrated in Fig. 3.6, the headway is the distance between the front of each vehicle in a travel lane, measured at a single point on the roadway.

The distance gap, as illustrated in Fig. 3.7, is the space between two vehicles. It is measured at a single point and is marked between the rear of the front vehicle and the front of the next vehicle.

Headway is the time between successive vehicles as they pass a point along a travel lane.

Measured from same point on vehicles (as illustrated in Fig. 3.8), such as the front of the vehicle, the headway between the vehicles is the difference between t_2 (the time V_2 arrives and the designated point) and t_1 (the time V_1 arrives at the designated point). Likewise, time gap, which is illustrated in Fig. 3.9, is the time difference between the passing of the rear of the front vehicle and the front of the next subsequent vehicle.

3.3.5   Speed-Flow-Density Relationship

The three traffic flow parameters of speed, flow, and density have general relationship that was first identified nearly a century ago.[3] The general relationship for uninterrupted flow is shown in the formula below:

$$q = uk$$

where q = flow rate, vehicles per hour
u = speed, mph/km/h
k = density (vehicles per mi/vehicles per km)

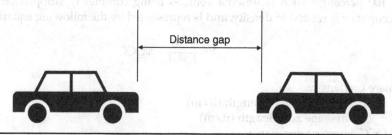

FIGURE 3.7   Vehicle gap diagram.

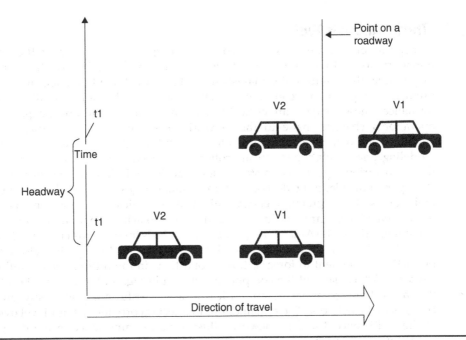

Figure 3.8 Vehicle headway.

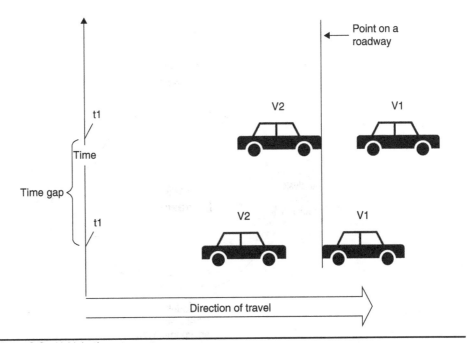

Figure 3.9 Vehicle time gap.

3.4   Traffic Analysis Tools

Transportation practitioners are frequently charged with analyzing the complex transportation network for a multitude of purposes. To undertake these analyses, they frequently turn to traffic analysis tools that allow them to model, simulate, and predict the impact of a broad range of actions on traffic flow and overall system performance. These analyses are critical to ensuring that any additions, expansions, or operational changes made to the network or specific facilities improve overall efficiency and help to meet the overall goals and objectives of the region. Analysis, modeling, and simulation (AMS) are collectively an assortment of tools and strategies that help various agencies and stakeholders evaluate design changes or operational strategies at the planning, design, and operational stages. Through the use of various tools and assets, the practitioner can evaluate how traffic flow might be managed and driver behavior might be influenced in real time to achieve operational and performance objectives. The AMS strategy of traffic analysis involves the creation of a model to analyze the supply and demand during a specified time period along with a predictive component to forecast travel conditions in the future. The overall framework of AMS consists of the components shown in Fig. 3.10. It is important to note that all of these components are critical to a successful analysis of any proposed changes to the network. The remainder of this section provides a high-level overview of the AMS concept and framework, illustrating its importance in the design and operation of the transportation system.

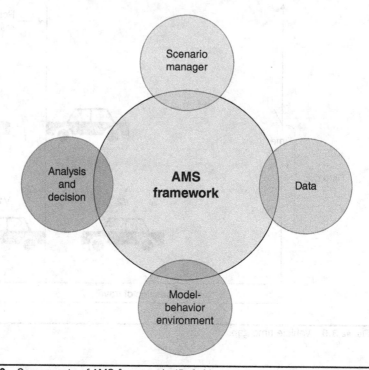

FIGURE 3.10   Components of AMS framework. (*Ref. 4.*)

The first component of the AMS framework is the scenario manager. The manager creates multiple scenarios from which the transportation analyst can choose (e.g., addition of capacity, lane closure due to incidents, change in traffic patterns, modification of signal timing plan). The scenario generator provides the necessary demand and supply updates to the transportation network simulator being used by the practitioner, which in turn replicates the real world in a simulation-based modeling environment. The second component of the AMS framework is data. The importance of data cannot be overstated. Whether historical or real-time in nature, data from multiple sources and modes generate the backbone of necessary inputs for analysis in a virtual environment using simulation. Without high-quality valid data, the AMS framework will not generate high-quality valid results.[3]

The model-based environment within the AMS framework creates a virtual simulated world for the network analysis. This simulation environment monitors the system, predicts future performance, and evaluates the impacts of various actions, including any dynamic ones that may be of interest to the practitioner. The practitioner then analyzes the results of the model to determine which actions or strategies are appropriate for the network. These strategies are compared against selected measures of effectiveness (MOEs) collected from network simulators. If the network simulator is being used for real-time operations, the practitioner will likely use a decision support system (DSS) to evaluate the simulation results and propose the best strategies for implementation.[3]

The AMS environment allows transportation agencies to manage their systems more effectively using smarter transportation networks, which are virtually impossible to measure through traditional planning alone. Simulation-based tools of transportation systems and mobility management, using both real-time and historical data, can be incorporated into the system analysis and can be combined with an evaluation and/or design of traffic flows, determination of the most reliable mode of operation supply and demand, and their interaction with and impact on the entire system.[3] The following sections outline elements needed in developing a modeling framework for AMS and demonstrate why AMS tools are becoming an important part of the decision-making process and the most appropriate method to analyze, model, and simulate traffic flow and operational strategies on a transportation network.

Traffic analysis and modeling tools can be generally grouped into a number of categories based on the level of detail required and the type of facility for which a practitioner might use them. Some of these tools are discussed elsewhere in this textbook in relation to specific topics:

- Sketch-planning tools—these tools evaluate alternatives or projects without performing a detailed traffic analysis and are appropriate for high-level analysis.
- Travel demand models—these models predict future travel demand based on existing conditions and projections of socioeconomic characteristics.
- Analytical/deterministic HCM-based tools—these tools evaluate the performance of isolated or small-scale facilities and are based on the HCM methodologies and procedures.[1]
- Real-time datasets—These datasets serve as the basis to analyze existing operations and estimate the effect of changes.

- Macroscopic simulation tools—These tools simulate traffic on a section-by-section basis[5] and are based on deterministic relationships of traffic network parameters (speed, flow, density). These tools were originally developed to simulate transportation subnetworks, such as freeways, corridors (including freeways and parallel arterials), surface-street grid networks, and rural highways.

- Microscopic simulation tools—these tools rely on car-following and lane-changing theories and simulate the movement of individual vehicles. They are particularly effective in analyzing congested conditions, complex geometric configurations of facilities, and system-level impacts of proposed transportation improvements that are beyond the limitations of other tool types.[4]

- Mesoscopic simulation tools—these tools combine the capabilities of both microscopic and macroscopic simulation models and consider the individual vehicle as the traffic flow unit, whose movement is governed by the average speed on a link. They typically have less fidelity than a microsimulation model, but provide more detail than a high-level planning analysis or sketch-planning tool.

- Traffic signal optimization tools—these tools develop optimal signal phasing and timing plans for isolated signal intersections, arterial streets, and signal networks.

- Ramp metering optimization tools—ramp meters are a unique signal application and a type of ramp control strategy. These tools are used to analyze ramp meter rates and the location of the downstream detector station. They are a type of ramp control strategy.

Each of the categories above has certain capabilities and limitations with regard to types of facilities that can be modeled by a tool, the phase of a particular transportation project (planning, design, operations/construction) during which the tool needs to be used, and the geographic scope of the study area (isolated locations, segments, corridors/small networks, region). For example, the HCM is the most widely used traffic analysis tool in the United States for evaluating isolated locations and roadway segments. The HCM procedures, some of which are discussed in Chap. 5, are appropriate and reliable for predicting whether a facility will be operating above or below capacity. The HCM procedures are static, macroscopic, and deterministic, but have limited capabilities in evaluating system-wide effects and dynamic traffic conditions, particularly in over-capacity conditions. Most of the HCM methods assume that the operation of a facility is not affected by traffic conditions on adjacent roadways. The HCM procedures become more complicated in analyzing queues, as they may extend upstream and affect other locations.

There are also some gaps in the HCM procedures as far as simulating complex operating strategies, such as those discussed in Chap. 8. However, some mesoscopic and microscopic simulation tools are theoretically capable of modeling the impacts of complex strategies, but their accuracy relies heavily on driver behavior models and compliance with any particular traffic control devices and messages, which may be difficult to calibrate and validate. The variety of these tools present challenges to the operating agencies as to which methodology or technique is appropriate for any one specific operating strategy. The purpose, the application area, the development cost/time, the required level of knowledge, hardware/software requirements, input parameters, and the expected output are some of the basic components that complicate the process of selecting the appropriate tool. Each category of tools has specific characteristics, input requirements, methodology, applicability, and limitations.

Simulation models are effective in capturing the dynamic evolution of traffic but require a significant amount of input data and manipulation of calibration parameters. Microsimulation typically requires significant computational time but tends to be accurate in modeling driver behavior if the significant effort to calibrate the model has been successful. Mesoscopic simulation, on the other hand, is less computationally intensive and reveals a less detailed modeling of driver behavior.[3] Additionally, practitioners and analysts should take other factors into account, such as selected and preferred performance measures, availability of real-time and historical data, and available evaluation resources. All these factors should be considered when determining the study area, and, in some cases, the study area should be considered when selecting possible performance measures, the appropriate analysis tools, and the evaluation resources required. Each traffic analysis or operational strategy has its own unique properties, so it is important to determine the adequate size for modeling them. Network sizes for freeways and arterials are categorized into three categories:

- Segment level (less than 1 mi)—these types of strategies are geared toward localized segments or intersections at a microscopic level. Typically, these are strategies that are lane-based and do not require extended roadway to simulate and analyze and require less effort in data collection.

- Corridor level (up to 5 mi)—these types of strategies usually require longer segments of roadway where merge/weave locations can be captured. The analysis models are usually microscopic in nature, and MOEs are typically associated with those used by engineers (e.g., average speed, travel time, travel time reliability). Typical corridor sections include a series of consecutive travel links on a major corridor as well as intersections, interchanges, parallel arterials (e.g., frontage roads), cross-streets, and entrance/exit ramps.

- Regional level (greater than 5 mi)—these types of strategies require larger networks to capture the full effect. The models are typically mesoscopic in nature in order to capture the regional effects of route choices and diversions given various network conditions and user classes (e.g., regular commuters, tourists). Mesoscopic models are node- and link-based, so they are most useful when considering the transportation network at a system level. MOEs from regional models usually are consistent with those used in regional planning (e.g., vehicle-miles traveled, travel time reliability).

3.5 Roadway Capacity

Transportation represents a service, and the transportation profession is charged with providing a service that meets the needs and expectations of the customer. Thus, it is important to understand to what extent the constructed system is capable of providing that service, and if that service is received by the system user. Transportation professionals typically capture these measures of transportation system performance using two concepts: level of service (LOS) and capacity. Both of these concepts represent the characteristics of the transportation facility and represent the supply provided to the

System Element	Definition
Point	A place along a facility where conflicting traffic stream cross, merge, or diverge; where a single traffic stream is regulated by traffic control; and/or where a significant change in the segment capacity occurs.
Segment	A length of roadway between two points for which traffic volumes and physical characteristics generally remain the same.
Facility	Lengths of roadways, bicycles paths, and pedestrian walkways comprised of a series of connected series of segments and points.
Corridor	A set of parallel transportation facilities designed to move people from two locations as a whole.
Area	An interconnected set of transportation facilities that serve movements of system users within a specific geographic area as well as between adjacent areas.
System	All transportation facilities and modes within a particular region whose purpose is to provide mobility for all system users.

TABLE 3.1   Transportation System Elements (*Ref. 1.*)

system users. The demand that the users place on the system is a separate topic, which is discussed in Chap. 7. This section introduces the concepts of capacity and LOS; and provides an overview of these measures for various types of transportation facilities, including freeways, multilane and two-lane highways, signalized intersections, and unsignalized intersections.

In order to discuss the concept of transportation system capacity, one needs to have a basic understanding of the vocabulary used by transportation professional to discuss the elements of the transportation system. The basic terms used in this context are provided in Table 3.1 along with definitions for each.[1] They essentially represent a series of elements that describe the transportation network in smaller and more refined components. They are important because they reflect the elements that practitioners analyze in terms of capacity for design and operational purposes.

3.5.1   Capacity

Capacity is defined as the maximum hourly flow that can be sustained on a uniform transportation system segment or pass a point during a specific period of time under prevailing conditions.[1] This quantitative value is independent of the demand on the system in the sense that it does not depend on the total number of system users who are demanding service on the element. Capacity is typically separated into vehicle capacity and person capacity. Vehicle capacity is the number of vehicles that can pass a point or through a uniform segment during a specific time period under prevailing conditions. Vehicle capacity is typically measured in vehicles per unit of time, such as vehicles per hour or passenger cars per hour. Person capacity is the number of persons that can pass a given point or through a uniform segment during a specific time period under prevailing conditions. Person capacity is typically measured in persons per unit of time, such as persons per hour. Flow is defined as the rate at which system users, typically vehicles, pass a certain point or travel through a segment, measured in vehicles per unit of time. Unlike capacity, flow is a function of the demand vehicles or persons place on the system and is independent of the facility.

3.5.2 Conditions Impacting Capacity

An important qualifying phrase in the definition of capacity is "under prevailing conditions." This phrase recognizes that a facility can have an ideal capacity and a practical capacity. The ideal capacity is that which can be expected under ideal conditions. However, the reality is that conditions on a facility are rarely ideal. In that regard, practical capacity reflects the capacity that can be expected given any conditions that might impact capacity: prevailing conditions. Table 3.2 presents the categories of conditions that can impact capacity: base, roadway, traffic, control, and technology. It provides a brief listing of specific factors under each category that can impact the capacity of a facility. Specific informations related to these factors are discussed within the context of the different types of facilities in the later sections of this chapter.

3.5.3 Level of Service

While capacity is a quantitative description of a facility, LOS is a qualitative term that represents the quality of transportation service that a user might experience on a facility. In other words, it embodies a variety of elements that describe a facility, including:

- Waiting time
- Freedom to maneuver
- Comfort of the system users
- Delay
- Speeds
- Travel times
- Safety
- Cost

Condition	Typical Impacting Factors
Base	• Good weather • Good and dry pavement conditions
Roadway	• Number of lanes • Lane widths • Shoulder widths and lateral clearances • Design speed • Horizontal and vertical alignments • Availability of exclusive turn lanes at intersections
Traffic	• Vehicle types (i.e., passenger vehicles, trucks, busses, recreational vehicles) • Directional and lane distribution • Driver population
Control	• Traffic signals • STOP and YIELD control • Other regulations
Technology	• Intelligent Transportation Systems (ITS)

TABLE 3.2 Typical Conditions Impacting Capacity (*Ref. 1.*)

Many of these elements are addressed elsewhere in this textbook, illustrating their inter-relationships with the ability for a transportation network to meet safety and mobility goals and provide a service to the traveling public. The LOS of a highway is typically designated a letter from A to F. LOS A represents the best operating conditions with an unrestricted ability to maneuver along a segment with little traffic or other conditions to impact progress. LOS F represents the worst operating conditions with congested lanes with too much traffic and other conditions that restrict one's ability to use the facility. Additional information related to LOS will be provided in later sections within the context of capacity.

The handbook used by transportation professionals for measuring capacity and LOS is the HCM. Developed by a standing committee of the Transportation Research Board, this document represents the cumulated wisdom of transportation researchers conducted over numerous decades.[1] The standing committee is charged with the periodic update of this document, and works to ensure that the latest research is included to better refine the methodology and the present new and emerging capacity-related topics to practitioners. The HCM covers two broad categories of facilities: uninterrupted flow facilities and interrupted flow facilities. The basic flow facilities for each of these categories are covered in the following sections to illustrate the methodology for determining the capacity of these facilities and understanding how the various factors impact capacity. The rest of these facilities are beyond the scope of the text, but in-depth detail regarding these analyses can be found in the HCM.

3.6 Capacity of Uninterrupted Flow Facilities

As discussed previously, uninterrupted flow facilities include freeway facilities, basic freeway segments, freeway weaving segments, freeway merge and diverge segments, multilane highways, and two-lane highways. For freeways, the HCM has specified that the base conditions under which capacity can be measured include:

- Good weather conditions
- Good visibility
- Good pavement conditions
- No traffic incidents
- No work zones
- No heavy vehicles in the traffic stream
- A driver population that is primarily made up of regular users of the facility
- 12-Ft lanes
- 6 ft of lateral clearance on the right side of the facility[1]

Under more restrictive conditions, one would expect more conservative driving behavior and traffic flow, yielding a lower capacity.

A basic freeway segment can be described using three performance measures:

- Density, which measures the congestion of traffic, measured in passenger cars per mile per lane (pc/mi/ln)
- Space mean speed, measured in miles per hour (mi/h)
- The volume-to-capacity ratio (v/c) that is a measure of the volume of traffic on the roadway normalized to the capacity of the roadway

LOS	Density (pc/mi/ln)
A	≤11
B	>11–18
C	>18–26
D	>26–35
E	>35–45
F	Demand exceeds capacity OR density > 45

TABLE 3.3 LOS Criteria for Basic Freeway Segments (*Ref. 1.*)

3.6.1   LOS, Density, Speed, and Flow Rates

The HCM measures LOS to specific densities, as illustrated in Table 3.3 and for which the speed-flow curves are illustrated in Fig. 3.11.

The speed flow curves are based on the equations presented in Table 3.4, illustrating the range of flows that exist for basic freeway segments for different speeds.

3.6.2   Computing LOS and Capacity for a Basic Freeway Segment

The steps for determining a facilitie's LOS or capacity for a signalized intersection basic freeway segment includes a series of computations that start with the FFS and refine that speed based on variations from the base conditions. A generalized process is illustrated in Fig. 3.12.

Step 1: Collect Input Data

To analyze a basic freeway segment for capacity and LOS, various data elements are required that describe the geometric and demand characteristics of the segment. The required input data are provided in Table 3.5.

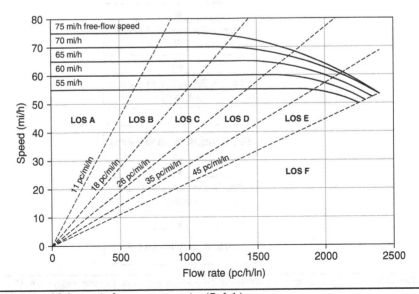

FIGURE 3.11 LOS for basic freeway segments. (*Ref. 1.*)

FFS (mi/h)	Flow Rate Range			Capacity
	Breakpoint	≥0≤Breakpoint	≥Breakpoint ≤Capacity	
75	1000	75	$75 - 0.00001107(v_p - 1000)^2$	2400
70	1200	70	$70 - 0.00001160(v_p - 1200)^2$	2400
65	1400	65	$65 - 0.00001418(v_p - 1400)^2$	2350
60	1600	60	$60 - 0.00001816(v_p - 1600)^2$	2300
55	1800	55	$55 - 0.00002469 (v_p - 1800)^2$	2250

TABLE 3.4 Equations Describing Speed Flow Curves for LOS for Basic Freeway Segments (*Ref. 1.*)

Step 2: Estimate and Adjust FFS

Once the input data have been collected, the FFS can be calculated using the following formula:

$$FFS = BFFS - f_{LW} - f_{LC} - 3.22 TRD^{0.81}$$

where FFS = free-flow speed
  BFFS = base FFS for the basic freeway segment (mph/h)
  f_{LW} = adjustment factor for lane widths (mi/h)
  f_{LC} = adjustment factor for lateral clearance (mi/h)
  TRD = total ramp density (ramps/mi)

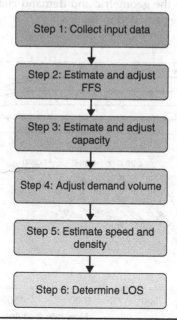

Step 1: Collect input data

Step 2: Estimate and adjust FFS

Step 3: Estimate and adjust capacity

Step 4: Adjust demand volume

Step 5: Estimate speed and density

Step 6: Determine LOS

FIGURE 3.12 LOS and capacity computational steps for basic freeway segments. (*Ref. 1.*)

Required Input Data	Data Elements
Freeway data	• Free-flow speed (FFS) • Number of mainline freeway lanes in one direction • Lane width • Right-side lateral clearance • Total ramp density • Terrain (i.e., level, rolling, mountainous, length and percent grade)
Demand data	• Demand during the analysis hour or daily demand • Presence of heavy vehicles • Peak hour factor (PFH) • Driver population factor
Length of analysis period	• The analysis period for the freeway analysis; typically the peak 15-min period with the peak hour

TABLE 3.5 Required Input Data for Basic Freeway Segments (*Ref. 1.*)

If the average lane width in the basic segment is less than 12 ft, then the adjustment factor for the reduced lane width needs to be used. As noted previously, if the lanes are narrower than typical, a driver may operate their vehicle in a more cautious manner to ensure they stay within the lane. The adjustment factors for average lane width are shown in Table 3.6.

If the clearance on the right side of the basic freeway segment is less than the typical 6 ft, then the FFS needs to be adjusted according to the factors provided in Table 3.7. Note that the more lanes the segment has, the less impact the reduced right-side clearance has on the FFS. Total ramp density is a measure of the impact of merging and diverging vehicles on FFS.

The practitioner can further adjust the FFS for a basic freeway segment to account for such conditions as work zones, weather, or local conditions. The formula for calculating this adjusted speed is the following:

$$FFS_{adj} = FFS \times SAF$$

where FFS_{adj} = the adjusted free-flow speed
FFS = free-flow speed
SAF = the speed adjustment factor

Typically, for basic freeway segments, the SAF is equal to 1.

Average Lane Width (ft)	Reduction in FFS, f_{LW} (mi/h)
≥12	0.0
≥11–12	1.9
≥10–11	6.6

TABLE 3.6 Adjustment to FFS for Average Lane Width, f_{LW} (*Ref. 1.*)

Right-Side Lateral Clearance (ft)	Lanes in One Direction			
	2	3	4	≥5
>6	0.0	0.0	0.0	0.0
5	0.6	0.4	0.2	0.1
4	1.2	0.8	0.4	0.2
3	1.8	1.2	0.6	0.3
2	2.4	1.6	0.8	0.4
1	3.0	2.0	1.0	0.5
0	3.6	2.4	1.2	0.6

TABLE 3.7   Adjustment to FFS for Right-Side Lateral Clearance, f_{LC} (Ref. 1.)

Step 3: Estimate and Adjust Capacity

Once the FFS is adjusted based on the various factors, the appropriate FFS curve is selected from Fig. 3.11. If the adjusted FFS does not fall exactly on one of the curves, the FFS should be rounded to the nearest 5 mi/h based on the following criteria[1]:

- ≥72.5 mi/h < 77.5: use FFS = 75
- ≥67.5 mi/h < 72.5: use FFS = 70
- ≥62.5 mi/h < 67.5: use FFS = 65
- ≥57.5 mi/h < 62.5: use FFS = 60
- ≥52.5 mi/h < 57.5: use FFS = 55

However, the capacity can also be calculated using the following formula:

$$c(\text{basic freeway segment}) = 2200 + 10 \times (\text{FFS}_{adj} - 50)$$

where c = capacity for a basic freeway segment
FFS_{adj} = the adjusted free-flow speed

Step 4: Adjust Demand Value

The next step is to adjust the demand volume by converting it to the flow rates expressed in passenger cars per hour as used in the speed-flow curves. The following equation is used to make this adjustment:

$$v_p = \frac{V}{\text{PHF} \times N \times f_{HV}}$$

where v_p = demand flow rate under equivalent base conditions (pc/h/ln)
V = demand volume under prevailing conditions (veh/h)
PHF = peak hour factor, which reflects variation in traffic flow within an hour
N = number of lanes in analysis direction
f_{HV} = adjustment factor for presence of heavy vehicles in traffic stream[1]

PCE	PCE by Type of Terrain	
	Level	Rolling
E_T	2.0	3.0

TABLE 3.8 Passenger Car Equivalents for Heavy Vehicles (*Ref. 1.*)

The operational characteristics of heavy vehicles are such that they have a negative impact on the traffic flow on a facility. The formula for calculating the heavy vehicle factors is as follows:

$$f_{HV} = \frac{1}{1 + P_T(E_T - 1)}$$

where f_{HV} = adjustment factor for presence of heavy vehicles in traffic stream
P_T = proportion of heavy vehicles in traffic stream
E_T = passenger-car equivalent (PCE) of a heavy vehicle in traffic stream

The PCEs for heavy vehicles are provided in Table 3.8.

Step 5: Estimate Speed and Density
The next step is to estimate the speed and density for the traffic stream. The following equation is used to calculate the density, using a speed determined using Table 3.4.

$$D = \frac{v_p}{S}$$

where D = density (pc/mi/ln)
v_p = demand flow rate (pc/h/ln)
S = mean speed of traffic stream under base conditions (mi/h)[1]

Step 6: Determine LOS
Once the density is calculated, it is used to determine the LOS from Fig. 3.7.

Example Problem An urban freeway with a base FFS of 75 mph has a demand volume of 4960 vph. It has three 12-ft lanes in each direction with a right-side lateral clearance of 5 ft. The total ramp density is 1.0. The traffic stream is comprised of 12% heavy vehicles and a PHF of 0.90. The terrain is level throughout the segment, and the mean speed of the traffic stream is 73 mph. What is the level of service for the facility?

Compute FFS

$$\text{FFS} = \text{BFFS} - f_{LW} - f_{LC} - 3.22\text{TRD}^{0.81}$$

Based on the given information:

$f_{LW} = 0.0$
$f_{LC} = 0.4$
$T_{RD} = 10$
$\text{FFS} = 75 - f_{LW} - f_{LC} - 3.22\,\text{TRD}^{0.84} = 75 - 0.0 - 0.4 - 3.22(1.0)^{0.84} = 71.93$

Assuming the SAF is 1, then the FFS = 70

Adjust demand value

$$v_p = \frac{V}{\text{PHF} \times N \times f_{HV}}$$

Based on the given information:

$$\text{PHF} = 0.90$$
$$N = 3$$
$$V = 4960 \text{ vph}$$
$$f_p = 1.0$$
$$P_T = 0.12$$
$$E_T = 2.0 \text{ (from Table 3.8)}$$

Calculate f_{HV}

$$f_{HV} = \frac{1}{1 + P_T(E_{T-1})} = \frac{1}{1 + 0.12(2.0 - 1)} = 0.89$$

Calculate v_p

$$v_p = \frac{V}{\text{PHF} \times N \times f_{HW}} = \frac{4.960}{0.30 \times 3 \times 0.89} = 2064 \text{ pcphpl}$$

Estimate Density

$$D = \frac{V_p}{S} = \frac{2.064 \text{ pcphpl}}{73 \text{ mph}} = 28.3 \text{ pcpmpl}$$

Determine LOS

Based on Fig. 5.1, the LOS is D for this facility.

3.7   Capacity of Interrupted Flow Facilities

Interrupted flow facilities include urban street facilities, urban street segments, signalized intersections, two-way stop-controlled intersections, all-way stop-controlled intersections, roundabouts, interchange ramp terminals, and off-street pedestrian and bicycle facilities. The procedure for a signalized intersection is described in the following sections in order to illustrate the process and the variety of factors that impact capacity. Analyses for additional interrupted flow facilities are included in the HCM.

3.7.1   Capacity and LOS of a Signalized Intersection

The steps for determining a facilitie's LOS or capacity for a signalized intersection basic freeway segment include a series of computations that start with the FFS and refine that speed based on variations from the base conditions. A generalized process is illustrated in Fig. 3.13. For the purpose of this introduction to intersection capacity analysis, the first six steps of the process will be discussed.

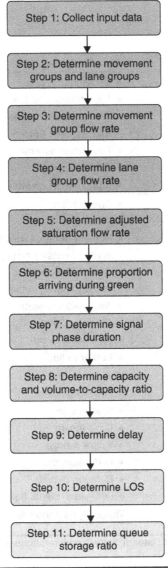

Figure 3.13   LOS and capacity computational steps for signalized intersections. (*Ref. 1.*)

Step 1: Collect Input Data

To analyze a signalized intersection for capacity and LOS, various data elements are required that describe the geometric and demand characteristics of the intersection. The required input data are provided in Table 3.9.

Step 2: Determine Movement Groups and Lane Groups

Once all of the necessary data have been collected, the next step is to determine the movement groups and lane groups for each intersection approach. Figure 3.14 illustrates the typical movement groups and lane groups that practitioners use for intersection capacity analysis.

Required Input Data	Data Elements
Traffic characteristics	• Demand flow rate of motorized vehicles • Right-turn-on-red flow rate • Permitted left-turn flow rate • Mid-segment 85th percentile speed • Pedestrian flow rate • Bicycle flow rate • Proportion of on-street parking occupied
Geometric design	• Street width • Number of lanes • Number of right turn islands • Width of outside through lane • Width of bicycle lane • Width of paved outside shoulder (or passing lane) • Total walkway width • Crosswalk width • Crosswalk length • Corner radius
Signal control	• Walk • Pedestrian clear • Rest in walk • Cycle length • Yellow change • Red clearance • Duration of phase serving pedestrians and bicycles • Pedestrian signal head presence
Other	The analysis period duration

TABLE 3.9   Required Input Data for Signalized Intersections (*Ref. 5.*)

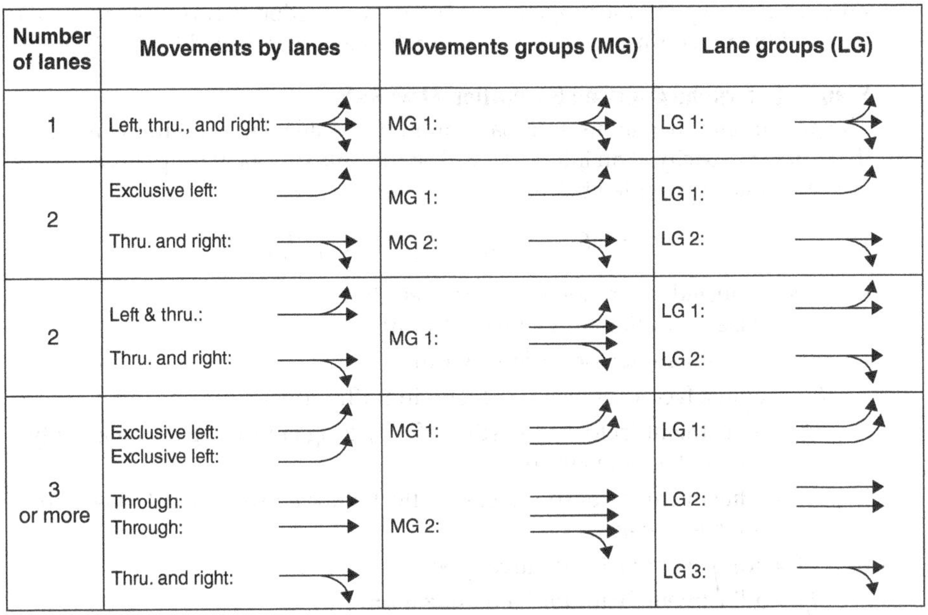

Number of lanes	Movements by lanes	Movements groups (MG)	Lane groups (LG)
1	Left, thru., and right:	MG 1:	LG 1:
2	Exclusive left:	MG 1:	LG 1:
	Thru. and right:	MG 2:	LG 2:
2	Left & thru.:	MG 1:	LG 1:
	Thru. and right:		LG 2:
3 or more	Exclusive left: Exclusive left:	MG 1:	LG 1:
	Through: Through:	MG 2:	LG 2:
	Thru. and right:		LG 3:

Figure 3.14 Typical movement groups and lane groups for analysis. (*Ref. 1.*)

When considering movement and lane groups, the practitioner should consider a number of rules. These rules include, but are not limited to:

- A turning movement that is served only by exclusive lanes but no shared lanes, it should be determined as a movement group.
- Exclusive left- or right-turn lane(s) should be determined as a separate lane group.
- Shared lanes should be determined to be a separate lane group.
- Any lanes that are not assigned to a movement group or a lane group should be combined into single movement or lane group, respectively.[1]

Step 3: Determine Movement Group Flow Rate

Once the movement groups have been designated, the practitioner needs to determine the flow rate for each movement group. Information on determining flow rates is provided earlier in this chapter. To address right-turns-on-red (RTOR), the RTOR flow rate is subtracted from the right-turn flow rate, regardless of whether the right turns occur from an exclusive or shared lane.[1]

Step 4: Determine Lane Group Flow Rate

Once the lane groups have been designated, the practitioner needs to determine the flow rates for each lane group. The process for determining the group flow rate is simplified if no shared lanes exist on each intersection approach. In those cases, the lane group flow rate is a one-to-one correspondence with movement group flow rate. If there are shared lanes, a more complex process is used to calculate the lane group flow rate, which is beyond the scope of this basic introduction to capacity analysis. Information and the process associated with this calculate are included in the HCM.[1]

Step 5: Determine Adjusted Saturation Flow Rate

The practitioner then adjusts the saturation flow rate to account for a variety of factors that impact capacity at an intersection. The formula for calculating this adjusted saturation flow rate is provided below:

$$S = S_0 f_w f_{HVg} f_p f_{bb} f_a f_{LU} f_{LT} f_{RT} f_{Lpb} f_{Rpb} f_{wz} f_{ms} f_{sp}$$

where s = adjusted saturation flow rate (veh/h/ln)

s_0 = base saturation flow rate (pc/h/ln)

f_w = adjustment factor for lane width

f_{HVg} = adjust factor for heavy vehicles in traffic stream

f_p = adjustment factor for existing of a parking lane and parking activity adjacent to lane group

f_{bb} = adjustment factor for blocking effect of local buses that stop within intersection area

f_a = adjustment factor for area type

f_{LU} = adjustment factor for lane utilization

f_{LT} = adjustment factor for left-turn vehicle presence in a lane group

f_{RT} = adjustment factor for right-turn vehicle presence in a lane group

f_{Lpb} = pedestrian adjustment factor for left-turn groups

f_{Rpb} = pedestrian-bicycle adjustment factor for right-turn groups

f_{wz} = adjustment factor for the presence of a work zone at the intersection

f_{ms} = adjustment factor for a downstream lane blockage

f_{sp} = adjustment factor for sustained spillback at the intersection[1]

Adjustment for Lane Width

The adjustment factor for lane width is provided in Table 3.10.

Adjustment for Heavy Vehicles and Grade

The formula for calculating the adjustment factor that accounts for heavy vehicles and grade at an intersection is as follows if the grade is negative (downhill on the approach):

$$f_{HVg} = \frac{100 - 0.79 P_{HV} - 2.07 P_g}{100}$$

Average Lane Width (ft)	Adjustment Factor (f_w)
<10.0	0.96
≥10.0–12.9	1.00
>12.9	1.04

TABLE 3.10 Lane Width Adjustment Factor (*Ref. 1.*)

and the following if the grade is positive (uphill on the approach):

$$f_{HVg} = \frac{100 - 0.79 P_{HV} - 2.07 P_g}{100}$$

where f_{HVg} = adjustment factor for heavy vehicles and the grade at the intersection
P_{HV} = percent heavy vehicles in the corresponding movement group (%)
P_g = the approach grade for the corresponding movement group[1]

Adjustment for Parking

The formula for calculating the factor associated with parking in the vicinity of the intersection is as follows:

$$f_p = \frac{N - 0.1 - \dfrac{18 N_m}{3600}}{N} \geq 0.05$$

where f_p = adjustment factor for parking in the vicinity of the intersection
N_m = parking maneuver rate adjacent to lane group (maneuvers/h)
N = number of lanes in lane group (ln)[1]

Adjustment for Bus Blockage

The formula for calculating the adjustment factor that accounts for blockages caused by buses is as follows:

$$f_{bb} = \frac{N - \dfrac{14.4 N_b}{3600}}{N} \geq 0.05$$

where f_{bb} = adjustment factor for bus blockage at the intersection
N_b = bus stopping rate on the subject approach (buses/h)
N = the number of lanes in lane group (ln)[1]

Adjustment for Area Type

The practitioner will need to modify the saturation flow rate depending on the area of a community in which the intersection is located. For example, in downtown areas, intersections are somewhat less efficient because of the high number of pedestrians or other geometric features that introduce increased headways. If the practitioner chooses to account for these conditions, the f_a used has a value of 0.90.[1]

Adjustment for Lane Utilization

For most circumstances, the lane utilization factor used to adjust the saturation flow rate is 1.0 if a lane group has one shared or one exclusive lane as part of the group.[1] For the purpose of this introduction to capacity calculations, it is assumed that the adjustment factor for lane utilization is 1.0. Additional information and the formula for calculating this adjustment factor are included in the HCM.[1]

Adjustment for Right Turns

The formula for calculating the adjustment factor that accounts for right turns at the intersection is as follows:

$$f_{RT} = \frac{1}{E_R}$$

where E_R = the equivalent number of through cars for a protected right-turning vehicle (=1.18).[1]

Adjustment for Left Turns

The formula for calculating the adjustment factor that accounts for left turns at the intersection is as follows:

$$f_{LT} = \frac{1}{E_L}$$

where E_L = the equivalent number of through cars for a protected left-turning vehicle (=1.05).[1]

Adjustment for Pedestrians and Bicycles

The presence of bicyclists and pedestrians at an intersection can create inefficiencies that reduce the saturation flow rate of a lane group. The conflict zone between these users and vehicles combined with the amount of green time during which conflicts exist in the zone impact the saturation flow rate. For the purpose of this introduction to capacity calculations, it is assumed that the adjustment factor for pedestrians and bicycles is 1.0. Additional information and the formula for calculating this adjustment factor is included in the HCM.[1]

Adjustment for Work Zone Presence

The presence of a work zone in the vicinity of an intersection can impact operations and reduce the overall saturation flow rate of an approach. The practitioner can account for the presence of a work zone if it is within 250 ft upstream of the stop line, then the practitioner can use a procedure for calculating this adjustment factor. For the purpose of this introduction to capacity calculations, it is assumed that the adjustment factor for work zone presence is 1.0. Additional information and the formula for calculating this adjustment factor is included in the HCM.[1]

Adjustment for Downstream Lane Blockage

Similar to a work zone, if a lane is blocked downstream of an intersection, the efficiency and saturation flow rate of the intersection is reduced. For the purpose of this introduction to capacity calculations, it is assumed that the adjustment factor for downstream lane blockage is 1.0. Additional information and the formula for calculating this adjustment factor is included in the HCM.[1]

Adjustment for Sustained Spillback

Spillback is used to describe the condition when a downstream intersection creates queues that spill back and impact an upstream intersection. For the purpose of this introduction to capacity calculations, it is assumed that the adjustment factor for sustained spillback is 1.0. Additional information and the formula for calculating this adjustment factor is included in the HCM.[1]

Step 6: Determine Proportion Arriving During Green
In this step, the practitioner determines what amount of the traffic demand arrives at the intersection during the green portion of signal cycle. This value is tied to delay and is calculated using the formula below:

$$P = R_p \left(\frac{g}{C} \right)$$

where P = proportion of vehicles arriving on green
$\quad R_p$ = platoon ratio
$\quad g$ = effective green time
$\quad C$ = cycle length

Step 7: Determine Signal Phase Duration
This step in the capacity analysis determines the length of the signal phase duration, which is based on the type of control, such as pre-time, semi-actuated, or fully actuated. Coordinated and uncoordinated control types are also factored into the determination. Additional details regarding the calculation of the signal phase duration are included in the HCM.[1]

Step 8: Determine Capacity and Volume-to-Capacity Ratio
The concept of volume-to-capacity ratio reflects the congestion level at the intersection and to what extent the demand on the intersection approaches the overall capacity of the intersection. It is calculated for each lane group and is a function of the demand flow rate and the capacity of the lane group. This step also assesses the critical volume-to-capacity ratio for the entire intersection. Additional details regarding the calculation of the volume-to-capacity ratio are included in the HCM.[1]

Step 9: Determine Delay
Delay is a fundamental performance measure across the spectrum of transportation systems. From the perspective of an intersection, delay is a measure of the average control delay experienced by all vehicles that arrive at an intersection during a designated analysis time period. In undersaturated conditions, delay is low because the intersection can handle the capacity that arrives during each cycle. In oversaturated conditions, queues build and cannot dissipate during a single signal cycle. Thus, delay increases significantly during oversaturation conditions. In general, delay is comprised of control delay, uniform delay, incremental delay, and initial queue delay.[1] Additional details regarding the calculation of delay and the various elements that make up the total intersection delay are included in the HCM.

Step 10: Determine LOS

The LOS of an intersection is determined for each lane group, each approach, and the intersection as a whole.[1] It is related to the conditions at the intersection (e.g., under-saturated vs. oversaturated) as well as what drivers will tolerate in terms of delay. Additional details regarding the determination of LOS are included in the HCM.

Step 11: Determine Queue Storage Ratio

The final step in the intersection analysis process is determining the ability of an inter-section to store a queue during the analysis period. Ideally, the signal timing plan should be able to handle demand without significant queues building up during each cycle. The queue storage ratio represents the amount of queue storage distance that is occupied at the point in the cycle when the last vehicle arrives at the back of the queue.[1] Additional details regarding the determination of the queue storage ratio are included in the HCM.

Example Problem   Calculate the adjusted saturation flow rate for an intersection lane group with two lanes with a base saturation flow rate of 1900 pc/h/ln and an average lane width of 9.8 ft. The facility has approximately 5% heavy vehicles, and the direction of traffic is a 4% downhill grade. The number of parking maneuvers each hour on the approach is 50, and the number of buses arriving is 25 in an hour. Assume that the area is in a central business district (CBD) and the adjustment factor is 0.90. Adjust for left turns and right turns at the intersection. Assume all other adjustment factors are 1.0.

$$s = s_0 f_w f_{HVg} f_p f_{bb} f_a f_{LU} f_{LT} f_{RT} f_{Lpb} f_{Rpb} f_{wz} f_{ms} f_{sp}$$

$$f_w = 0.96 \text{ (Table 3.10)}$$

$$f_{HVg} = \frac{100 - 0.79 P_{HV} - 2.07 P_g}{100} = \frac{100 - 0.79(0.05) - 2.08(0.04)}{100} = 0.99$$

$$f_p = \frac{N - 0.1 - \dfrac{18 N_m}{3600}}{N} \geq 0.05 \; f_p = \frac{N - 0.1 - \dfrac{18(50)}{3600}}{2} = 0.825$$

$$f_{bb} = \frac{N - \dfrac{14.4 N_b}{3600}}{N} \geq 0.05 \; f_{bb} = \frac{N - \dfrac{14.4(25)}{3600}}{N2} = 0.95$$

$$f_{RT} = \frac{1}{E_R} = \frac{1}{1.18} = 0.85$$

$$f_{LT} = \frac{1}{E_L} = \frac{1}{1.05} = 0.95$$

$$S = S_0 f_w f_{HVg} f_p f_{bb} f_a f_{LU} f_{LT} f_{RT} f_{Lpb} f_{Rpb} f_{wz} f_{ms} f_{sp}$$

$$S = (1900)(0.96)(0.99)(0.825)(0.95)(0.9)(1.0)(0.85)(0.95)(1)(1)(1)(1)(1) = 1029 \text{ pcphl}$$

3.8   Case Studies

3.8.1   SHRP2—Capacity Solutions

As discussed in Chap. 1, transportation practitioners continue to struggle to meet the demand placed on the transportation network. With the number of vehicle miles being traveled increasing each year and limited resources to expand the physical

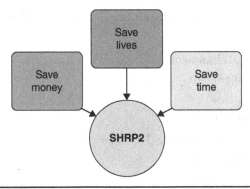

FIGURE 3.15   Objectives of SHRP2 Program. (*Ref. 7.*)

capacity of facilities, agencies are looking at innovative approaches to enhance capacity within existing strategies. The second Strategic Highway Research Program (SHRP2) was authorized in 2005 by the Safe, Accountable, Flexible, Efficient Transportation Equity Act: A Legacy for Users (SAFETEAL-LU)[6] and extended in 2012 by Moving Ahead for Progress in the 21st Century (MAP-21).[7] Throughout the course of the program, over 100 research projects addressed critical state and local challenges related to the transportation infrastructure.[8] The four themes of SHRP2 were safety, renewal, capacity, and reliability. Additionally, all of the projects funded by SHRP2 were intended to help transportation agencies, practitioners, and their stakeholders address three critical objectives to save lives, money, and time (see Fig. 3.15). The SHRP2 program recognized the connection between planning and operations. The cornerstone of the capacity projects is PlanWorks, which is a web-based resource for agencies to collaboratively work with regional stakeholders to deliver better transportation projects. The focus is to facilitate that collaboration and ensure that projects meet environmental, community, and mobility needs of the system users.[9] Other specific topics addressed through the capacity projects include the integration of freight transportation into highway capacity planning and decision, freight demand modeling, and expedited project delivery. All of these approaches work to ensure that capacity-related projects meet the needs of all system users, shorten construction time, improve safety of travelers and workers, decrease congestion, and enhance system reliability.

3.8.2   Roadway Improvements and Operational Capacity

The *Freeway Management and Operations Handbook* (FMOH) published by the Federal Highway Administration (FHWA) is a comprehensive document recognizing the importance of effective management and operations of the transportation network.[10] The reference manual provides information on a broad range of topics and strategies agencies undertake to better operate their network to meet the regional goals and objectives. These topics include innovative operational strategies the work to optimize the existing network footprint, many of which are discussed in Chap. 8. These topics include active transportation and demand management, ATM, integrated corridor management, managed lanes, and regional integration. In addition to these operational strategies, the FMOH examines specific roadway operational improvements that are directly tied to capacity and design features. These features include, but are not limited to:

- Horizontal alignment
- Vertical alignment
- Auxiliary lanes
- Shoulder widening
- High occupancy vehicle (HOV) lanes
- Acceleration lanes
- Deceleration lanes
- Climbing lanes
- Clear recovery zones
- Accident refuge areas
- Escape ramps
- Widening travel lanes
- Weaving segments
- Ramp configurations[9]

Each of these design features has the potential to add capacity to a facility depending on the existing geometric footprint and current operational characteristics. They represent the intersection of design and operations and reflect the ongoing effort to identify practical design alternatives that enhance capacity when combined with operational strategies to improve the overall management and operations of the network.

3.9   Summary

It is important to note that capacity analysis is only one part of the broader scope of transportation network assessment. As discussed in other chapters in this book, the transportation professional is charged with analyzing numerous aspects of the network for planning, design, and operations across a spectrum of issues. Other analyses consider such factors as noise, air quality, and economic impact. Multimodal planning analysis and system performance are also critical efforts that are related to capacity. These other analyses reinforce the reality that virtually every aspect of transportation is interrelated, and that virtually no element of the network can be analyzed in a vacuum. The practitioner needs to understand the interrelationships of these aspects of the network and work collaboratively to ensure that the system functions to meet the safety and mobility goals and objectives of the impacted jurisdiction.

Glossary of Acronyms

AADT—average annual daily traffic

ADT—average daily traffic

AMS—Analysis, modeling, and simulation

ATM—active traffic management

DSS—decision support system

FFS—free-flow speed

FHWA—Federal Highway Administration

HCM—Highway Capacity Manual

ITS—Intelligent Transportation Systems

k—density

LOS—level of service

MPO—metropolitan planning organization

PCE—passenger-car equivalent

PHF—peak hour factor

q—flow rate

RTOR—right-turn-on-red

SHRP2—Strategic Highway Research Program 2

SMS—space mean speed

TMS—time mean speed

TTI—Texas A&M Transportation Institute

u—speed

V—flow rate

V_{15}—peak 15-minute volume

Exercises

3.1 Calculate the PHF for a facility with an hourly flow rate of 4295 vehicles/hour and a peak 15-minute volume of 1095 vehicles.

3.2 Calculate the PHF for a facility with an hourly flow rate of 5394 vehicles/hour and a peak 15-minute volume of 1450 vehicles.

3.3 What is the peak 15-minute volume on a facility with a PHF of 0.97 and an hourly flow rate of 6840 vehicles/hour?

3.4 What is the peak 15-minute volume on a facility with a PHF of 0.94 and an hourly flow rate of 5375 vehicles/hour?

3.5 What is the hourly flow rate on a facility with a PHF of 0.91 and a peak 15-minute volume of 876 vehicles?

3.6 What is the hourly flow rate on a facility with a PHF of 0.89 and a peak 15-minute volume of 927 vehicles?

3.7 The speed of 10 vehicles were measured as spot speeds at the midpoint of a 0.75-mile (1.207 km) section of roadway. Calculate the TMS and SMS for the vehicles assuming each vehicle traveled the entire section of roadway at a uniform speed. The speeds collected were as follows:

Vehicle	Speed (mph)
1	66
2	63
3	70
4	72
5	65
6	64
7	65
8	69
9	64
10	65

3.8 The speed of 10 vehicles were measured as spot speeds at the midpoint of a 0.85-mile (1.368 km) section of roadway. Calculate the TMS and SMS for the vehicles, assuming each vehicle traveled the entire section of roadway at a uniform speed. The speeds collected were as follows:

Vehicle	Speed (mph)
1	75
2	74
3	76
4	78
5	85
6	75
7	74
8	72
9	73
10	77

3.9 The speed of 10 vehicles were measured as spot speeds at the midpoint of a 0.5-mile (0.805 km) section of roadway. Calculate the TMS and SMS for the vehicles, assuming each vehicle traveled the entire section of roadway at a uniform speed. The speeds collected were as follows:

Vehicle	Speed (mph)
1	69
2	70
3	70
4	68
5	72
6	75
7	71
8	79
9	75
10	74

3.10 The speed of 10 vehicles were measured as spot speeds at the midpoint of a 0.75-mile (1.207 km) section of roadway. Calculate the TMS and SMS for the vehicles, assuming each vehicle traveled the entire section of roadway at a uniform speed. The speeds collected were as follows:

Vehicle	Speed (mph)
1	55
2	60
3	61
4	58
5	54
6	55
7	56
8	57
9	54
10	55

3.11 An urban freeway with a base free-flow speed of 70 mph has a demand volume of 6750 vph. It has four 11-ft lanes in each direction with a right-side lateral clearance of 4 ft. The total ramp density is 1.2. The traffic stream is comprised of 8% heavy vehicles and a PHF of 0.94. The terrain is rolling throughout the segment, and the mean speed of the traffic stream is 68 mph. What is the level of service for the facility? What is the capacity?

3.12 An urban freeway with a base free-flow speed of 65 mph has a demand volume 4120 vph. It has three 12-ft lanes in each direction with a right-side lateral clearance of 6 ft. The total ramp density is 0.8. The traffic stream is comprised of 9% heavy vehicles and a PHF of 0.90. The terrain is level throughout the segment, and the mean speed of the traffic stream is 67 mph. What is the level of service for the facility? What is the capacity?

3.13 An urban freeway with a base free-flow speed of 75 mph has a demand volume of 6480 vph. It has five 11-ft lanes in each direction with a right-side lateral clearance of 3 ft. The total ramp density is 1.5. The traffic stream is comprised of 7% heavy vehicles and a PHF of 0.92. The terrain is rolling throughout the segment, and the mean speed of the traffic stream is 74 mph. What is the level of service for the facility? What is the capacity?

3.14 An urban freeway with a base free-flow speed of 70 mph has a demand volume of 4670 vph. It has three 10-ft lanes in each direction with a right-side lateral clearance of 3 ft. The total ramp density is 1.0. The traffic stream is comprised of 5% heavy vehicles and a PHF of 0.91. The terrain is rolling throughout the segment, and the mean speed of the traffic stream is 69 mph. What is the level of service for the facility? What is the capacity?

3.15 For an urban freeway, how many 12 ft lanes in each direction are needed to achieve LOS D on a freeway with a peak hour traffic volume of 5725 vph and with a PHF = 0.96? The traffic stream is comprised of 8% heavy vehicles and the location is rolling terrain. The right-side lateral clearance is 4 ft, and interchanges are spaced approximately 1.5 mi apart. The base free-flow speed is 70 mph.

3.16 Calculate the adjusted saturation flow rate for an intersection lane group with two lanes with a base saturation flow rate of 1900 pc/h/ln and an average lane width of 12 ft. The facility has approximately 2% heavy vehicles, and the direction of traffic is a 3% uphill grade. The number of parking maneuvers each hour on the approach is 75, and the number of buses arriving is 15 in an hour. Assume that the area is not in a CBD and the adjustment factor is 1.0. Adjust for left turns and right turns at the intersection. Assume all other adjustment factors are 1.0.

3.17   Calculate the adjusted saturation flow rate for an intersection lane group with three lanes with a base saturation flow rate of 1900 pcphpl and an average lane width of 12.8 ft. The facility has approximately 7% heavy vehicles, and the direction of traffic is a 4% uphill grade. The number of parking maneuvers each hour on the approach is 60, and the number of buses arriving is five in an hour. Assume that the area is not in a CBD and the adjustment factor is 1.0. Adjust for left turns and right turns at the intersection. Assume all other adjustment factors are 1.0.

3.18   Calculate the adjusted saturation flow rate for an intersection lane group with three lanes with a base saturation flow rate of 1900 pc/h/ln and an average lane width of 9.5 ft. The facility has approximately 10% heavy vehicles, and the direction of traffic is a 2.6% uphill grade. The number of parking maneuvers each hour on the approach is 125, and the number of buses arriving is 35 in an hour. Assume that the area is in a CBD and the adjustment factor is 0.9. Adjust for left turns and right turns at the intersection. Assume all other adjustment factors are 1.0.

References

1. *Highway Capacity Manual,* 6th Edition. Transportation Research Board, National Academy of Science, Washington, D.C., 2016.
2. *Traffic Flow Theory: A State-of-the-Art Report.* Organized by the Committee on Traffic Flow Theory and Characteristics (AHB45), http://tft.eng.usf.edu/docs/revised_monograph_2001.pdf (accessed June 2018).
3. Greenshields, B. "The Photographic Method of Studying Traffic Behavior." *Proceedings of the Thirteenth Annual Meeting of the Highway Research Board.* December 1933, Highway Research Board, Washington, D.C., 1934.
4. Kuhn, B., K. Balke, T. Lomax, J. Shelton, P. Songchitruksa, I. Tsapakis, M. Waisley, et al. *Planning and Evaluating Active Traffic Management Strategies.* NCHRP 03-114 Draft Final Guidebook. Unpublished. 2016.
5. Jeannotte, K., A. Chandra, V. Alexiadis, and A. Skabardonis. *Traffic Analysis Toolbox Volume II: Decision Support Methodology for Selecting Traffic Analysis Tools.* Report FHWA-HRT-04-039. Federal Highway Administration, U.S. Department of Transportation, Washington, D.C., June 2004.
6. "SAFETEA-LU, Safe Accountable Flexible Efficient Transportation Equity Act: A Legacy for Users." Federal Highway Administration, U.S. Department of Transportation, https://www.fhwa.dot.gov/safetealu/ (accessed January 28, 2017).
7. "MAP-21: Moving Ahead for Progress in the 21st Century." Federal Highway Administration, U.S. Department of Transportation, https://www.fhwa.dot.gov/map21/ (accessed January 28, 2017).
8. "About SHRP2," website, SHRP2 Solutions, Federal Highway Administration, U.S. Department of Transportation, https://www.fhwa.dot.gov/goshrp2/About (accessed June 2018).
9. "Capacity Solutions," website, SHRP2 Solutions, Federal Highway Administration. U.S. Department of Transportation, https://www.fhwa.dot.gov/goshrp2/Solutions/Capacity/List (accessed June 2018).
10. Hatcher, S., M. McGurrin, M. Vasudevan, L. Burgess, D. Haase, S. Levine, and G. Havinovski. *Freeway Management and Operations Handbook.* Report FHWA-HOP-17-031, Noblis, Inc., for Federal Highway Administration, U.S. Department of Transportation, Washington, D.C., July 2017.

CHAPTER 4

Traffic Control

4.1 Introduction

A fundamental component of any transportation system is the process of controlling traffic on that system. In addition to designing the physical elements of a facility, the transportation professional is responsible for designing the traffic control system that helps facilitate safe and efficient operations on the facility. The concept of traffic control covers a broad range of devices and topics, each of which plays an integral part in helping system users navigate the various facilities they encounter. It is critical for any transportation professional to understand traffic control, the various elements of this broad topic, and how traffic control supports safe and efficient mobility for all users. This chapter provides a discussion on the various devices and approaches to controlling traffic, including traffic control devices (TCDs); traffic signals, operations, and timing; and regional traffic signal operations programs.

4.2 Traffic Control Devices

For over 80 years, the Manual on Uniform Traffic Control Devices for Streets and Highways (MUTCD) has been the national standard for TCDs in the United States (US).[1] As illustrated in Figs. 4.1 and 4.2, early traffic signals and pedestrian signals look nothing like the ones used today. Additional examples of early warning signs for railroad grade crossings are shown in Figs. 4.3 and 4.4, both of which resemble to some extent the ones currently used to warn travelers of the presence of a railroad grade crossing. Over time, the transportation profession has worked to streamline and standardize the look and use of traffic control used on public rights of way. Since its initial introduction, the MUTCD has worked to provide uniformity in the traffic control system to help all system users navigate the transportation system safely.

The first edition of the MUTCD was published in 1935 by the American Association of State Highway Officials, which is now known as the American Association of State Highway and Transportation Officials (AASHTO). Since that time, the document has evolved to address the changing transportation landscape and the evolving needs of the users of that complex landscape. Since 1971, the Federal Highway Administration (FHWA) has administered the document and coordinates the periodic update of the document through the Code of Federal Regulations.[2] As technology evolves and new research results emerge, FHWA works with the National Committee on Uniform Traffic Control Devices (NCUTCD) to modify the MUTCD to ensure it meets the needs of the traveling public and represents the most current technology and knowledge available. The current version of the MUTCD is located online

Figure 4.1   Early traffic signal. (© *Texas A&M Transportation Institute [TTI]*.)

Figure 4.2   Early traffic signal with pedestrian indications. (© *TTI*.)

Figure 4.3   Early advance warning sign for railroad crossing. (© *TTI*.)

Figure 4.4   Early sign for railroad crossing. (© *TTI*.)

(https://mutcd.fhwa.dot.gov/) so that all transportation professionals responsible for the planning, design, construction, operations, maintenance, and enforcement as well as research of the transportation network always have ready access to the latest standards.

4.2.1   Definition, Purpose, and Principles

TCDs encompass a broad range of objects and elements that are found on the transportation network. Specifically, TCDs include all signs, signals, markings, and other devices that are used to regulate, warn, or guide traffic.[1] In general, these devices are those placed on, over, or adjacent to any public or private street, highway, or facility that accommodates the flow of vehicles, pedestrians, or bicycles. These facilities can include toll roads and private roads as well, so long as they are open to use by the public. Consider all of the devices that you have ever seen in your travels that provide some type of information related to the transportation system. The list of those devices is long, they have different types of messages, can be a number of different colors and color combinations, and they address a broad range of information they convey to users. Some of that information is very specific and direct, while some of that information may be subtle. Some of it may be about specific regulations, while some may serve as a warning to users about upcoming conditions. However, all of that information is important, and the uniformity of that information helps ensure that system users understand the message every time they see the device. The MUTCD provides guidance on how to design and place those devices to ensure their message is appropriately conveyed. Figure 4.5 illustrates the five key principles of TCDs. The MUTCD emphasizes that the design, placement, operation, maintenance, and uniformity of TCDs are essential to ensuring that each device meets these five principles.[1] It is important to note that the MUTCD sets the standards for TCDs, while state and local laws are needed to require road users to obey regulatory devices and regulations on the roadway.

The MUTCD uses several specific words to indicate the strength of the guidance provided. The four types of guidance provided in the MUTCD are shown in Table 4.1

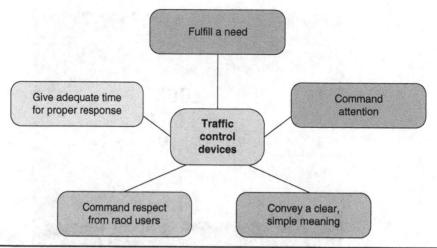

Figure 4.5   Principles of traffic control devices. (*Ref. 1.*)

Guidance	Definition	Verb Text
Standard	A statement of required, mandatory, or specifically prohibitive practice regarding a TCD.	Shall
Guidance	A statement of recommended, but not mandatory, practice in typical situations, with deviations allowed if engineering judgment or engineering study indicates the deviation to be appropriate.	Should
Option	A statement of practice that is a permissive condition and carries no requirement or recommendation.	May
Support	An informational statement that does not convey any degree of mandate, recommendation, authorization, prohibition, or enforceable condition.	—

Table 4.1   Guidance Levels in MUTCD (*Ref. 1.*)

along with verbs used in the text to indicate how the transportation professional is to proceed when applying the guidance.

The MUTCD contains guidance on all TCDS that fall into the following categories:

- Signs
  - Regulatory signs, barricades, and gates
  - Warning signs and object markers
  - Guide signs for conventional roads, freeway, and expressways
  - Toll road signs
  - Preferential and managed lane signs and general information signs
  - General service signs, specific service signs, tourist-oriented directional signs, changeable message signs, recreational and cultural interest are signs, and emergency management signing

- Markings
- Highway traffic signals
- TCDs for low-volume roads
- Temporary traffic control
- Traffic controls for school areas
- Traffic control for railroad and light rail transit grade crossings
- Traffic control for bicycle facilities

The information addresses the design, placement, operation, maintenance, uniformity, responsibility, and the authority for placement of TCDs in the transportation network.

4.2.2 Design

The MUTCD provides specific guidance related to the design of TCDs. This guidance covers a broad range of elements of the design, including size, shape, color, composition, message, lighting, and contrast. All of these elements, when combined appropriately, are intended to draw attention to the device so that travelers can see the device clearly, process the message appropriately, and take appropriate action.[1] Recall that in Chap. 2, the system user is one of the three elements of the roadway system, and specific characteristics and factors impact how that user interacts with the roadway environment. The uniformity of TCDs plays into these characteristics by helping minimize the amount of time a driver needs to process the information provided and make appropriate decisions related to their control, guidance, and navigation on the network.

One design element included in the MUTCD is the color of TCDs. Thirteen colors are designated for use for TCDs, with 11 of them being specifically identified as have a particular meaning. Table 4.2 provides the list of colors along with their meanings and examples of that color in use. The examples provided are all traffic signs that one might see along a roadway facility. However, these colors are also used for pavement markings, such as on a roadway centerlines and edge lines.

A key element to the use of color is the combination of specific colors with a particular sign shape. Along with color, the shape of a sign can alert system users to the type of information displayed on the sign.[3] The sign, shape, and color combinations used in the MUTCD are provided in Table 4.3.

The MUTCD addresses a broad range of applications of TCDs. However, work zones present additional challenges due to the temporary nature of the traffic control and the unfamiliar conditions associated with construction. Workers are typically present, and operational conditions are frequently atypical. Various resources are readily available to transportation professionals to ensure the best design and operations of work zones across a broad range of applications. Much of that information centers on the appropriate design, installation, and operation of TCDs within work zone. The National Work Zone Safety Information Clearinghouse[4] is a comprehensive collection of information on roadway construction zone safety. Additionally, FHWA has a work zone management program that provides resources for professionals who focus on effective work zone traffic management to minimize traffic delays, maintain motorist and worker safety, and maintain access while ensuring the timely completion of construction.[5]

Color	Meaning	Example
Black	Regulation	ONLY
Blue	Road user services guidance, tourist information, and evacuation route	INFO
Brown	Recreational and cultural interest area guidance	BOAT LAUNCH AREA (RW-080)
Coral	Unassigned	—
Fluorescent pink	Incident management	—
Fluorescent yellow-green	Pedestrian warning, bicycle warning, playground warning, school bus and school warning	
Green	Indicated movements permitted, direction guidance	FREEWAY ENTRANCE
Light blue	Unassigned	—

TABLE 4.2   Color Code Standard for Traffic Control Devices (*Refs. 1 and 3.*)

Color	Meaning	Example
Orange	Temporary traffic control	FLAGGER AHEAD (W20-7a)
Purple	Lanes restricted to use only by vehicles and registered electronic toll collection (ETC) accounts	Toll Pass ONLY ↓
Red	Stop or prohibition	STOP
White	Regulation	SPEED LIMIT 50
Yellow	Warning	

TABLE 4.2   Color Code Standard for Traffic Control Devices (*Refs. 1 and 3.*) (*Continued*)

Shape/Color	Meaning
Round/red	Regulatory
Diamond/yellow	Warning
Rectangle/green	Guide
Square/blue	Services
Diamond/orange	Construction
Square/brown	Recreation
Pentagon/fluorescent yellow-green	School zone
Diamond/fluorescent pink	Incident management

TABLE 4.3   Meaning of Sign, Shape, and Color Combination of Traffic Control Devices (*Ref. 3.*)

4.3   Traffic Signals

When drivers approach an intersection of two roadways, they are faced with one of four general methods of intersection control. They will encounter a situation where the basic rules of the road apply, a YIELD sign, a STOP sign, or a traffic signal.[6] The use of these methods of control is a function of a variety of factors, including but not limited to the location of the intersection, its overall design, the number of roads or "legs" at the intersection, the width of the roadways (i.e., number of lanes), and the amount and type of traffic moving through the intersection (i.e., vehicles, bicycles, pedestrians). Since traffic control of any type interrupts the flow of traffic at the intersection, the general concept is to implement the lowest form of control as possible while ensuring the safe and efficient operation at the intersection. The transportation engineer has a variety of alternatives at their disposal to help improve the safety and operation of an intersection without installing a traffic signal. These options include, but are not limited to:

- Installation of warning signs and/or flashing beacons in advance of the intersection
- Relocation of stop lines to improve sight distance
- Installation of roadway lighting to improve visibility at night
- Revision of the geometrics at an intersection to address various operational issues
- Restriction of certain movements, perhaps during specific times of the day
- Installation of a roundabout[1]

Many of these strategies can address problems at a YIELD or STOP sign-control intersection. If after the installation of these devices or application of these strategies does not improve the intersection to the extent desired, the next step is the consideration of the installation of a traffic signal.

4.3.1   Traffic Signal Warrants

Traffic signals are the highest form of intersection control that transportation engineers work with on a regular basis. They are typically the last resort to control an intersection for safety and efficiency. Since signals interrupt the flow of traffic for extended

Warrant Number	Title
Warrant 1	Eight-hour vehicular volume
Warrant 2	Four-hour vehicular volume
Warrant 3	Peak hour
Warrant 4	Pedestrian volume
Warrant 5	School crossing
Warrant 6	Coordinated signal system
Warrant 7	Crash experience
Warrant 8	Roadway network
Warrant 9	Intersection near a grade crossing

TABLE 4.4 MUTCD Traffic Signal Warrants (*Ref. 1.*)

periods—thereby possibly reducing the efficiency of the intersection—the transportation professional must conduct an engineering study to determine if a signal is warranted. The MUTCD standard requires a transportation professional to perform an engineering study to assess whether the traffic conditions, pedestrian characteristics, or physical characteristics at an intersection warrant a traffic signal.[1] However, it is important to note that even if an intersection satisfies a warrant, the transportation professional should use engineering judgment to decide whether to install a signal. The nine warrants included in the MUTCD are provided in Table 4.4.

A review of these warrants indicates that they focus on a variety of conditions: vehicular traffic moving through the intersection, pedestrian traffic moving through the intersection, crashes at the intersection, and the presence of other factors that impact the operation of the intersection. Prior to conducting a traffic signal warrant analysis, the transportation professional must gather relevant data to ensure they have the information required for the analyses. This data might include:

- Vehicular volumes for each traffic movement for each approach across a variety of time periods
- Classification of data with respect to vehicular volumes
- Pedestrian volumes and information on nearby facilities that might serve children, the elderly, or individuals with disabilities
- Crash statistics, including diagrams of collisions (1 year minimum, 3–5 year preferred)
- A comprehensive diagram of the intersection[6]

Once the transportation engineer has gathered the appropriate data, they can conduct a warrant analysis to determine whether a signal is warranted at the intersection. If one is warranted, the engineer should then use engineering judgment to determine whether the signal is the best option. Engineering judgment is defined in the MUTCD as follows:

"...the evaluation of available pertinent information, and the application of appropriate principles, provisions, and practices...for the purpose of deciding upon the applicability, design, operation, or installation of a traffic control devices."[1]

In other words, the transportation engineer should assess all information—not just the warrant analysis—to determine whether a signal should be installed. This assessment holds for all TCDs as well, not just signals. Additional details associated with traffic signal warrants, including the specific thresholds for conditions that warrant a signal, are provided in Chap. 4C of the MUTCD.[1]

4.3.2 Traffic Signal Operations

A traffic signal is designed to assign right of way to different movements at an intersection to avoid conflicting movements. As with overall intersection control, the less interference with the flow of vehicles and other users at the intersection the more efficient the operations. Every traffic signal functions by means of a traffic signal controller unit. Essentially, a controller unit is a computer that is installed near the intersection in a special cabinet. The controller contains the timing plans for the intersection and is connected to the signal equipment in the field. It is also connected to any detection technology in the field that provides information on traffic approaching or at the intersection.

To understand how traffic signals work and how to design them appropriately, the transportation engineer first needs to understand the vocabulary associated with signals and signal timing. Table 4.5 provides definitions for a number of terms frequently used in the design and operation of traffic signal systems and timing plans.

As noted above, a traffic signal cycle is one complete sequence of indications serving all movements at an intersection. As illustrated in Fig. 4.6, a cycle provides each movement (through movements and turning movements) to move through the intersection. A phase is a part of this cycle that is allocated to any combination of traffic movements. In this example, the cycle is comprised of four phases, each allowing either turning vehicle or through vehicles to travel through the intersection.

Each phase of a cycle is divided into three intervals: the green interval, the yellow change interval, and the red clearance interval. As illustrated in Fig. 4.7, the intervals occur in a specific sequence and indicate to the driver how to proceed through the intersection. The green interval is the segment of the phase during which vehicles have the right-of-way through the intersection. The yellow change interval warns traffic approaching the intersection that the right-of-way for that direction is about to end.[6] The driver can expect that the signal will change to red when the yellow interval ends. The red clearance interval is used at the end of the yellow change interval to allow any vehicles that may be proceeding through the intersection when the yellow change interval ends to leave the intersection before the next phase begins. It is important to note that not all jurisdictions use a red clearance interval after the yellow change interval. Its use is frequently a matter of regional or agency policy. The discussion related to the complexities and approaches to determining yellow clearance and red clearance interval is beyond the scope of this textbook. A common approach is presented later in this chapter, but the reader should be aware that several methods exist to determine both the yellow change and red clearance intervals.

Traffic signals can operate in several modes, each of which assigns right of way to intersection users in different ways. Four broad methods of control are described in Table 4.6. As evidenced by the descriptions, each control type functions differently with regard to how it assigns right-of-way to movements and utilizes different data from the intersection.

In general, pre-timed operations have cycle lengths and phase durations of predetermined length, though cycle lengths might change based on the time of day.

Term	Definition
Actuation	Initiation of a change in or extension of a traffic signal phase through the operation of any type of detector.
Conflict monitor	A device used to detect and respond to improper or conflicting signal indications and improper operating voltages in a traffic controller assembly.
Cycle	One complete sequence of all signal indications at a traffic signal.
Cycle length	The time required for one complete sequence of signal indications.
Cycle split	The segment of the cycle length allocated to each phase or interval that may occur.
Dark mode	The lack of all signal indications at a signalized location.
Detector	A device used for determining the presence or passage of vehicles or pedestrians.
Dual-arrow signal section	A type of signal section designed to include both a yellow arrow and a green arrow.
Emergency-vehicle traffic control signal	A special traffic control signal that assigns the right-of-way to an authorized emergency vehicle.
Flashing mode	A mode of operation in which at least one traffic signal indication in each vehicular signal face of a highway traffic signal is turned on and off repetitively.
Interval	The part of a signal cycle during which signal indications do not change.
Interval sequence	The order of appearance of signal indications during successive intervals of a signal cycle.
Major street	The street normally carrying the higher volume of vehicular traffic.
Minor street	The street normally carrying the lower volume of vehicular traffic.
Pedestrian change interval	An interval during which the flashing UPRAISED HAND signal indication is displayed.
Pedestrian clearance interval	The time provided for a pedestrian crossing in a crosswalk, after leaving the curb or shoulder, to travel to the far side of the traveled way or to a median.
Pedestrian signal head	A signal head, which contains the symbols WALKING PERSON (symbolizing WALK) and UPRAISED HAND (symbolizing DON'T WALK), that is installed to direct pedestrian traffic at a traffic control signal.
Permissive mode	A mode of traffic control signal operation in which left or right turns are permitted to be made after yielding to pedestrians, if any, and/or opposing traffic if any.
Phase	A part of the traffic signal time cycle allocated to any combination of traffic movements.
Platoon	A group of vehicles or pedestrians traveling together as a group, either voluntarily or involuntarily, because of traffic signal controls, geometrics, or other factors.
Preemption	The transfer of normal operation of a traffic control signal to a special control mode of operation.
Primary signal face	One of the required or recommended minimum number of signal faces for a given approach or separate turning movement, but not including near-side signal faces requires as a result of the far-side signal faces exceeding the maximum distance from the stop line.
Priority control	A means by which the assignment of right-of-way is obtained or modified.

TABLE 4.5 Traffic Signal Vocabulary (*Refs. 1, 6, and 7.*)

Term	Definition
Protected mode	A mode of traffic control signal operation in which left or right turns are permitted to be made when a left or right GREEN ARROW signal indication is displayed.
Red clearance interval	An interval that follows a yellow change interval and precedes the next conflicting green interval.
Right-of-way	The permitting of vehicles and/or pedestrians to proceed in a lawful manner in preference to other vehicles or pedestrians by the display of a sign or signal indications.
Saturation flow rate	The equivalent hourly rate at which vehicles can traverse an intersection approach under prevailing conditions, assuming a constant green indication at all times and with no lost time, noted in vehicles per hour or vehicles per hour per lane.
Separate turn signal face	A signal face that exclusively controls a turn movement and that displays signal indications that are applicable only to the turn movement.
Shared turn signal face	A signal face, for controlling both a turn movement and the adjacent through movement, that always displays the same color of circular signal indication that the adjacent through signal face or faces display.
Signal coordination	The establishment of timed relationships between adjacent traffic control signals.
Signal face	An assembly of one or more signal sections that is provided for controlling one or more traffic movements on a single approach.
Signal head	An assembly of one or more signal faces that is provided for controlling traffic movements on one ore more approaches.
Signal housing	That part of a signal section that protects the light source and other required components.
Signal indication	The illumination of a signal lens or equivalent device.
Signal lens	That part of the signal section that redirects the light coming directly from the light source and its reflector, if any.
Signal louver	A device that can be mounted inside a signal visor to restrict visibility of a signal indication to a certain lane or lanes, or to a certain distance from the stop line.
Signal phase	The right-of-way, yellow change, and red clearance intervals in a cycle that are assigned to an independent traffic movement or combination of movements.
Signal section	The assembly of a signal housing, signal lens, if any, and light source with necessary components to be used for displaying one signal indication.
Signal system	Two or more traffic control signals operating in signal coordination.
Signal timing	The amount of time allocated for the display of a signal indication.
Split	A percentage of the cycle length allocated to each of the various phases in a signal sequence.
Supplemental signal face	A signal face that is not a primary signal face but which is provided for a given approach or separate turning movement to enhance visibility or conspicuity.
Yellow change interval	The first interval following the green or flashing arrow interval during which the steady yellow signal indication is displayed.

TABLE 4.5 Traffic Signal Vocabulary (*Refs. 1, 6, and 7.*) (*Continued*)

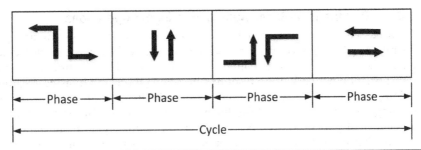

Figure 4.6   Basic traffic signal cycle.

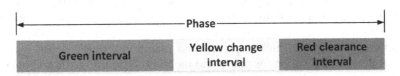

Figure 4.7   Traffic signal phase intervals.

Control Type	Description
Pre-timed operation	A type of traffic signal control operation in which none of the signal phases function on the basis of actuation.
Semi-actuated operation	A type of traffic control signal operation in which at least one, but not all, signal phases function on the basis of actuation.
Full-actuated operation	A type of traffic control signal operation in which all signal phases function on the basis of actuation.
Adaptive traffic signal control operation	The dynamic adjustment of signal timing to smooth traffic flow along coordinated routes by the continuous monitoring of arterial traffic conditions and queuing at intersections.

Table 4.6   Types of Traffic Signal Control (*Refs. 6 and 8.*)

For example, the cycle lengths and phase durations might be longer during the day when more traffic moves through the intersection. Shorter lengths and phase durations might be used at night when traffic is lighter. For actuated operations, the signals respond to short-term fluctuations in traffic demands, altering cycle and phase lengths in response to changes in traffic demand. They require the installation of detectors at approaches to provide the data to the controller. For full-actuated signals, each phase is guaranteed a minimum green, and the green time is extended every time a vehicle passes over a detector at or in advance of the intersection. These extensions can occur until the maximum green time is met, or no actuations occur.

4.3.3 Performance-Based Approach to Signal Operations

As discussed later in Chap. 8 of this textbook, transportation system management and operations (TSMO) is a critical approach to managing the existing infrastructure investment. Agencies have invested billions of dollars over decades into building a complex transportation network. With resources becoming more and more scarce, the transportation professional is charged with the responsibility of optimizing the performance of existing systems to limit or delay the need for expansion. Traffic signal operations are an elemental part of TSMO. A comprehensive traffic signal management plan helps ensure that an agency has incorporated signal operations into their overall TSMO efforts. Transportation professionals need to have a clear understanding of how their signal systems are operating, and performance measures help increase that understanding. Performance measures can help an agency determine whether a signal system helps meet the regional goals and objectives for the overall transportation network.

The first step in developing a comprehensive performance-based traffic signal management plan is to first understand the overall regional goals and objectives for the transportation agency. Understanding those goals and objectives helps the transportation engineer design, build, operate, and maintain a traffic signal system that helps meet the regional vision for safety and mobility. Typically, goals and objectives look to improve the overall region in terms of safety (i.e., improve the safety of the transportation system) and/or mobility (i.e., reduce congestion by making the transportation infrastructure more efficient). Additionally, they are likely to reflect on sustainability (i.e., enable more efficient and reliable transit trips) and livability (i.e., expand safer accessibility to bicycles and pedestrians). The transportation engineer can work to develop a traffic signal management program that supports these goals and objectives. Examples of signal timing policy and strategies related to overall regional transportation policies are provided in Table 4.7. For example, if one regional transportation policy focuses on pedestrian and bicycle accessibility, then the signal timing plan should incorporate pedestrian and bicycle-focused timing strategies in areas where those system users are more prevalent, such as near schools, parks, or any area with high pedestrian/bicycle traffic. Similar timing strategies can be incorporated into the signal timing plan to clearly link timing policy to the overall regional goals and objectives.

A critical step in the development of a traffic signal management plan is to understand the current state of the existing traffic signal system. One method for gaining this comprehensive understanding is to conduct a traffic signal operations self-assessment. The objective of this exercise is to document how an agency's signal system currently performs as well as to identify opportunities for improving its policies and practices with respect to signal operations. It can also serve as a baseline or benchmark against which improvements can be measured. Typical questions included in a self-assessment fall into the categories of management, signal operations, timing practices, traffic monitoring and data collection, and maintenance.[9]

Once an agency has a grasp of current traffic signal operations and practices, it can then determine its capabilities to improve those operations. One approach to assessing those capabilities is through the use of the traffic signal capability maturity framework (CMF).[10] This framework is an online support tool designed to help transportation agencies identify their current capabilities with respect to traffic signal program management and to identify a set of actions to improve those capabilities to better manage their signal systems, thereby working to address the complex transportation mobility challenges in their region. The traffic signal CMF is best described as a matrix defining

Transportation Policy	Setting	Signal Timing Strategy
Pedestrian/ bicycle-focused	Downtowns, schools, universities, dense multiuse development, parks, or any location with high pedestrian/ bicycle traffic	• Shorten cycle lengths to reduce wait times. • Extend pedestrian crossing timing. • Add bicycle/pedestrian detection. • Use exclusive pedestrian phasing. • Include leading pedestrian interval.
Emergency vehicle-focused	Transit corridors, along transit routes, near transit stations or crossings	• Signal preemption for high-importance transit modes (e.g., rail). • Signal priority for strategic transit modes and routes. • Signal coordination based on transit vehicle speeds. • Extend pedestrian crossing timing. • Use exclusive pedestrian phasing. • Use leading pedestrian interval.
Transit-focused	Key roadways and routes to and from hospitals, fire stations, and policy stations	Signal preemption for high-importance vehicles.
Automobile- focused/ freight-focused	Locations with high automobile or truck/ freight traffic, facilities of regional importance, freight corridors, ports, or intermodal sites.	• Avoid cycle failure. • Maintain progression on coordinated systems as well as possible to avoid unnecessary stops and delay. • Use appropriate cycle lengths. • Ensure appropriate pedestrian signal timing to allow safe multimodal use of the roadway network.
Low-volume locations or periods	Locations with low-traffic volumes or during off-peak travel periods	• Ensure efficient signal timing operations. • Consider flashing operation if conditions allow. • Use appropriate resting state for the signal with no traffic demand. • Allow skipping of unnecessary movements. • Use half, third, or quarter cycle lengths relative to other coordinated signalized intersections. • Allow pedestrian actuations to temporarily length a cycle length, removing an intersection out of coordination, if pedestrian and vehicular volumes are low.

TABLE 4.7 Examples of Signal Timing Policy and Strategies (*Ref. 6.*)

process improvement areas and levels—from Level 1 (low-level) to Level 4 (optimized high-level)—of capability across six dimensions of process improvement. Those dimensions are:

- Business processes
- Systems and technology
- Performance measurement

- Organization and workforce
- Culture
- Collaboration

Following a self-assessment process, specific actions are identified to increase capabilities across the desired process areas of relevance to traffic management. Table 4.8 provides an overview of the traffic signal CMF, including the six dimensions, descriptions of those dimensions within the traffic signal management context, and sub dimensions that provide additional detail and refinement of the capabilities of agencies.

The framework looks at the agency's ability to monitor, manage, and control traffic signal systems and its ability to implement institutional architectures and business processes that make traffic signal management a success for the region.[11] Broadly, the framework assesses the capability to efficiently manage the traffic signal system. The capability levels and the actions are focused and defined from a traffic signal system manager's perspective. The actions may require other agencies to be the responsible party, which is intended to foster multiagency collaboration and dialogue about traffic signal management at the regional level. A multi-stakeholder approach is recommended to review the framework and identify improvement actions. Typical stakeholders include city and state traffic managers in the region, selection of traffic operators, transportation planners, and transit operators.

An effective traffic signal management plan (TSMP) sets forth a regional approach to help ensure good basic service that aligns with regional TSMO goals and objectives. Figure 4.8 illustrates the three critical elements of an effective TSMP, one that provides good basic service: design, operations, and maintenance.[12] These interrelated elements work in concert to enhance the reliability of the traffic signal program. Good basic service fits within the overall context of TSMO as it emphasizes the concept of prioritizing the most important elements of traffic signal operations using limited resources. It depends upon several key tenets:

- Clearly articulated objectives
- Expert, committed staff
- Processes that are well-documented and optimized for effectiveness
- Systematic processes related to hardware and software procurements
- Availability of capital and operating funds on a predictable basis
- Meaningful performance measurement of the program[12]

Other elements of a TSMP that help ensure effective implementation include management and administration strategies; interagency communication and collaboration; and an action plan that sets out a framework for moving forward with improvements and securing resources to do so.

Performance measures are necessary to help determine whether a traffic signal management plan helps meet regional goals and objectives. As illustrated in Fig. 4.9, an analysis of the strategies and tactics can be compared against the objectives to determine to what extent they advance the goals and objectives. Performance measures associated with traffic signal systems typically fall into four categories: capacity, progression, multimodal, and maintenance. Typical performance measures within these categories

Dimension or Process Improvement Area	Description	Sub Dimensions
BUSINESS PROCESSES	Processes that link planning, design, operations, and maintenance activities to resource management and budgeting decisions in consideration of operational objectives that identify and respond to the needs of stakeholders.	Strategic planning Operations and maintenance Programming and budgeting Resource allocation
SYSTEMS AND TECHNOLOGY	How agencies use their systems and technologies to make strategic and tactical decisions related to the operations and performance of their traffic signal systems.	Continuity of service procurement Systems engineering and interoperablity Operational flexibility state of good repair
PERFORMANCE MEASUREMENT	An agency's ability to use a performance-based approach to manage its traffic signal system, including the ability to define performance measures, acquire performance data, and utilize performance measures in the planning, design, operations, and maintenance of traffic signal operations and maintenance programs.	Performance measure definition Performance measure utilization
ORGANIZATION AND WORKFORCE	Developing and ensuring that agency staff has the knowledge, skills, and abilities necessary to achieve the goals and objectives defined by the agency.	Staff development program structure

TABLE 4.8   FHWA's Traffic Signal Management Capability Maturity Framework (™CMF) (*Ref. 10.*)

Dimension or Process Improvement Area	Description	Sub Dimensions
CULTURE	The technical understanding, leadership, outreach, and legal authority of agencies to implement actions necessary to improve operations and maintenance of traffic signal systems.	Outreach leadership
COLLABORATION	The ability of an agency to form relationships with other regional partners and stakeholders (e.g., public safety agencies, local governments, metropolitan planning organizations (MPOs), and the private sector) to address regional traffic signal operational issues and needs.	Data sharing external stakeholders

TABLE 4.8   FHWA's Traffic Signal Management Capability Maturity Framework (™CMF) (*Ref. 10.*) (*Continued*)

FIGURE 4.8   Good basic service components of traffic signal management program. (*Ref. 12.*)

are shown in Table 4.9.[13] An agency should map specific performance measures to regional goals and objectives and establish target improvements to determine how well the TSMP is working to meet them. Regular review of signal performance can be used for a variety of purposes, including incorporating the performance measures into agency business processes and prioritizing investment in signal system improvements.

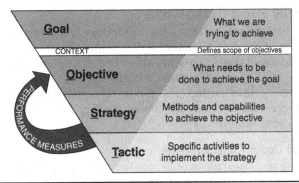

Figure 4.9 Goals, context, objectives, strategies, and tactics (GOST) pyramid. (*Ref. 12.*)

Performance Measure Category	Performance Measures
Capacity	• Cycle length • Green time and capacity • Count and volume • Volume-to-capacity ratio • Degree of intersection saturation • Green occupancy ratio and red occupancy ratio
Progression	• Percent on green, arrival type • Coordination • Platoon/flow profile • Estimated queue length • Oversaturation severity index • Input-output delay • Maximum vehicle delay • Estimated vehicle Highway Capacity Manual (HCM) delay • Platoon characteristics • Coordination optimization potential • Phase termination diagram
Multimodal	• Pedestrian actuation rate • Pedestrian actuation to service time • Estimated pedestrian HCM delay • Pedestrian conflicting volume • Preempt duration • Preemption event diagram • Priority time to green • Pedestrian demand
Maintenance	• Maintain communication systems • Maintain detection systems • Evaluation performance of a corridor signal system • Evaluate performance of a corridor signal system

Table 4.9 Typical Traffic Signal Outcome-Based Performance Measures (*Ref. 13.*)

4.3.4 Traffic Signal Timing Basics

The process of developing a signal timing strategy involves a series of steps that identifies the needs at the intersection and determines the minimal amount of green time needed to service all movements and all users of the intersection. Figure 4.10 represents an outcome-based approach to timing traffic signals,[14] which follows the concept discussed in the previous section. The following sections provide details related to this multistep process for developing a timing strategy for an intersection through the use of a step-by-step example.

Initial Signal Timing Considerations

The following steps provide overall insight into the initial signal timing considerations assembled by the transportation engineer.

Step 1: Define the Operating Environment   The first step in the outcome-based process of designing a traffic signal is to establish the operating environment for the signal. This environment can refer to different considerations, such as whether a system of signals operates across jurisdictional boundaries or the specific environment at the intersection.[14] The environment can be the physical location of the signal (i.e., rural, suburban, urban) or other features about the area surrounding the signal that may impact operations. For example, the intersection may be near major traffic generators requiring the need to accommodate a broad range of users. Also, the signal may be near a railroad grade crossing, be located on a high-capacity transit route, or have other geometric constraints such as nearby driveways, all which may create specific needs or challenges with respect to the timing plan. The classification of the roadway directly relates to the specific mobility objectives (i.e., access vs. speed), which in turn impacts the operating objectives of the signal.[14] Additionally, the transportation engineers need to understand the overall characteristics of the network, whether the signal is part of a grid network or a corridor, and how the signal will operate (isolated vs. coordinated). All of these factors can influence the overall timing plan and how

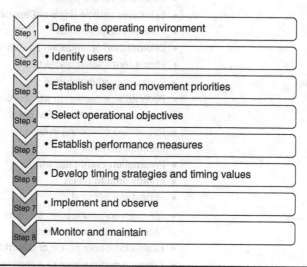

Step 1	• Define the operating environment
Step 2	• Identify users
Step 3	• Establish user and movement priorities
Step 4	• Select operational objectives
Step 5	• Establish performance measures
Step 6	• Develop timing strategies and timing values
Step 7	• Implement and observe
Step 8	• Monitor and maintain

FIGURE 4.10   Signal timing plan process. (*Ref. 14.*)

the signal accommodates the users while working to achieve regional safety and mobility objectives.

Step 2: Identify Users   The primary purpose of the intersection is to assign the right-of-way to users to permit them to pass through the intersection. The second critical step in the timing process is the understanding of the mix of users navigating through the intersection and their specific traffic patterns.[14] The transportation engineer needs to identify the type and number of users accessing the intersection in order to accommodate them in the timing plan. These users include the following:

- Pedestrians
- Bicycles
- Light vehicles
- Heavy vehicles
- Emergency vehicles
- Transit vehicles

This information can typically be gathered through volume counts at the intersection. Turning movements associated with these users, as well as related information such as the intersection's proximity to a fire station or hospital or whether it serves as a primary transit route are also important elements to include in the information related to users.

Step 3: Establish User and Movement Priorities   Once the transportation engineer knows the specific users navigating through the intersection, they must then establish a prioritized approach to serving the needs of the users. These priorities typically consider any relevant jurisdictional standards and policies along with the intersection's operational environment.[14] Critical movements need to be identified and specific movement patterns need to be assessed to ensure the resulting timing plan yields the most efficient operation possible. Specific traffic patterns and characteristics that may be considered in this step include, but are not limited to:

- The proportion of turning vehicles at the intersection
- Corridor directionality
- Peak hour, weekday, and weekend characteristics
- Lane usage
- Origin-destination information
- Trends, including crashes, incidents, planned special events, work zones, or other recurring and nonrecurring congestion events[14]

All of this information is collected and analyzed to determine a prioritized list of the most important movements and users to serve in order at the intersection, which impacts the selected timing plan.

Data Collection
Having a full understanding of the conditions at an intersection requires data. Only with comprehensive and detailed data about the physical conditions at the intersection,

the users, and the operational history can a transportation engineer begin to time a traffic signal to safely and efficiently manage the traffic through the intersection. The type of data needed to begin the timing design process includes, but it is not limited to:

- Field data such as operational operations and bottleneck considerations
- Traffic counts, both 24-hour weekly counts and turning movement counts
- Other traffic characteristics such as vehicular speed, travel time, delay, and queue lengths
- Intersection geometry and existing TCDs
- Existing signal timing
- Crash history[14]

This assortment of data, when combined with the initial timing considerations, sets the framework for selecting the appropriate timing plan.

Operational Objectives and Performance Measures

The following steps address the process of identifying and selecting operational objectives and performance measures for the traffic signal under development. The overall intent of this effort is to ensure that the resulting timing plan helps the operating agency meet its safety and mobility goals for the community.

Step 4: Select Operational Objectives   The outcome-based process for developing a signal timing plan relies on selecting the appropriate operational objectives to yield the desired outcome. Specific operational objectives should also link to regional safety and mobility goals and objectives to ensure that they help an agency meet them. Table 4.10 outlines typical objectives that an agency might select for traffic signal operations based

Operational Objective Category	Operational Objectives
Vehicle-specific objectives	Vehicle safety
	Vehicle mobility—capacity allocation
	Vehicle mobility—corridor progression
	Vehicle mobility—secondary progression
	Environmental impact mitigation
	Queue length management
	Vehicle and driver costs
Pedestrian-specific objectives	Pedestrian safety
	Pedestrian mobility
	Pedestrian accessibility
Bicycle-specific objectives	Bicycle safety
	Bicycle mobility
Transit-specific objectives	Transit safety
	Transit mobility
	Transit accessibility

TABLE 4.10   Traffic Signal Operational Objectives (*Ref. 14.*)

regional goals, policies, and/or intersection users. They are categorized based on whether they are vehicle-, pedestrian-, bicycle-, or transit-specific objectives.[14]

The selection of the operational objectives for the traffic signal has a direct impact on the remaining activities associated with the development and implementation of a signal timing plan. The objectives translate into performance measures, which direct the strategies and ongoing monitoring and evaluation of the signal to ensure it meets the operational objectives on an ongoing basis.

Step 5: Establish Performance Measures   For each operational objective, the transportation professional needs to select one or more performance measure to use to assess whether the traffic signal is working to meet the objective. It is important to note that some objectives are qualitative in nature, while some are clearly quantitative and easier to assess. Furthermore, some objectives are measured from the users' perspective, while others are measured at the system level and may be less obvious to the traveling public. Typical performance measures are discussed previously in this chapter. An important criterion for selecting a performance measure is ensuring that the operating agency has the ability to collect the data necessary to utilize that measure in its overall analysis of the traffic signal. Overall, the performance measures should clearly relate to the desired outcomes for the system, charting a clear path forward for the transportation professional in terms of data collection, analysis, and reporting of the performance of the traffic signal.[14]

Signal Timing Strategies and Plans

The design of a traffic signal is a process involving a number of elements, such as the selection, design, and placement of detection technologies; the selection and installation of the signal cabinet and its related equipment, and the installation of the displays to support the signal timing plan and the users at the intersection. The specific design of the traffic signal is beyond the scope of this textbook, but various documents and guidebooks exist that can provide detailed information about this aspect of traffic signals. The step discussed in this section is the selection of the signal timing strategy for the intersection and the development of the timing plan.

Step 6: Develop Timing Strategies and Timing Values   As discussed previously, there are numerous traffic signal parameters related to the design of a timing strategy and overall timing plan. Some of these parameters may be impacted by regional policy while others may be a function of the specific intersection operational considerations discussed previously. Once a transportation engineer has determined that a traffic signal is needed at an intersection, they need to review all of the data collected to start the process of developing a signal timing plan.

Typical numbering convention assigns a phase number to each movement at an intersection. This numbering is shown in Table 4.11. While agencies can vary from this

Phase	Movement	Phase Number
Even	Through movement, major street	2 and 6
	Through movement, minor street	4 and 8
Odd	Major street left turn	1 and 5
	Minor street left turn	3 and 7

TABLE **4.11**   Traffic Signal Phase Numbering (*Ref. 14.*)

numbering scheme depending on local preference or policy, it is a good practice to use consistent numbering throughout the jurisdiction to avoid confusion.

An important factor to consider is how to accommodate left turns at the intersection. Five types of left-term phasing exist for traffic signals. These are:

- Permitted left-turn phasing (left turns yield to conflicting vehicle and pedestrian movements)

- Protected left-turn phasing (left turns proceed without conflicting movements)

- Protected-permitted left turn phasing (left turns have both permitted and protection intervals in the phase)

- Split phase (all movements on an approach are provided right-of-way at the same time)

- Prohibited left-turn phase (left turns are prohibited at the intersection)[14]

The use of one or all of these phases is typically included in local jurisdiction policies or procedures for traffic signal operations. Each of these phase options has advantages and challenges with respect to safety and efficiency. Additionally, the left-turn phase can be served at different places in the cycle. The three left-turn phase sequences are:

- Lead-lead sequence (the opposing left-turn phase in each direction occurs prior to the through phase)

- Lag-lag sequence (the opposing left-turn phase in each direction occurs after the through phase)

- Lead-lag sequence (the opposing left-turn phases in each direction occur at different times relative to the through phase)

The use of these sequences can be based on a variety of factors, including regional preference, the presence of and storage available in a left-turn bay, and the size of the intersection. For illustration purposes, a sample intersection is illustrated in Fig. 4.11, and the hourly volume counts collected for this intersection are provided in Table 4.12 along with the phases using the typical phase numbering sequence. In this intersection, the north-south roadway is the major roadway at the intersection given the design and the volumes.

Identify Lane Groups Once the volume data have been collected along with the schematic of the intersection, the transportation professional needs to identify the lane groups at an intersection. It is important to recognize that the signal timing strategy is related to the lane configuration at the intersection and the associated movements assigned to specific lanes. Figure 4.12 illustrates the relationship between the number of lanes at the intersection along with the movements by lane and group.[15]

For the sample intersection shown, the lane groups are presented in Table 4.13. In the northbound and southbound directions, the left turns have a dedicated lane. Thus, they are a separate lane group than the through movements. In the eastbound and westbound directions, all of the movements travel through the intersection from a single lane. Thus, there is one-lane group for each direction.

Compute Volume to Saturation Flow Ratio The saturation flow rate is a number that reflects the maximum number of vehicles in a movement that can move through an intersection,

Figure 4.11 Sample intersection.

Movement	Hourly Volume
NBLT (1)	325 vph
NBTR (6)	1015 vhp
SBLT (5)	375 vph
SBTR (2)	1200 vhp
WB (4)	525 vph
EB (8)	492 vph

Table 4.12 Sample Intersection Hourly Volumes

assuming that the traffic signal indication is always green and no time is lost when vehicles start through the intersection from a complete stop. For the sample intersection, the saturation flow rates for the individual movements are shown in Table 4.14.

To calculate the volume to saturation flow ratio, the following equation is used:

$$y = \frac{v_i}{s_i}$$

where y = volume to saturation flow ratio
v_i = volume of lane group i, vph
s_i = saturation flow rate for lane group i, vph

For the sample intersection, the v/s ratios are shown in Table 4.15.

Number of lanes	Movements by lanes	Movements groups (MG)	Lane groups (LG)
1	Left, thru., & right:	MG 1:	LG 1:
2	Exclusive left:	MG 1:	LG 1:
	Thru. & right:	MG 2:	LG 2:
2	Left & thru.:	MG 1:	LG 1:
	Thru. & right:		LG 2:
3 or more	Exclusive left: Exclusive left:	MG 1:	LG 1:
	Through: Through:	MG 2:	LG 2:
			LG 3:
	Thru. & right:		

FIGURE 4.12   Lane and movement group designation. (*Ref. 15.*)

SBTR (2)	SBLT (5)
NBLT (1)	NBTR (6)
EB (8)	WB (4)

TABLE 4.13   Sample Intersection Lane Groups

Movement	Saturation Flow Rate
NBLT	1805 vph
NBTR	3610 vhp
SBLT	1805 vph
SBTR	3610 vhp
WB	1800 vph
EB	1800 vph

TABLE 4.14   Sample Intersection
Saturation Flow Rates

Movement	Hourly Volume	Saturation Flow Rate	v/s Ratio
NBLT (1)	325 vph	1805 vph	0.18
NBTR (6)	1015 vhp	3610 vhp	0.28
SBLT (5)	375 vph	1805 vph	0.21
SBTR (2)	1200 vhp	3610 vhp	0.33
WB (4)	525 vph	1800 vph	0.29
EB (8)	492 vph	1800 vph	0.27

Table 4.15   Sample Intersection v/s Ratios

Find Critical Movements at Intersection   Various approaches to signal phasing exist, from which the transportation engineer selects a pattern. A number of factors play into the selection of the phasing pattern, including local policy, safety, traffic demands, and efficiencies. In general, the least amount of disruption at the intersection is preferred to minimize delay as vehicles move through the intersection. Drivers prefer to spend the least amount of time stopped at an intersection as possible.

After the transportation engineer has calculated the *v/s* ratios, they then need to identify the critical movements at the intersection. This information is important because the phase duration must be long enough to satisfy the demand of the critical movements. The critical movements are a function of the phasing pattern to be used and conflicting movements. Conflicting movements are any vehicle movements that normally cannot receive green simultaneously at the intersection. For example, as illustrated in Table 4.16, the eastbound through movement conflicts with the northbound through movement (the westbound and southbound through movements also conflict). The other movements that are conflicting at the sample intersection are marked with a check.

The next step is to identify critical movements for various phase sequence alternatives. The first option is the phase sequence for leading left turns. As illustrated in Table 4.17, the engineer compares the opposing left turns for the major roadway, the through movements for the major roadway, and the total movements for the

EB (8)	SBTR (2)	SBLT (5)	SBTR (2)	WB (4)
→	↓	↳	↓	↕↔
↑	↰	↑	↑	↔↕
NBTR (6)	NBLT (1)	NBTR (6)	NBTR (6)	EB (8)
✓	✓	✓	⊘	⊘

✓ conflicting movement
⊘ nonconflicting movement

Table 4.16   Sample Intersection Conflicting Movements

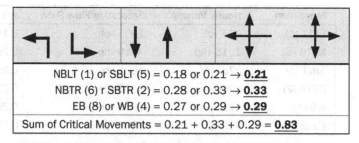

NBLT (1) or SBLT (5) = 0.18 or 0.21 → **0.21**			
NBTR (6) r SBTR (2) = 0.28 or 0.33 → **0.33**			
EB (8) or WB (4) = 0.27 or 0.29 → **0.29**			
Sum of Critical Movements = 0.21 + 0.33 + 0.29 = **0.83**			

TABLE 4.17   Critical Movements, Leading Left Turns

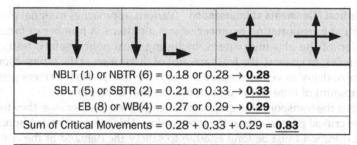

NBLT (1) or NBTR (6) = 0.18 or 0.28 → **0.28**			
SBLT (5) or SBTR (2) = 0.21 or 0.33 → **0.33**			
EB (8) or WB(4) = 0.27 or 0.29 → **0.29**			
Sum of Critical Movements = 0.28 + 0.33 + 0.29 = **0.83**			

TABLE 4.18   Critical Movements, Split Phasing

minor roadway. In this example, the critical movements are the southbound left turns, the southbound through movements, and the westbound movements since these movements each have the largest v/s ratio when compared to the opposing direction.

As noted previously, split phasing is when all movements in a particular direction are provided the right-of-way together. To determine to critical movements with split phasing, Table 4.18 illustrates how the v/s ratios for all movements in each direction are analyzed. In the example intersection, the critical movements for split phasing are the northbound through movement, the southbound through movement, and the westbound movement.

Frequently, an overlap phase can be used to improve the efficiency of the intersection when one turning movement is greater than the other. This practice allows a movement to operate during more than one phase. The transportation engineer also needs to determine which movements can overlap at the intersection. For overlap phasing, the v/s ratios for conflicting movements need to be compared to identify the critical movements. In Table 4.19, the conflicting movements are added together to determine the critical combination of movements for overlap phasing.

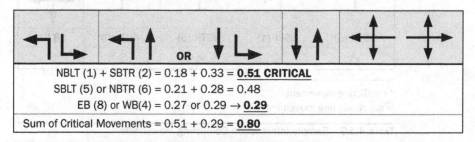

NBLT (1) + SBTR (2) = 0.18 + 0.33 = **0.51 CRITICAL**			
SBLT (5) or NBTR (6) = 0.21 + 0.28 = 0.48			
EB (8) or WB(4) = 0.27 or 0.29 → **0.29**			
Sum of Critical Movements = 0.51 + 0.29 = **0.80**			

TABLE 4.19   Critical Movements, Overlap Phasing

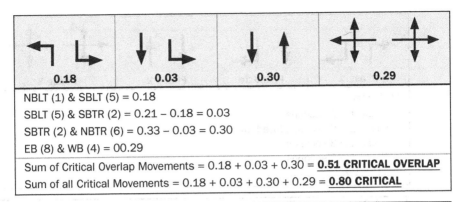

0.18	0.03	0.30	0.29

NBLT (1) & SBLT (5) = 0.18

SBLT (5) & SBTR (2) = 0.21 – 0.18 = 0.03

SBTR (2) & NBTR (6) = 0.33 – 0.03 = 0.30

EB (8) & WB (4) = 00.29

Sum of Critical Overlap Movements = 0.18 + 0.03 + 0.30 = **0.51 CRITICAL OVERLAP**

Sum of all Critical Movements = 0.18 + 0.03 + 0.30 + 0.29 = **0.80 CRITICAL**

TABLE 4.20   Critical Movements, Overlap Phasing Allocation

Once the critical movements for overlap phasing are determined, the transportation engineer needs to determine which movements will overlap and how the flow ratio will be distributed across the movements. In the sample intersection overlap phasing has been shown in Table 4.20.

The v/s ratio needs to be allocated to the movements to ensure all movements are served. In this example, the critical movements are the northbound left turn (0.18 v/s) and the southbound through movement (0.33 v/s). However, it is important to note that the southbound left movement has a higher v/s than the left (0.21). In allocating the critical v/s ratio, the first phase would consist of allocating 0.18 to the opposing lead left movement. However, the southbound left movement is underserved with this allocation. Thus, the overlap phase of the southbound left movement and the southbound through movements needs to serve the remaining portion of the turning movement (0.03). Then, the remaining southbound through movement of 0.30 is used, which also handles the northbound through movement.

Determine Cycle Length   A traditional method for calculating the cycle length is Webster's model,[16] which is shown in the following formula:

$$C = \frac{1.5L + 5}{1.0 - Y}$$

where C = optimum cycle length (seconds)

$\quad\quad\quad Y$ = critical lane volume divided by the saturation flow, summed over all phases in the cycle

$\quad\quad\quad L$ = lost time per cycle (seconds)

Lost time is the time at the beginning and end of a signal phase that is lost because of start-up delays and the yellow clearance interval. Generally, the lost time is equal to the change interval, though there is typically no lost time in an overlapped phase. The total lost time for the sample intersection and the cycle phases is shown in Table 4.21.

As noted previously, the yellow change interval warns traffic that the right-of-way for that direction is about to end,[6] while the red clearance interval is often used to allow any vehicles that may be proceeding through the intersection when the yellow change interval ends to leave the intersection before the next phase begins. It is important to note that not all jurisdictions use a red clearance interval after the yellow change interval. The practices associated with timing yellow and red clearance intervals vary and their

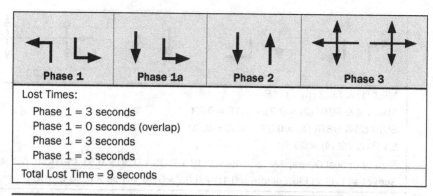

| Lost Times: |
| Phase 1 = 3 seconds |
| Phase 1 = 0 seconds (overlap) |
| Phase 1 = 3 seconds |
| Phase 1 = 3 seconds |
| Total Lost Time = 9 seconds |

TABLE 4.21 Total Lost Time

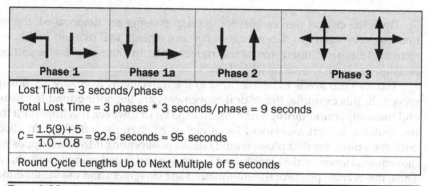

| Lost Time = 3 seconds/phase |
| Total Lost Time = 3 phases * 3 seconds/phase = 9 seconds |
| $C = \dfrac{1.5(9)+5}{1.0-0.8} = 92.5$ seconds ≈ 95 seconds |
| Round Cycle Lengths Up to Next Multiple of 5 seconds |

TABLE 4.22 Cycle Length Calculation

discussion is beyond the scope of this textbook. For the purposes of basic traffic signal timing, the yellow clearance interval can be assumed to be between 3 and 7 seconds, while an all-red clearance interval can be assumed to be 1 to 2 seconds. The cycle length calculation for the sample problem is shown in Table 4.22, assuming the lost time per phase is equal to the yellow clearance interval, which is 3 seconds.

Determine Green Time as Fraction of Cycle   Once the cycle length is determined, the proportion of that cycle that will be green needs to be determined. The process for determining that proportion is a function of the length of the yellow clearance interval and the number of phases in the cycle and is calculated as a fraction of the cycle. For the purpose of the sample intersection timing, Table 4.23 illustrates the calculation of the total yellow and green times.

Determine Green Time as Fraction of Cycle   The green time must then be distributed to all of the movements in the cycle and their corresponding v/s ratios. The formula for distributing the green time to the movements is as follows:

$$\frac{g_i}{C} = \frac{\left(\frac{v}{s}\right)_i}{\sum \left(\frac{v}{s}\right)_{\text{Critical Movements}}} * \text{Total}\,\frac{G}{C}$$

Yellow time calculation

$$\frac{Y}{C} = \frac{3}{95} = .032 \text{ per phase}$$

Total yellow = 0.032 per phase * 3 phases = 0.10

Total green time (fraction of cycle)

$$\frac{G}{C} = 1 - 0.10 = 0.90$$

TABLE 4.23 Total Yellow and Green Time Calculation

where g_i/C = green ratio for movement i

v/s_i = volume to saturation flow ratio for movement i

Total G/C = total green for cycle ratio

For the sample intersection, the g/C calculations for the movements are shown in Table 4.24. The sum of volume to saturation flow ratios used in the equation is that for the overlap phase sequence in Table 4.20.

The resulting G/C ratios are then assigned to the appropriate overlap phases for the complete sequence as shown in Table 4.25. The resulting critical movements equal the total green time.

Once the g/c ratios are determined, the transportation engineer needs to check to ensure that minimum green requirements are met. Minimum green requirements typically vary by policy or practice, but no green interval can be shorter than the minimum green requirement set by the local jurisdiction. The process for checking the minimum green is straightforward: multiply the shortest g/c for the corresponding movement by the cycle length. If the phase green is longer than the required minimum green, then the signal timings can be finalized. If the shortest phase green is too short, then it must be extended to accommodate the longer minimum green. Any additional time needed to have the cycle length round up to a 5-second increment can be distributed across the yellow intervals. The calculations for the final phase timings are calculated in the same manner.

$$NBLT = \left(\frac{0.18}{0.80}\right) * 0.90 = 0.20 \text{ Critical Movement}$$

$$SBLT = \left(\frac{0.21}{0.80}\right) * 0.90 = 0.24$$

$$NBTR = \left(\frac{0.28}{0.80}\right) * 0.90 = 0.32$$

$$SBTR = \left(\frac{0.33}{0.80}\right) * 0.90 = 0.37 \text{ Critical Movement}$$

$$EB/WB = \left(\frac{0.29}{0.80}\right) * 0.90 = 0.33 \text{ Critical Movement}$$

TABLE 4.24 Total Yellow and Green Time Calculation

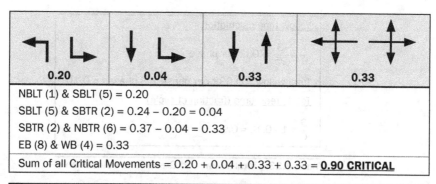

0.20	0.04	0.33	0.33

NBLT (1) & SBLT (5) = 0.20

SBLT (5) & SBTR (2) = 0.24 − 0.20 = 0.04

SBTR (2) & NBTR (6) = 0.37 − 0.04 = 0.33

EB (8) & WB (4) = 0.33

Sum of all Critical Movements = 0.20 + 0.04 + 0.33 + 0.33 = **<u>0.90 CRITICAL</u>**

TABLE 4.25 G/C Ratios for Overlap Phase Sequence

Interval	Fraction of Cycle	Seconds
Phase 1	0.20	19
Phase 1a	0.04	4
Yellow	0.032	3
Phase 2	0.33	31
Yellow	0.032	3
Phase 3	0.33	31
Yellow	0.032	3+1
Total	1.00	94 + 1 = 95

TABLE 4.26 Final Signal Timings

For the sample intersection used throughout this section the final signal timings are presented in Table 4.26.

The process of designing and timing traffic signals and traffic signal systems, along with coordination, is a complex process. The process described in this textbook is intended to present the overall general concept of determining critical movements and allocation of right-of-way proportionate to those movements. Additional strategies are available in a number of resource guides, handbooks, and manuals, which are beyond the overall scope of this introductory text.

Implementation and Maintenance

Once the transportation engineer has developed a timing plan for an intersection, they need to take that plan, implement it in the field, regularly monitor the signal to ensure it is operating properly, and periodically evaluate the performance of the signal to determine if changes need to be made to better optimize the outcomes of the operation. The following sections describe the overall process associated with signal timing implementation and operation.

Step 7: Implement and Observe If the traffic signal is connected to a central system, the timing plan can be transferred via the communication network in place. If the signal operates in isolation and is not connected to a central system, then the engineer or signal technician needs to enter the timing plan directly into the signal controller in the field.

Prior to implementation, the transportation engineer needs to confirm that all of the critical elements of the timing plan have been defined and approved as part of the signal timing development process.[14] These elements include general, uncoordinated, and coordinated parameters that control all movements at the signal depending on the nature of the intersection.

All of the elements are then compiled into an electronic or paper file in preparation for implementation. The transportation engineer or signal technician then transmits the timing plan into the controller, depending on the communication network for the signal system. After transmission, the technician should ensure that the plans are uploaded correctly into the controller.

Once the signal timing plan has been implemented, the transportation engineer should observe the signal in operation to determine if it is operating properly. This observation can involve observing traffic operations at the specific intersection(s) where the plan was installed, or driving through the intersection or corridor to observe operations as a system user.[14] Through these observations, the transportation engineer might determine that adjustments are needed to refine the operation of the signal, most if not all of which can be accomplished in the field in the controller. Regardless of the adjustments made, the engineer needs to consider the overall operational objectives of the signal system when making any changes in the field. More complex changes involving multiple signals will need additional analysis prior to implementation. Any adjustments made in the field need to be documented on paper, electronically, and in any software models used by the agency, to indicate the final "as-built" design of the timing plan.[14]

Step 8: Monitor and Maintain Once the signal timing plan becomes operational, the agency needs to establish an ongoing monitoring and evaluation process to periodically assess the operational performance of the signal. Traffic volumes and system users change over time, so installing a timing plan and never revisiting the signal does not yield optimal performance. Monitoring of the signal takes on a variety of activities to ensure that operational objectives are being met. These activities include, but are not limited to:

- Monitoring of signal operations
- Monitoring of signal and other field equipment
- Ongoing review of agency policies and national standards
- Ongoing response to requests and enquiries from the public[14]

Monitoring of traffic signal operations helps an agency sustain its outcome-based performance of the system. Periodic evaluation of individual signals as well as the complete signal system ensures that the operating agency is aware of changes in performance; provides the opportunity to make operational changes to better meet the needs of the system users; and ensures that the signal system works to meet regional safety and mobility goals and objectives. Documenting the monitoring and evaluation efforts allows the agency to share performance data with regional decision makers and the public and helps those stakeholders see the value in a well-designed and well-performing traffic signal system.

4.4   Regional Traffic Signal Operations Programs

The practice of establishing a regional traffic signal operation program (RTSOP) is an effective approach to signal operations when signal systems span large areas or cross multiple jurisdictions. It falls within the broader context of TSMO by targeting the signal systems, which can negatively impact mobility and safety when not operated in an optimal manner. This strategy for signal management is also beneficial in the current context of limited resources and budgets. When resources are limited, opportunities to optimize performance tend to take a back seat to more immediate needs such as maintenance to keep the system operating, particularly in smaller jurisdictions that operate only a few dozen signals. Transportation agencies recognize the benefits of an RTSOP, which leverages agency strengths and works with other partnering stakeholder agencies to enhance and optimize traffic signal operations on a regional basis.[17]

The purpose of an RTSOP is to establish a formal framework that guides partner agencies through the various activities required to operate traffic signal systems on a regional basis. By fostering collaboration across jurisdictional boundaries, it improves customer service to the traveling public; helps elevate major traffic signal system projects to the transportation improvement plan (TIP) for the region; leverages community resources to help meet regional goals; improves practices and efficiencies across the various jurisdictions; and strengthens cooperative relationships among all of the regional partners.[17] The critical elements of a RTSOP that foster effective and collaborative operations include the following:

- Integration, allocation, and management of resources
- Documentation and exchange of information
- Sharing of equipment
- Pooling of funding
- Training, development, and integration of personnel
- Integration of systems
- Integration of signal operations into each partner institution

While each RTSOP is unique based on the specific partner agencies, regional goals and objectives, and characteristics of the traffic signal network, commonalities exist across most programs. These commonalities most often include the fact that they create a culture of cooperation, develop successful partnerships between the participating stakeholder agencies, and allow for the evolution of the organizational structure of the program over time to better meet the needs of the region.[17]

As noted previously, an RTSOP establishes a framework that guides the collaborative management of the traffic signal system by all of the regional partners. A typical framework for an RTSOP is illustrated in Fig. 4.13, which demonstrates the importance of continuous improvement in throughout the entire process. General descriptions of these individual steps are included in Table 4.27. It is important to note that in the RTSOP context, these steps are undertaken by all partnering agencies that are included in the program.

Once an RTSOP is in place, the stakeholder agencies need to ensure that the program is sustainable. A long-term successful program is an integral part of broad

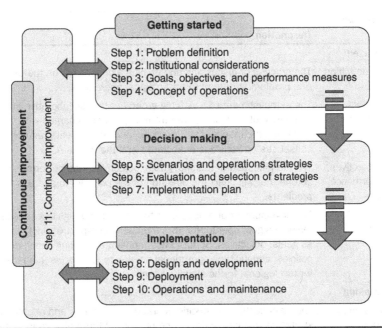

Figure 4.13 Regional traffic signal management and operation program framework. (*Ref. 17.*)

regional TSMO program. Key elements of a sustainable program include, but are not limited to:

- Leadership from the stakeholder agencies to champion the program and work to ensure its long-term commitment to meeting regional goals and objectives

- Ongoing self-assessment and evaluation of regional traffic signal operations to identify opportunities to enhance system efficiency and effectiveness

- The ongoing collection of relevant data and the assessment of signal system performance measures against targets to chart progress

- Ongoing training program for stakeholder staff to develop knowledge, skills, and abilities to support traffic signal system operations and to promote innovative solutions

- Commitment by all stakeholder agencies to pursue funding mechanisms to support the program at all levels and through collaborative partnerships in identifying sources for that funding

- Ongoing public involvement and outreach to disseminate information related to the program, related performance measures, the program's impact on meeting regional goals and objectives, and the gathering of public feedback into the continual improvement process[17]

Overall, a successful RTSOP brings together the regional transportation partners to address traffic signal system challenges in a collaborative, organized, and comprehensive manner. The program leverages partnerships to implement strategies that help

RCTOP Framework Step	Description
Getting Started	
1: Problem definition	The process of discussing and gaining a consensus on the extent and severity of a problem(s) related to traffic signal operations.
2: Institutional considerations	The establishment of a working group or other collaborative structure, comprised of representatives from all partners, charged with the responsibility of guiding the management process, and which meets regularly to gain consensus on activities associated with the program.
3: Goals, objectives, and performance measures	The identification of regional goals, objectives, and performance measurement criteria that will chart the direction of the program to address the identified problems.
4: Concept of operations	The development of a document that provides a high-level description of regional signal operations from the user's perspective. Includes such elements as goals, objectives, performance measures, existing conditions, practices, policies, capabilities, operational scenarios, strategies, plans, and procedures for the regional traffic signal system.
Decision Making	
5: Scenarios and operations strategies	The identification of specific operational scenarios and related operational strategies that can address one or more of the problems identified previously.
6: Evaluation and selection of strategies	The evaluation of operational scenarios and strategies with the intent to select the most appropriate for working to address the identified problem(s) which can help meet goals and objectives.
7: Implementation plan	The development of a plan to implement the selected operational strategy or strategies selected and which incorporates all activities conducted throughout the entire process along with all details associated with the deployment of that strategy, including capital and operating costs, programming priorities, scheduling, infrastructure needs, maintenance, and costs.
Implementation	
8: Design and development	The establishment of an executable project plan to implement the strategy(ies) select, including details on how the plan will be implemented to address the goals and objectives of the strategy(ies) and the region.
9: Deployment	The process of executing the project plan to deploy the strategy(ies), which involves interagency agreements and collaboration of all participating agencies.
10: Operations and maintenance	The ongoing operation and maintenance of the strategy(ies) by the appropriate stakeholders, including the clear identification of related activities, roles, and responsibilities for the specific operating plans and procedures.
Continuous Improvement	
11: Continuous improvement	The process of continually monitoring and evaluating the traffic signal system to assess the impacts of the deployed strategy(ies), comparing those impacts and resulting performance measures to stated goals, and objectives, and determining if changes or modifications need to be made to the strategy(ies) and its operating plans and procedures.

TABLE 4.27   RTSOP Framework Steps (Ref. 17.)

meet regional safety and mobility goals and objectives through a continual improvement process. To that end, it is an integral part of a broader TSMO program, which is discussed in Chap. 7.

4.5 Case Studies

The following case studies illustrate examples of state and local agencies addressing the challenge of traffic control in their jurisdictions. They represent a range of approaches that work to improve the operations of the transportation network and help agencies meet mobility and safety needs for the traveling public.

4.5.1 Traffic Signal Management Plan—Utah

The Utah Department of Transportation (UDOT) established a TSMP in 2016 to marry the strategic goals of UDOT with the need to ensure the smooth flow of traffic on the transportation network.[18] The document lays out its purpose, which is to accomplish the following:

- Provide a framework for UDOT to sustain and advance the state's traffic signal system through maintenance, design, and operation.
- Illustrate the connection between the UDOT traffic signal system and the overall mobility goals of the State and its partner agencies.
- Establish the groundwork for future operational funding for the traffic signal system.
- Outline succession planning.

The TSMP describes the overall vision for UDOT, its mission, and its goals, which are shown in Fig. 4.14. The UDOT's core values include innovation, dedication, integrity, public responsiveness, passion, and fiscal responsibility, with emphasis areas including integrated transportation, collaboration, education, transparency, and quality.[18]

The goal for UDOT traffic signal systems is to move toward world-class traffic signal operations, which support the Department's vision, mission, and goals. To that end,

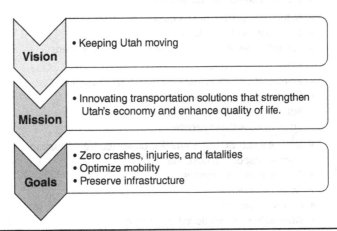

FIGURE 4.14 UDOT vision, mission, and goals. (*Ref. 18.*)

UDOT establishes the following as the critical objectives of the traffic signal system in the state:

- Safe signal operations
- Efficient and optimized signal timing and coordination
- Consistency in the quality of operations
- Comprehensiveness in coverage[18]

The UDOT TSMP outlines the relationship between traffic signal management in the state and the overall state vision for mobility, and includes detailed plans for maintenance, design, operations, and management and administration. The performance measures associated with these plans are presented in Table 4.28. Each performance measure is cross-referenced with the UDOT strategy it supports, a target performance measure, and the timing for reading that performance target. Additionally, for each topic, the UDOT TSMP outlines an enabling action plan that describes the existing condition associated with the topic, the future condition, an action plan to improve the condition, and the timing for the action plan.[18]

4.5.2   Regional Traffic Signal Operations Program—Denver, Colorado

The Denver Regional Council of Governments (DRCOG) administers the regional traffic signal operations program for the Denver region, also known as the Regional Traffic

TSMP Topic	Performance Measures
Maintenance	• Percent of functional detection • Percent of preventative maintenance vs. reactive maintenance • Time to respond to emergency calls • Ground performance measures (PMs) including malfunction management unit (MMU) testing • Aerial PMs • Ongoing funding for proactive signal equipment replacement and maintenance • Signal maintenance budget online
Design	• Automated system health monitoring • Communications to detection • Percent of signals communicating to central system
Operations	• Minor phase max-out • Percent of detection installed that detect bicycles • Percent of signals arriving on green • Automated volumes • Improve pedestrian service
Management and administration	• Best practice vs. UDOT practice on subjective evaluation • Time to respond to customer • Time to close out request • Types of inquiries • New work orders • Work orders closed during the month

TABLE 4.28   UDOT TSMP Performance Measures (*Ref. 18.*)

Signal System Improvement Program (TSSIP).[19] The region has had the TSSIP in place since 1994, and the transportation management area currently covers 38 different operating agencies responsible for more than 3,800 traffic signals.

The Denver TSSIP outlines the regional goals and objectives for the traffic signal system, which serve as the benchmark against which the program measures improvements. The goal of the program is to ensure that the Denver region's traffic signal system will operate in safe manner that maximizes the efficient use of the arterial street network.[19] The signal system objectives that support this goal are:

- To minimize stops on the arterial system
- To minimize the stop time at intersections
- To maximize the reliability of the traffic signal system equipment

To meet these goals and objectives, the TSSIP outlines regional management strategies in four specific areas: operations, maintenance, design, and public communications. Table 4.29 provides a summary of the specific strategies included in these areas, all of which are intended to provide mobility benefits to a broad range of system users,

Focus Area	Strategy
Operations	• Address signal coordination timing on a corridor-by-corridor basis without regard to jurisdictional boundaries. • Optimize cycle lengths, splits, and offsets of coordination timing plans on a 3- to 5-year basis that work to achieve specific objectives. • For weekday operations, provide three time-of-day coordinating timing plans. Weekend operations and other special coordination timing plans to be evaluated and implemented where needed. • Monitor and manage the traffic signal systems to ensure reliable, coordinated operations for key signals. • Implement advanced function signal timing, from a variety of options, where needs and engineering analysis demonstrate a technical- and cost-effectiveness.
Maintenance	• Where warranted, implement and maintain a traffic signal system with specific base-level traffic signal control requirements. • Provide controllers that are compatible with the traffic signal system and provide functionality that supports the other maintenance and support strategies. • Where warranted, implement and maintain a traffic signal system with the specific advanced-level traffic signal control requirements. • Maintain the field infrastructure under their control in working order to support other operations and maintenance strategies.
Design	• Use communications design practices that support center-to-center communications that directly support shared traffic monitoring and operations.
Public communications	• Acknowledge when a public comment has been received and that it is being addressed by the appropriate agency. • When discussing coordinating timing with the public, highlight that the plans are developed in partnership with the operating agency, its neighboring jurisdictions, and DRCOG. • DRCOG conducts an evaluation of each signal coordination timing plan implemented, calculates the arterial progression index, and provides a summary of the evaluation results to the public, decision makers, and operators impacted by the improvement.

TABLE 4.29 Denver TSSIP Strategies (*Ref. 19.*)

including drivers, passengers, truckers, service vehicles, bicyclists, and pedestrians throughout the region.

The TSSIP contains a comprehensive system inventory that represents the current state of the signal systems across the region. Specific information included in assessment includes a traffic signal inventory; an accounting of controller type and signal system type by operating agency; system communications media; coordination methods by operating agency; and other details that provide a snapshot of the current state of the signal systems currently in operation. Based on the current inventory, the TSSIP lists specific projects which are needed by operating agency and which emerged from stakeholder meetings during the update process. Finally, the document contains an implementation plan for specific projects, and prioritizes those included based on the criticality of the need; the capability of the project to advance the regional goals and objectives; their cost-effectiveness; the importance of the corridor; strategic communications links; and local priorities and synergies among projects.[19]

4.6 Summary

As discussed throughout this chapter, traffic control is a critical element of the transportation system. Without a consistent traffic control system, both in terms of design and operation, the ability to safely and efficiently manage the network would be difficult. The transportation professional needs to understand the fundamentals of traffic control and how to design and operate traffic control systems so that they help agencies meet regional goals and objectives and help ensure the optimization of the transportation network.

Glossary of Acronyms

AASHTO—Association of State Highway and Transportation Officials

CMF—capability maturity framework

DRCOG—Denver Regional Council of Governments

ETC—electronic toll collection

FHWA—Federal Highway Administration

HCM—Highway Capacity Manual

MMU—malfunction management unit

MPO—metropolitan planning organization

MUTCD—Manual on Uniform Traffic Control Devices

NCUTCD—National Committee on Uniform Traffic Control Devices

PM—performance measure

RTSOP—regional traffic signal operation program

TCD—traffic control device

TIP—transportation improvement plan

TMC—transportation management center

TSMO—transportation systems management and operations

TSMP—traffic signal management plan

TSSIP—Traffic Signal System Improvement Program

UDOT—Utah Department of Transportation

Exercises

4.1   Write a paper (no more than 10 pages) on the importance of the uniformity of traffic control devices. Describe the five principles of traffic control devices and which each principle is important to the message they convey.

4.2   Write a paper (no more than 5 pages) on one particular traffic control device that you have seen that you think could be improved. Explain why you think it is lacking, how it might not meet one of the five principles of a traffic control device, and which specific principle(s) could be better met if it is improved.

4.3   Write a paper (no more than 5 pages) on the difference between a standard, guidance, and option with respect to the use of traffic control devices. Provide examples of each.

4.4   Describe the difference between pre-timed and actuated traffic signal control. Explain when a transportation engineer would implement each.

4.5   Flow rates are given below for each lane group of an intersection. Determine the minimum cycle and phase splits using the Webster method. Lost time is equal to the sum of the yellow intervals, which are 3 seconds each. The minimum green for each phase is 15 seconds. Prepare a traditional signal timing plan with the cycle length given as a multiple of 5 seconds and the phases in multiples of 0.01 cycle.

Lane Group	NBTR	SBTR	EBTR	WBTR
Flow Ratio				

4.6   Flow rates are given below for each lane group of an intersection. Determine the minimum cycle and phase splits using the Webster method. Lost time is equal to the sum of the yellow intervals, which are 3 seconds each. The minimum green for each phase is 15 seconds. Prepare a traditional signal timing plan with the cycle length given as a multiple of 5 seconds and the phases in multiples of 0.01 cycle.

Lane Group	NBLT	SBLT	NBTR	SBTR	EBTR	WBTR
Flow Ratio						

4.7   Flow rates are given below for each lane group of an intersection. Determine the minimum cycle and phase splits using the Webster's method. Lost time is equal to the sum of the yellow intervals, which are 3 seconds each. The minimum green for each phase is 15 seconds. Prepare a traditional signal timing plan with the cycle length given as a multiple of 5 seconds and the phases in multiples of 0.01 cycle.

Lane Group	NBLT	SBLT	NBTR	SBTR	EBTR	WBTR
Flow Ratio						

4.8   Flow rates are given below for each lane group of an intersection. Determine the minimum cycle and phase splits using the Webste's method. Lost time is equal to the tum of the yellow intervals, which are 3 seconds each. The minimum green for each phase is 15 seconds. Prepare a traditional signal timing plan with the cycle length given as a multiple of 5 seconds and the phases in multiples of 0.01 cycle.

Lane Group	NBLT	SBLT	NBTR	SBTR	EBLT	WBLT	EBTR	WBTR
Flow Ratio								

4.9   Flow rates are given below for each lane group of an intersection. Determine the minimum cycle and phase splits using the Webster's method. Lost time is equal to the sum of the yellow intervals, which are 3 seconds each. The minimum green for each phase is 15 seconds. Prepare a traditional signal timing plan with the cycle length given as a multiple of 5 seconds and the phases in multiples of 0.01 cycle.

Lane Group	NBLT	SBLT	NBTR	SBTR	EBLT	WBLT	EBTR	WBTR
Flow Ratio								

4.10   Flow rates are given below for each lane group of an intersection. Determine the minimum cycle and phase splits using the Webster's method. Lost time is equal to the sum of the yellow intervals, which are 3 seconds each. The minimum green for each phase is 15 seconds. Prepare a traditional signal timing plan with the cycle length given as a multiple of 5 seconds and the phases in multiples of 0.01 cycle.

Lane Group	NBLT	SBLT	NBTR	SBTR	EBLT	WBLT	EBTR	WBTR
Flow Ratio								

4.11   Write a paper (no more than 5 pages) reviewing three different traffic signal management plans for three different-sized cities. Compare and contract the documents and their strategies for signal management.

4.12   Write a paper (no more than 5 pages) comparing two different regional traffic signal operations programs from the United States. Compare and contrast the documents and their approaches to addressing regional goals and objectives.

References

1. *Manual on Uniform Traffic Control Devices for Streets and Highways, 2009 Edition (Including Revision 1 dated May 2012 and Revision 2 dated May 2012).* Federal Highway Administration, U.S. Department of Transportation, Washington, D.C., 2009.
2. 23 Code of Federal Regulations 255, https://www.ecfr.gov/cgi-bin/text-idx?SID=a2583ef3fa3a41e5b157549f8dd705ab&mc=true&node=pt23.1.655&rgn=div5#se23.1.655_1603, (accessed March 2018).
3. *United State Road Symbol Signs.* Report FHWA-OP-02-084, Federal Highway Administration, U.S. Department of Transportation, Washington, D.C., 2002.
4. "National Work Zone Safety Information Clearinghouse," https://www.workzone-safety.org/ (accessed March 2018).
5. "Work Zone Traffic Management." Federal Highway Administration, U.S. Department of Transportation, https://ops.fhwa.dot.gov/wz/traffic_mgmt/index.htm (accessed March 2018).

6. *Traffic Engineering Handbook,* 7th Edition. Institute of Transportation Engineers, Washington, D.C., 2016.

7. *Traffic Control Devices Handbook,* 2nd Edition. Institute of Transportation Engineers, Washington, D.C., 2013.

8. Kuhn, B., K. Balke, and N. Wood. *Active Traffic Management (ATM) Implementation and Operations Guide.* Report FHWA-HOP-17-056, Federal Highway Administration, U.S. Department of Transportation, Washington, D.C., 2017.

9. *Traffic Signal Operations Self Assessment.* National Transportation Operations Coalition, Washington, D.C., http://www.ite.org/selfassessment/ (accessed March 2018).

10. "Welcome to the Business Process Frameworks for Transportation Operations-Traffic Signal Management Capability Maturity Framework Tool," U.S. Department of Transportation, Federal Highway Administration, https://ops.fhwa.dot.gov/tsmoframeworktool/available_frameworks/traffic_signal.htm (accessed March 2018).

11. *Traffic Signal Management Capability Maturity Framework Factsheet.* Report FHWA-HOP-16-028, U.S. Department of Transportation, Federal Highway Administration, Washington, D.C., February 2016.

12. Fehon, K., and P. O'Brien, *Traffic Signal Management Plans— An Objectives- and Performance-based Approach for Improving the Design, Operations, and Maintenance of Traffic Signal Systems.* Report FHWA-HOP-15-038. Leidos and DKS Associates for Federal Highway Administration, U.S. Department of Transportation, Washington, D.C., 2015.

13. Day, C., D. Bullock, H. Le, S. Remias, A. Hainen, R. Freije, A. Stevens, et al. *Performance Measures for Traffic Signal Systems: An Outcome-Oriented Approach.* Purdue University, West Lafayette, IN, 2014.

14. Urbanik, T., A. Tanaka, B. Lozner, E. Lindstrom, K. Lee, S. Quayle, S. Beaird, et al., *NCHRP Report 812: Signal Timing Manual, 2nd Edition.* National Cooperative Highway Research Program, Transportation Research Board, Washington, D.C., 2015.

15. *Highway Capacity Manual 2010.* Transportation Research Board, National Academies of Science and Engineering, Washington, D.C., 2010.

16. Webster, F.V., *Traffic Signal Settings. Road Research Technical Paper No. 39. H.M. Stationary Office,* London, 1958.

17. Koonce, P., K. Lee, and T. Urbanik, *Regional Traffic Signal Operations Programs: An Overview.* Report FHWA-HOP-09-007. Kittelson & Associates, Inc. for Federal Highway Administration, U.S. Department of Transportation, Washington, D.C., October 2009.

18. *Utah Department of Transportation Traffic Signal Management Plan.* Utah Department of Transportation, 2016, http://www.udot.utah.gov/main/uconowner.gf?n=29256708738824069 (accessed March 2018).

19. *Traffic Signal System Improvement Program, 2013 Update.* Denver Regional Council of Governments, Denver, CO, 2013.

CHAPTER 5

Transportation Safety

5.1 Introduction

Working to ensure the safety of the transportation system is one of the most important responsibilities of the transportation professional. Since the invention of the automobile, safety on the road network has been a challenge. For example, as the Interstate system expanded, Americans took to the open road to see the country. Early transportation practitioners saw the need for providing highway rest areas, like the one shown in Fig. 5.1, to provide opportunities for drivers to stop and rest on long road trips. Today, these rest areas serve a vital role in highway safety not only for private citizens but also for the freight community. Long-haul truck drivers are subject to federal regulations governing hours of service. Because of these limits, drivers must find safe and convenient locations to park and rest. Roadside rest areas help serve that purpose. Without the accessibility to these areas, commercial truck drivers may be inclined to continue driving or park in unsafe location, such as the highway shoulders, exit ramps, or vacant lots.[1] As truck traffic continues to increase on the freeway network, this safety challenge will continue to grow. The transportation professional is always working to address such challenges through such innovations as uniform traffic control devices (TCDs), high-mast lighting, breakaway sign supports, and other roadside and roadway features that make navigating the transportation safer. Motor vehicle laws have also helped reduce roadway deaths with requirements for child restraints, graduated driver licensing, minimum drinking age laws, and distracted driving laws. However, fatalities in motor vehicle crashes in the United States still top 35,000 each year, and nearly every citizen can expect to be impacted in some way by a traffic crash in their lifetime.[2] This number of roadway deaths is unacceptable and continues to take a significant toll on society, both in terms of human and economic loss. Traffic safety must be eliminated as a public health issue to ensure the long-term livability of society. This chapter discusses the comprehensive approach to addressing safety in all phases of transportation, from planning to operations. The overall objective is to help transportation professionals and traffic safety experts ensure safety is a fundamental component of everything they do on a daily basis.

5.2 Safety Challenges and Programs

The direction for addressing safety in transportation is charted by the Federal Highway Administration (FHWA) Office of Safety, which has as its mission to lead the highway community in making the roadways safer. The challenges associated with the mission,

FIGURE 5.1 Early highway rest area. (© *Texas A&M Transportation Institute [TTI]*.)

which are in the forefront of the responsibilities of the transportation professional, are evident in the focus areas of the Office. These program areas include:

- The Highway Safety Improvement Program (HSIP)
- Intersection safety
- Local and rural road safety
- Pedestrian and bicycle safety
- Roadway departure safety
- The Roadway Safety Data Program (RSDP)
- Speed management[3]

These programs illustrate specific areas that bear specific attention because of the risks encountered by system users in these situations. Clearly, roadway safety is a complex challenge that should be attacked from all angles to eliminate roadway deaths.

5.2.1 Highway Safety Improvement Program

The cornerstone of the transportation safety initiatives in the United States is the HSIP. A cornerstone of the core Federal-aid safety program, the HSIP provides funding to states to help them address their safety challenges. The purpose of the program is to reduce traffic fatalities and serious injuries on all public roads, and the program has

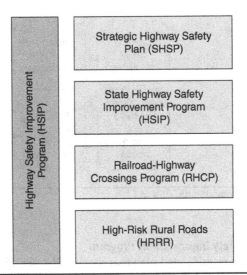

Figure 5.2   Highway Safety Improvement Program components.

four components as shown in Fig. 5.2.[4] The Strategic Highway Safety Plan (SHSP) is a plan required of all states that puts forth a statewide coordinated safety plan to address highway fatalities and serious injuries. The State HSIP represents the specific projects, activities, plans, and reports that are undertaken at the state level to improve safety. When jurisdictions are faced with hazards at railway-highway crossings, the Railroad-Highway Crossings Program (RHCP) provides funds for their elimination. Finally, for those states that see an increase in the fatality rate on rural roads, they are required to spend a portion of HSIP funds on rural roads. Collaboratively, all of these programs advance the mission of the FHWA Office of Safety and provide resources to states to address safety across their network. The following sections provide a brief overview of each of these programs and examples of how they help practitioners address safety in their transportation networks.

Strategic Highway Safety Plan

The SHSP is a statewide coordinated safety plan that is used by state transportation agencies to identify key safety needs across the state.[5] Each state develops its own SHSP with input and collaboration with stakeholder partners. These stakeholders include local, State, Federal, and Tribal agencies or governing bodies, private sector safety stakeholders, and other public agencies or advocacy groups who have a vested interest in public safety. Together, these partners develop a multiyear comprehensive plan that is intended to establish statewide safety goals and objectives in key emphasis areas and which focus on engineering, education, enforcement, and emergency medical services (EMS). The SHSP has four interrelated components, as illustrated in Fig. 5.3. The development and implementation of the SHSP incorporate a continuous improvement program and engage stakeholders and ensure that the document is regularly updated to reflect the changing safety needs of the state.

FIGURE 5.3   SHSP components. (*Ref. 4.*)

State Highway Safety Improvement Program

The state HSIP is a multifaceted plan that specifically identifies projects, activities, plans, and reports that support the SHSP and the goals and objectives included in that document. Specific safety-related projects are included in this plan, and practitioners use the planning process, as illustrated in Fig. 5.4, to identify countermeasures for safety challenges and prioritize projects in order of importance. Systemic safety analysis is part of the HSIP, and transportation agencies use a variety of tools, procedures, and guides to make consistent and sound investment decisions for safety-related projects.

Railroad-Highway Crossings Program

Railroad grade crossings present a unique challenge to transportation agencies from the perspective of safety. Crossings like the one shown in Fig. 5.5 inherently mix multiple modes (e.g., vehicles, bicycles, pedestrians) with the proverbial immovable object: a train. Since the inception of this program in 1987, fatalities at these crossings have decreased by over 57 percent in spite of the fact that vehicle miles traveled (VMT) on roadways in the United States has increased along with an increased in traffic on freight and passenger rail lines.[6] The program sets aside funds that are available to state DOTs to eliminate hazards at railway-highway crossings. Crossings that are eligible include public crossings that include roadways, bike trails, and/or pedestrian paths. Projects

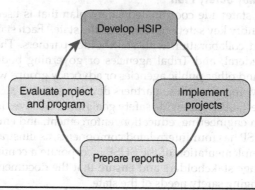

FIGURE 5.4   State HSIP process. (*Ref. 4.*)

Figure 5.5 Railroad-highway grade crossing in Texas. (© *Jim Lyle, TTI.*)

might incorporate such safety-related countermeasures as separation, relocation, protective devices, or appropriate signing.[6]

High-Risk Rural Roads

Nearly half of all highway fatalities each year occur on rural roadway. What is particularly troublesome about this statistic is that the fatality rate per 100 million VMT is more than double for rural roadways than for urban roadways.[7] In other words, fatalities on rural roadways are overrepresented when compared to urban fatalities or all fatalities combined. With less traffic on this segment of the transportation network, one would assume that crash rates are lower. However, the reality is that one is more likely to die in a rural roadway crash than in a crash on an urban freeway. The High-Risk Rural Roads (HRRR) program provides opportunities for state agencies to examine their network of rural roads, much like the one presented in Fig. 5.6, to determine if specific roadways pose significant safety risks to the traveling public. These roads, if they are identified in the state's SHSP, may qualify for funding to help reduce those risks through countermeasures.

5.2.2 Intersection Safety

Intersections represent a significant safety challenge to transportation professionals. By design, intersections introduce conflict into a roadway system since they are the location where opposing traffic meets and requires some manner of control of these conflict points. Over the past several years, approximately one-quarter of traffic fatalities and half of all traffic injuries are attributed to intersections.[8] This is a staggering statistic (as illustrated in Fig. 5.7) and represents a major focus area for improving safety, which is frequently tied to both design and operations. However, these factors are also intertwined with human factors (see Chap. 2). Understanding how these three elements are interrelated is essential to addressing the safety challenge at intersections.

FIGURE 5.6   Rural roadway with curve (© *TTI.*)

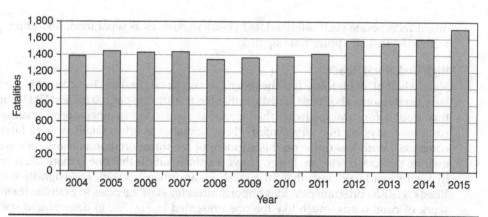

FIGURE 5.7   National fatalities at intersections (2001–2015). (*Ref. 9.*)

Strategies for addressing intersection safety approach the challenge from different perspectives, many of which are engineering in nature. For example, many intersection improvements can enhance safety focus on the vulnerable users of the traffic stream, such as pedestrians and bicyclists. Specifically, these users are at risk at intersections because of the conflicts that can occur with motor vehicles. As shown in Fig. 5.8, approximately 20 percent of intersection fatalities involve a pedestrian or bicyclist. Specific treatments and intersection additions that can enhance safety for these users at intersection like that shown in Fig. 5.9 include, but are not limited to:

- Advanced stop lines to separate the pedestrians and bicyclists from vehicles
- Installation of improved crossing zones

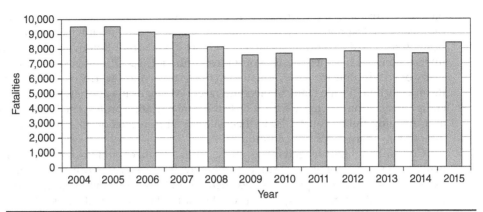

FIGURE 5.8   National pedestrian and bicyclist fatalities at intersections (2001–2015). (*Ref. 10.*)

FIGURE 5.9   Rural intersection. (© *TTI.*)

- Addition of pushbuttons for pedestrians
- Roadway features to increase awareness of pedestrians and bicyclists in the intersection median barriers, such as signs, median barriers, bollards, and refuge islands
- Improved intersection lighting and removal of obstructions to enhance visibility
- Improved signal timing and traffic signal enhancements to benefit these users[8]

Innovative designs can also enhance safety at the conflict points that are inherent in intersections. These designs include roundabouts; U-turn–based designs such as the median U-Turn and the Restricted Crossing U-Turn; crossover-based designs such as the Diverging Diamond Interchange and the Displace Left Turn intersection; and other designs such as the Continuous Green T, Offset T, Quadrant Roadway, and Jughandle intersections. Each of these designs provides solutions to specific intersection challenges, many of which come from the reduction in the number and severity of conflict points at the intersection.[8] While many of these intersection designs may be new to communities, comprehensive outreach and education to the transportation professionals, stakeholders, and traveling public can facilitate their successful introduction into the collection of intersection alternatives in a community.

Conventional four-legged intersections, both signalized and unsignalized, can also benefit from safety-related improvements as well. For signalized intersections, some examples that address specific issues include, but are not limited to, retroreflective borders on traffic signal backplates, providing all red clearance intervals, illumination, and specific intersection phasing. Unsignalized intersections, and rural intersections in particular (see Fig. 5.10), can benefit from oversized advance intersection warning signs and stop signs, removal of obstructions that might limit sight distance, flashing beacons, and retroreflective sheeting on sign posts.[8] All of these elements increase the conspicuity of the intersection and can improve the overall safety of the intersection. The transportation professional implements a broad range of safety improvements at intersections to address specific challenges, most of which are flexible and can integrate with regional goals and objectives.

5.2.3   Local and Rural Road Safety

The safety on local and rural roads continues to be a problem for transportation agencies. Over the past decade, the number of fatalities on rural facilities has decreased significantly as have fatalities for urban facilities. However, fatalities are disproportionately higher in the rural setting. Approximately 19 percent of Americans live in rural areas in

Figure 5.10   Rural intersection with safety improvements. (© *TTI*.)

Factor	Challenge with Rural Road Safety
Physical characteristics	Frequently lack shoulders and clear zones that provide recovery area for roadway departures
Behavioral issues	Higher travel speeds, reduced seat belt use, and higher rates of impaired driving are more common
Emergency medical services (EMS) response	The response time to incidents for EMS is increased in rural areas because of the reduced likelihood of witnesses to the crash and the long distances EMS must travel to reach the scene; increased time for victims to receive medical care
Data, expertise, and funding	Local agencies often have limited access to crash data; have varying level of expertise; and rural road issues have to compete with urban improvements for funding

TABLE 5.1 High-Risk Rural Road Safety Factors (*Ref. 12.*)

the country, yet fatalities on rural roadways account for approximately half of all fatalities nationwide.[11] A variety of factors contribute to the rural roadway safety problem experienced today, as described in Table 5.1. Most HRRR are located on the local road system that is operated by a local government. Engineering and safety expertise is often limited at the local government level, presenting challenges with identifying the appropriate countermeasure or improvement needed to address a rural road safety problem as well as securing the funding to implement the improvement.

Local operating agencies can utilize a variety of tools to identify HRRR safety issues and appropriate treatments to help mitigate the problem. These resources include the *Highway Safety Manual* (HSM),[13] the Safety Analysis online tool,[14] the Crash Modification Factor (CMF) Clearinghouse,[15] a Road Safety Audit (RSA), and training offered through Local Technical Assistance Programs (LTAP) and Tribal Technical Assistance Programs (TTAP) as well as other national-level training offerings. Safety treatments that can improve the safety and operations of rural locations cover a broad range of application scenarios, include, but not limited to:

- Horizontal curves
- Signalized and unsignalized intersections
- Applications for the non-motorized user
- Pavement and shoulder resurfacing
- Pavement markings
- Roadside elements
- Signing
- Vertical curves

When analyzing the need for safety improvements on rural roads, the transportation professional should follow a structured process to identify the best alternatives for the situation. The steps associated with the HRRR safety enhancement analysis are illustrated in Fig. 5.11.

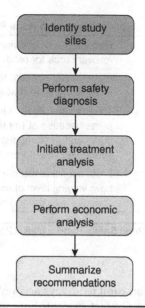

FIGURE 5.11   HRRR safety enhancement analysis process.

Transportation professionals should conduct an HRRR safety enhancement analysis for specific sites or site types that might benefit from safety modifications. They should then perform a safety diagnosis, using various descriptive statistics related to safety, to determine common crash types and those features or conditions that might contribute to those crashes. The next step is to conduct a treatment analysis to determine which safety treatments have the potential to enhance safety on the facility or selected site based on the common crash types previously identified. The transportation professional should then conduct an economic analysis to evaluate the economic feasibility of a selected treatment. As noted previously, funding is a major constraint in the ability to improve HRRR, emphasizing the importance of understanding the benefits and costs of an improvement. The final step is the assembly of a list of recommended candidate safety treatments for consideration. The implementing agency can then assess those treatments within the broader context of the agency and regional goals and objectives as well as needs to select the appropriate improvement project to address the safety challenge.[12]

Figure 5.12 illustrates a rural highway that has had several safety-related elements added, including an advance warning sign for an upcoming intersection and a reduced advisory speed. The reduced speed is provided on both a plaque on the advance warning sign as well as horizontal signing on the pavement. These treatments bring attention to the intersection and warn drivers to slow down and anticipate vehicles entering the roadway at the intersection.

5.2.4   Pedestrian and Bicycle Safety

As noted previously, pedestrian and bicycle safety is a major challenge in today's transportation environment. Annual fatalities of these system users top 16 percent of all traffic fatalities, with 65,000 pedestrians and 48,000 bicyclists being injured on roadway

Figure 5.12 Rural highway with safety improvements. (© *TTI*.)

crashes each year.[16] Working to ensure the safety of these transportation system users at intersections, like that pictured in Fig. 5.13, helps foster the livability of communities by offering safe travel options beyond the automobile. These modes also promote personal and public health, thereby reinforcing their importance as a viable transportation alternative that should be safe and convenient.

Figure 5.13 Intersection with pedestrians. (© *TTI*.)

Numerous approaches exist that enhance the safety of the transportation system for pedestrians and bicyclists. For example, the Every Day Counts (EDC-4) program promotes several safety countermeasures to enhance pedestrian safety: road diets, pedestrian hybrid beacons, pedestrian refuge islands, raised crosswalks, and crosswalk visibility enhancements.[17] These countermeasures offer several benefits, including improved safety, a targeted investment, and an enhanced quality of life for pedestrians of all ages and abilities. Similarly, a variety of actions on the part of operating agencies can enhance the safety of bicyclists.

The selection and design of bicycle facilities (i.e., shared roadway with regular lane width, wide curb lane, bike lane, separated path or lane) can foster safer bicycle travel when facilities compatible with the roadway network are implemented, as illustrated in Fig. 5.14.[18] Other factors that can enhance bicyclist safety include ensuring good maintenance of bicycle facilities; the provision of safe and convenient bicycle parking; offering connectivity to transit services; the implementation of greenways and shared-use paths to foster bicycling and connectivity in a community; and accommodation of bicyclists in work zones.

Transit agencies can also play a role in the enhancement of pedestrian safety and access in the transit network.[19] Internally, transit agencies can ensure that pedestrian safety is part of the overall culture of the organization with all levels of employees considering pedestrian safety issues into their daily responsibilities. Pedestrian training for transit operators can also help ensure that passenger safety is a priority on the system. Policies, services, and facilities can also be updated to meet the needs of their customers while enhancing pedestrian safety. Working in partnership with other local agencies, transit agencies can implement some engineering solutions to enhance pedestrian safety as part of the transit network. These improvements which could be applied to

Figure 5.14   Bicycle facility. (© *Jim Lyle, TTI.*)

FIGURE 5.15   Mid-block transit stop with pedestrian access. (© *Jim Lyle, TTI.*)

transit stops like that one provided in Fig. 5.15 might include, though not exhaustive, the following:

- Improved sidewalk design with an adequate width, a smooth, stable, and slip-resistant surface, and the provision of a buffer between the pedestrian and vehicle traffic

- Enhancement of roadway crossings near transit with marked crosswalks, median islands, curb extensions, and pedestrian warning signs and signals

- Safety treatments at pedestrian crossings of rail systems, including traditional gate/flasher/bell assemblies; active or passive warnings; fending; or grade crossings

- Enhanced transit vehicle design with such features as collision avoidance technology; pedestrian detection technology (see Fig. 5.16); strobe lights on top of buses; door safety interlocks; and right rear wheel safety guards

- Improved transit stop locations and design elements that improve the safety and comfort of pedestrian; including stop placement in relation to an intersection; bus stop design; loading zone type; shelters and other pedestrian waiting facilities; and identification and wayfinding signs[19]

Figure 5.16 Pedestrian detection technology on a transit vehicle. (© *TTI*.)

Transportation professionals have a number of tools at their disposal to both diagnose the pedestrian and bicycle safety problems within their purview and to identify potential solutions. A number of these tools are described in Table 5.2, each focusing on one of the system user categories and offering specific processes and resources to address the safety challenge. However, design alone cannot maximize the safety of bicycling or pedestrian facilities. Accommodating both bicyclists and pedestrians should follow a comprehensive approach that incorporates the elements of engineering, education, enforcement, encouragement, and evaluation. This approach brings all of the stakeholder groups to the table and helps ensure that form a comprehensive and stepwise approach to enhancing safety for these users.

5.2.5 Roadway Departure Safety

When a driver loses control of a vehicle and leaves the roadway, the consequences of any crash that might occur can be significant. For over six decades, transportation professionals have worked to reduce the negative impacts of roadway departure, such as the early crash tests like the one shown in Fig. 5.17 designed to develop crashworthy barriers that reduce the likelihood of a fatality. If a driver hits an obstacle on the side of the roadway, such as a bridge rail or another fixed object, roadside safety hardware can make that roadside more forgiving, thereby increasing their chances of surviving a crash.

In recent years, over 18,000 fatalities on roadways in the United States involved a roadway departure where the vehicle crossed an edge line, crossed a centerline, or left the traveled way. This number amounts to over half of all transportation crash fatalities nationwide: a sobering figure that presents a major safety concern for State and local transportation agencies.[20] To that end, the FHWA has developed a three-pronged strategic

Tool	Description
Bikesafe 2014: Bicycle Safety Guide and Countermeasure Selection System	An expert system that can be used to select engineering, enforcement, and/or education treatments and activities that might help mitigate known bicycle-related crash problems or help achieve specific performance objectives.
Pedsafe 2013: Pedestrian Safety Guide and Countermeasure Selection System	An expert system that can be used to select engineering, enforcement, and/or education treatments and activities that might help mitigate known pedestrian-related crash problems or help achieve specific performance objectives.
Bicycle Road Safety Audit	A formal safety examination by an independent, experiences, and multidisciplinary team of an existing or future roadway or off-road facility intended to assess the safety of cyclists and to suggest a multimodal approach to improving the safety of cyclists and all roadway users.
Pedestrian and Bicyclist Crash Analysis Tool	A software tool intended to assist pedestrian and bicycle coordinators, planners, and engineers at all levels of government in addressing crash problems involving these user groups.
Pedestrian Road Safety Audit	A formal safety examination by an independent, experiences, and multidisciplinary team of an existing or future roadway or off-road facility intended to assess the safety of pedestrians and to suggest a multimodal approach to improving the safety of pedestrians and all roadway users.

TABLE 5.2 Tools to Diagnose and Solve the Pedestrian and Bicycle Safety Problem (*Ref. 16.*)

approach to addressing the roadway departure safety issue through countermeasures. As illustrated in Fig. 5.18, the first thrust area is to keep vehicles on the roadway. In the event that a vehicle leaves the roadway, the second thrust area focuses on giving the driver the opportunity to recover safely and reenter the roadway when possible. Finally, in the event that a driver cannot recover, the third thrust area works to reduce the severity of any crash that occurs. Combined, these areas of focus work to reduce crashes, injuries, and fatalities associated with roadway departures. Furthermore, this approach complements other safety initiatives within FHWA and discussed in elsewhere in this section, including local and rural safety, the RSDP, and speed management.

The transportation professional can implement a number of focused countermeasures that work to reduce crashes related to roadway departures. Structured around the three key thrust areas discussed previously, these countermeasures are described in Table 5.3. Examples of some of these countermeasures are described in the following sections.

Roadway Delineation

Navigating curves can be challenge for drivers, particularly if they approach them at too high speed or if the curve is unexpected. Delineation, or the placement of TCDs to draw attention to the curve, is a safety countermeasure that has proven to be successful

Figure 5.17   Early crash test of roadside barriers. (© *TTI.*)

at reducing crashes on curves. As illustrated in Fig. 5.19, this delineation alerts drivers of the upcoming curve through the installation of such TCDs as post-mounted delineation chevrons and warning signs to reduce speed.[21] The warning signs can be installed with or without flashing beacons, which can be particularly beneficial during nighttime hours. The objective of this and other similar countermeasures is to work to accomplish the first step in keeping the vehicles on the roadway.

Pavement Edge

In the event that a vehicle begins to leave the roadway, the edge treatment on the pavement can help keep the driver from losing complete control of the vehicle. A pavement edge on highways with a sharp dropoff has been attributed to many serious crashes and fatalities. In an effort to help drivers maintain or regain control of their vehicle when leaving the pavement, a graduated pavement technique called SafetyEdge[SM] can

Figure 5.18   Countermeasures to address roadway departure safety. (*Ref. 20.*)

Thrust Area	Countermeasures
Keep vehicles on the roadway (see Fig. 5.19)	• Improve pavement friction • Install rumble strips and rumble stripes to alert drivers • Enhance delineation on horizontal curves • Improve nighttime visibility
Provide for safe recovery (this approach minimizes the sharp dropoff that occurs when height differences between a paved road and the adjacent roadside exist. Fig. 5.20)	• Install SafetyEdge[SM] technology to shape the edge of the pavement to help reduce the loss of vehicle control at the edge of the pavement • Create a clear zone: an unobstructed and traversable roadside area that allows a driver to stop safely or regain control once they leave the roadway
Reduce crash severity (Fig. 5.21)	• Install barriers, sign supports, and work zone devices to reduce the potential severity of crashes on the roadside should a vehicle leave the roadway and hit the device

TABLE 5.3 Effective Countermeasures to Reduce Crashes Related to Roadway Departures (*Ref. 20.*)

FIGURE 5.19 Horizontal curve delineation. (© *TTI.*)

be installed as a low-cost safety countermeasure[22] to reduce the sharp pavement dropoff and reduce the number of rural run-off road crashes on paved roads or unpaved shoulders. As illustrated in Fig. 5.20, a smooth pavement edge that gradually tapers to the unpaved shoulder can help improve safety on these types of roadways. This approach minimizes the sharp dropoff that occurs when height differences between a paved road and the adjacent roadside exist.

Roadside Crash Hardware

In the event that a driver leaves the pavement, the presence of median barriers can help reduce the severity of a roadside crash. Median barriers, which run longitudinally along the roadway facility in the median, separate traffic traveling in opposite directions. The objective of installation of the barrier is to redirect a vehicle that might strike it and keep that vehicle from heading into oncoming traffic. Figure 5.21 illustrates a more recent innovation in median barrier technology called a cable barrier. This type of barrier is a cost-effective means of reducing the severity of crossover crashes that occur on high-speed roadways, and the unique design of the cable barrier results in less impact force

FIGURE 5.20   Installation of road pavement and striping. (© *Jim Lyle, TTI.*)

Figure 5.21 Roadside cable barrier. (© *Jim Lyle, TTI.*)

when struck.[23] These barriers are particularly beneficial for operating agencies in that they are adaptable to a variety of median designs and slopes and can be installed using less invasive construction techniques, thereby reducing their overall costs.

Pavement Friction

Pavement friction is an essential element in a driver being able to keep their vehicle in the travel lane as they navigate a horizontal curve. When pavement is in poor condition, particularly when it is wet, it can contribute to a roadway departure crash. Research has shown that pavement safety performance can be improved through such low-cost safety improvements as chip seal, slurry seal, microsurfacing, diamond grinding, grooving, micro-milling, and high-friction surfacing, to name a few.[24] High-friction surface treatments are especially effective at high-crash areas or on severe curves that experience wet weather crashes. Rumble strips installed on a roadway's center line or the shoulder produce noise and vibration when the vehicle travels over them. The intent is to alert the driver that they are leaving the traveled way. Rumble stripes are painted with a retroreflective coating to alert drivers with an audible noise but to also increase the nighttime visibility of the edge of the pavement. Horizontal curves can also benefit from low-cost countermeasures to improve their safety. Such treatments include pavement markings to delineate the curve and alert drivers to reduce speeds; signing to warn drivers of upcoming curves; pavement and shoulder improvements; and delineation, visibility, and pavement improvements at intersection in curves.[25] Finally, transportation professionals can improve the visibility of the roadway during nighttime hours by installing and adequately maintaining retroreflective signs, pavement markings, and roadway lighting. All of these countermeasures work to improve roadway conditions and inform the driver to reduce the likelihood that a vehicle leaves the roadway.

Roadside Clear Zone

If a vehicle leaves the roadway, it does not necessarily mean that a crash will occur. The transportation professional can design the roadside to reduce the likelihood of a crash by providing the driver with the opportunity to regain control of their vehicle. Additionally, creating a clear zone of space beyond the pavement can help a driver regain control of their vehicle. Finally, installing crashworthy roadside hardware helps reduce the likelihood of injury or fatality should a vehicle strike the device. All of these approaches to roadway departure safety help reduce crashes that occur when a vehicle leaves the roadway. Developing a roadway departure safety implementation plan can help states develop a comprehensive and systematic approach to implementing low-cost treatments to address specific types of roadway departure crashes and enhance the overall safety of their system.

5.2.6   Roadway Safety Data Program

To effectively manage a transportation network, an operating agency needs to understand the current status of its system. As discussed in Chap. 8, transportation systems management and operations (TSMO) has emerged as the modern approach to addressing mobility and safety issues by capitalizing on the infrastructure investment through optimization. A key element of a TSMO program is being able to assess the performance of the system. Data are essential to understanding performance. The RSDP Toolbox offers resources to help agencies develop or strengthen their roadway safety data program for use in their safety management program.[26] With an RSDP, an agency can determine what safety data to collect, how to collect and maintain that data, ensure that the quality of that data is maintained, and determine how to integrate with other sources for effective analysis. Once an agency has the data, it can analyze it using various analysis tools that are then used to inform investment decisions to address safety challenges. The overall steps and rationale for a comprehensive roadway safety data program is presented in Fig. 5.22.

As with other agency programs, a roadway safety program requires a comprehensive management plan, which incorporates the elements of data collection, data analysis, and strategic decision making to enhance overall safety on the network. The RSDP is an effective tool that an agency can use to accomplish this important aspect of TSMO.

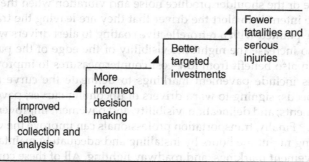

Figure 5.22   Roadway Safety Data Program rationale. (*Ref. 26.*)

5.2.7 Speed Management

Nearly one-third of all traffic fatalities are related to the excessive use of speed, either traveling in excess of the posted speed limit or driving too fast for the conditions. The FHWA encourages states to develop speed management programs to work to address this critical safety concern. Since speed-related crashes occur on all levels of roadways, agencies at all levels should develop and implement strategies to address crashes in their jurisdiction. Transportation professionals can also work to integrate speed management into other critical safety-related programs such as roadway departure, intersection, and pedestrian and bicyclist safety focus areas.

One elemental approach that operating agencies undertake to manage speed is the process of setting speed limits.[27] It is critical that speed limits be appropriate for a facility and reflect the maximum reasonable and safe speed for normal conditions. Ideally, the speed limit posted on a facility should be determined to be acceptable by most drivers. While practitioners cannot account for all drivers with very high and very low risk tolerances, if most drivers believe that a speed is appropriate, they will obey it. If they believe the speed is too low, then they are likely to violate the limit imposed on them. The Manual on Uniform Traffic Control Devices (MUTCD) sets national standards for signing for speed limits and advisory speeds, but emphasizes the requirement that speed limits shall be established on the basis of an engineering study.[28] A variety of methods and practices are readily available to transportation professionals in setting speed limits. Four of these methods include the engineering approach based on either operating speed or road risk; an expert system (e.g., the web-based tool USLIMITS2[29]); the use of optimal speeds; and injury minimization.[30] Other special situations that the practitioner should consider with respect to setting speed limits, particularly to address unique conditions, include:

- Advisory speeds
- Nighttime speed limits
- School zone speed limits
- Work zone regulatory speeds
- Truck speed limits
- Minimum speed limits
- Variable speed limits
- Transition zone speed limits
- Seasonal or holiday speed limits

Additionally, it is important to recognize that the practitioner should not set a speed limit for a facility and never change it. Periodic reevaluation of speed limits helps ensure that the limit continues to reflect the reasonable speed for the conditions. As the roadway environment evolves over time, such as changes in land use, geometry, or other conditions, the speed limit may need to be modified.

Traffic calming is a design approach that can work to manage speed in certain areas of a community. A formal definition that has been developed by FHWA and ITE is provided below:

The primary purpose of traffic calming is to support the livability and vitality of residential and commercial areas through improvements in non-motorist safety, mobility, and comfort. These objectives are typically achieved by reducing vehicle speeds or volumes on a single street or a street network. Traffic calming measures consist of horizontal, vertical, lane narrowing, roadside, and other features that use self-enforcing physical or psycho-perception means to produce desired effects.[31]

Practitioners can implement any number of traffic calming applications to reduce speeds and thereby enhance the safety and livability of a community. Examples are provided in Table 5.4. It is important to note that implementing agencies should work closely with stakeholder agencies and community groups to develop such applications and to ensure that any potential negative ramifications of these strategies are mitigated appropriately.

The list of traffic calming countermeasures is extensive, and many jurisdictions across the country have implemented a variety of strategies to address speeding and other safety challenges related to speeding. One particular intersection design that can benefit speed management is the roundabout. As illustrated in Fig. 5.23, a roundabout is a circular intersection that replaces a conventional intersection and eliminates the need for a traffic signal or conventional stop control at an intersection.

Traffic Calming Category	Traffic Calming Example
Horizontal deflection	• Lateral shift • Chicane • Realigned intersection • Traffic circle • Small modern roundabout and mini-roundabout • Roundabout
Vertical deflection	• Speed hump • Speed cushion • Speed table • Offset speed table • Raised crosswalk • Raised intersection
Street width reduction	• Corner extension • Choker • Median island • On-street parking • Road diet
Routing restriction	• Diagonal divider • Full closure • Half closure • Median barrier • Forced turn island

TABLE 5.4 Traffic Calming Applications (*Ref. 31.*)

Figure 5.23   Roundabout. (© *Jim Lyle, TTI.*)

Roundabouts can be used in both rural and urban locations, and they are an effective means of moving vehicles through an intersection safely and efficiently as the inherent design helps lower speeds and reduce conflict points between vehicles.[32] Because of the reduced speeds, crash severity at roundabouts tends to be less than that a conventional intersections.

5.3   Vulnerable Populations

From a safety perspective, the transportation professional needs to pay particular attention to vulnerable populations. Statistics show that certain segments of the population are overrepresented in safety-related crash data, emphasizing the importance of working to reduce safety risks for those groups. Some of these groups include older drivers, younger drivers, motorcyclists, young children, and persons with disabilities. For example, motor vehicle crashes are the leading cause of death for young persons in the United States, and this group of drivers is overrepresented in the crash statistics.[33] On the other end of the spectrum, older drivers experience deterioration in a variety of skills essential to driving that deserve special attention.[34] Motorcycles also represent a unique challenge as they lack a protected compartment for the rider and passenger, making them more vulnerable to injury.[35] Table 5.5 provides characteristics about some of these vulnerable populations that put them at risk and possible countermeasures to help reduce collisions involving these groups.

While this list is not exhaustive, it illustrates the unique challenge that these practitioners face when working to address safety on the roadway networks. When developing strategic plans to address safety across the broad range of situations, operating

Vulnerable Population	Characteristics	Approaches, Strategies, and Countermeasures
Younger drivers[33]	• Have less experience • Tend to make poor judgments about hazards in the driving environment • Tend to make poor judgments about their own hazardous actions • Likely to be a passenger in a vehicle driving by a younger driver	• Implement or improve graduated driver licensing systems • Publicize, enforce, and adjudicate laws pertaining to young drivers • Assist parents in managing their teens' driving • Improve young driver training • Employ school-based strategies
Older population[34]	• Reductions in strength, flexibility, and range of motion that can negatively impact driving • Deterioration of cognitive functions (working memory, selective attention, processing speed) and visual functions (visual acuity, contrast sensitivity, and glare sensitivity) can impact ability to process roadway information quickly • May have difficulty judging the speed of approaching vehicles[19]	• Plan for an aging population within agency • Improve the roadway and driving environment to better accommodate the special needs of older drivers • Identify older drivers at increased risk of crashing and intervene • Improve the driving competency of older adults in the general driving population • Reduce the risk of injury and death to older drivers and passengers involved crashes
Children as pedestrians	• May have difficulty choosing where it is safety to cross the street • May have difficulty deciding when it is safe to cross the street • May have difficulty seeing (and being seen by) drivers of all types of vehicles because of less peripheral vision and being smaller than adults • May have difficulty judging the speed of approaching vehicles • May need more time to cross a street than adults[19]	• Enhance public awareness about the need to improve safety for child pedestrians while promoting the health and environmental benefits of walking • Modify the behavior and attitudes of both pedestrians and drivers to improve sharing the road • Modify the physical environment to better support pedestrian traffic • Develop and conduct effective safe-walking programs[36]
Motorcycles[35]	• Lack a protected vehicle compartment • Operating a motorcycle is more demanding than operating a passenger vehicle • Visibility of motorcycles to drivers of motor vehicles is often a challenge	• Incorporate motorcycle-friendly roadway design, traffic control, construction, and maintenance policies and practices • Improve motorcycle licensing and rider training programs to teach and measure skills and behaviors required for crash avoidance • Increase the visibility of motorcyclists • Increase motorcycle rider safety awareness • Increase safety enhancements for motorcyclists

TABLE 5.5   Vulnerable Populations, Characteristics, and Possible Countermeasures

Vulnerable Population	Characteristics	Approaches, Strategies, and Countermeasures
Persons with disabilities	<ul><li>May be more affected by surface irregularities in the pavement and changes in slope or grade</li><li>May need more time to cross a street than people without disabilities</li><li>May have trouble seeing (and being seen) by drivers of all types of vehicles due to seated position (for people using wheelchairs)</li><li>Visually impaired pedestrians may have trouble detecting yielding vehicles or communicating visually with drivers in crossing at unsignalized crosswalks[19]</li></ul>	<ul><li>Design sidewalks to accommodate wheelchairs and construct with a smooth, durable material</li><li>Build and maintain sidewalks in urban areas along all major arterial streets, in commercial areas, and where the public is invited</li><li>Include curb cuts at all crosswalks and install ramps to accommodate wheelchairs, elderly pedestrians, persons with mobility limitations, etc</li><li>Keep street furniture out of the normal travel path to the extent possible</li><li>May benefit from pedestrian signal information provided in multiple formats (audible, tactile, and visual) and incorporate accessible pedestrian push buttons[37]</li></ul>

TABLE 5.5   Vulnerable Populations, Characteristics, and Possible Countermeasures (*Continued*)

agencies need to make a deliberate effort to consider these populations in plans and programs for safety-related countermeasures. Incorporating them in planning, design, and operations efforts can support regional safety goals and objectives and work to reduce crashes, injuries, and fatalities in their jurisdictions. The following sections discuss some unique vulnerable populations that present a challenge for transportation agencies.

5.3.1 Motorcycles

In recent years, motorcycle fatalities have increased on the nation's highways and they are disproportionately represented in fatality statistics. Fatalities involving a motorcyclist were 28 times more likely to occur than fatalities involving an occupant of a passenger car.[38] Speeding and impairment are frequently cited as contributing factors to these crashes and resulting fatalities. From an infrastructure perspective, transportation agencies can work to help reduce the likelihood and severity of crashes involving motorcycles. For example, practitioners can work to develop road-sides on rural facilities that are more forgiving to motorcyclists since they tend to prefer rural roads. Additionally, some road conditions, while necessary for a variety of practical reasons, present challenges for motorcyclists. These conditions—whether as a result of a work zone or inherent in the roadway—might include steep pavement crowns, no shoulders, steel plates, grooved pavement, sealants, or loose material. Providing advance warning to riders (see Fig.5.24) that these conditions exist helps enhance their awareness and they are more likely to be cautious and drive

FIGURE 5.24 Motorcyclists as vulnerable users. (© *Jim Lyle, TTI.*)

at an appropriate speed through the impacted area. Advance warning of geometric features such as curves and roundabouts, even if advisory signs are not necessarily needed, can also alert riders to upcoming changes in the geometry of the facility.

Some European countries have also developed infrastructure countermeasures that not only benefit motorcycles, but which also improve operations and safety for all vehicles on the roadway network. These examples include:

- Work zone activities and warnings that specifically target motorcyclists
- Maintenance practices that particularly benefit motorcyclists, including pavement quality and debris and litter removal
- Traffic control device sign design and placement that makes the roadside more forgiving for motorcyclists
- Design and application of pavement markings that are textured or have anti-skid characteristics
- Design of motorcycle-friendly barriers that help shield a boy sliding on the pavement from posts[39]

All of these treatments and countermeasures as well as a general awareness of the unique needs of motorcycles can help agencies address the safety challenges surrounding motorcyclists on their roadways.

5.3.2 Children

In addition to children as pedestrians being vulnerable users, children are also vulnerable in the vehicle. Fatalities associated with safety belts and child safety seats continue to be of concern for most state DOTs. The first Federal standards that addressed child restraints went into effect in the early 1970s.[40] However, crash tests were not required for child restraints until the 1980s. Crash data indicate that children are more likely to survive a crash if they are properly secured into a child restraint or a booster seat like the one shown in Fig. 5.25. Countermeasures targeting infants and children in child restraints and booster seats that have proven effective include, but are not limited to:

- Implementation of child restraint laws that cover seating position, vehicles, and ages
- Short-term, high-visibility enforcement of child restraint laws
- Community outreach and communications in support of enforcement
- Inspection stations
- Child restraint distribution programs

Countermeasures such as these can increase proper use and help decrease fatalities of children involved in vehicle crashes.

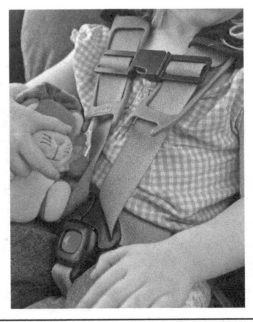

Figure 5.25 Children as passengers. (© *TTI*.)

5.3.3 Highway Workers

As discussed elsewhere in this textbook, the maintenance of the transportation network is essential to its overall effective operation. The necessary evil associated with maintenance is the work zone. Every year, thousands of work zones are active across the country providing necessary and critical improvement to the infrastructure. However, these work zones also present risks to both the traveling public and the workers in those work zones because of daily changes in traffic patterns, narrowed lanes, and other construction-related activities that can potentially increase the occurrence of crashes, injuries, and even fatalities.[41] In recent years, work zone fatalities have increased 7 percent, many of which are fatalities of highway workers. The National Work Zone Safety Information Clearinghouse provides a broad range of resources and tools to transportation practitioners to implement various countermeasures to improve work zone safety for everyone.[42] Examples of countermeasures include such applications as truck-mounted attenuators to protect workers in a moving convoy (see Fig. 5.26), and effective traffic control for even the smallest, short-duration work zone (see Fig. 5.27). An emerging trend that bears additional focus is the occurrence of nighttime work zones. In an effort to optimize the performance of the transportation network and to reduce the impact of work zones on the traveling public, many construction and maintenance efforts take place at night (see Fig. 5.28). While the number of vehicles moving through the work zone is drastically reduced at night, the safety of the workers may be more at risk due to lack of visibility. Unique countermeasures are available to mitigate the visibility issue such as nighttime lighting, mobile warning lights, effective speed control, and high-visibility apparel.[42]

Figure 5.26   Work convoy. (© *TTI.*)

Figure 5.27 Active work zone. (© *TTI.*)

Figure 5.28 Nighttime work zone. (© *Jim Lyle, TTI.*)

Figure 5.29   Driver using a handheld device. (© *Jim Lyle, TTI.*)

5.3.4   Distracted Drivers

Perhaps one of the most critical safety issues emerging today on the transportation network is distracted driving. With the rapid advancement of technology, the use of that technology while operating a motor vehicle causes a distraction that can be fatal (see Fig. 5.29). Transportation agencies are grappling with this safety challenge in a variety of ways, identifying countermeasures and other effective mechanisms to reduce distracted driving. State governments have passed legislation that specifically penalizes driving while distracted, many categorizing distracted driving as negligent driving.[43] Other strategies include the development of public outreach campaigns that coincide with efforts to raise awareness of distracted driving, and reducing roadside distractions that may exacerbate the problem. All of these countermeasures work to influence the safety culture in the United States, which helps reinforce socially acceptable and unacceptable behavior among peers.

5.4   Planning for Safety

The most effective way that a State agency can incorporate safety in their planning activities is to develop a SHSP. This plan, which is required as part of the HSIP, is a statewide-coordinated plan that sets forth an integrated framework for addressing the safety challenges that are paramount to reducing crashes, serious injuries, and fatalities on public roads.[44] Various resources are available for State agencies to develop a successful SHSP; implement SHSP strategies and track and monitor progress; promote the SHSP and engage stakeholder groups and community leaders to gain buy-in; and collect data and analyze performance to chart progress and to update and modify the SHSP as appropriate. Table 5.6 provides a description of the foundational requirements for an SHSP. Note that the plan emphasized a multidisciplinary approach that emphasizes collaboration, coordination, and consensus building to incorporate safety into the overall planning process and the integrate safety into all phases of an agency's processes.

Requirement	Description
A consultative approach	The planning process must include key multidisciplinary stakeholders, which should be consulted early in the planning process to help facilitate improved coordination across the diverse group.
Coordination with other transportation plans	The relevant transportation plans within a State should be developed in a cooperative process and have consistent safety goals and objectives that support a performance-based highway safety program.
Data-driven problem identification	The SHSP must analyze and make effective use of the best available safety data to identify critical highway safety problems and safety improvement opportunities.
Consideration of additional safety factors	States must consider additional safety factors when establishing their emphasis areas and strategies.
A performance-based approach	Plans should support a performance-based approach by adopting performance-based goals and include multiyear objectives to encourage monitoring of the status and progress of implementation efforts.
Use of effective strategies and countermeasures	Must describe a program of strategies to reduce or eliminate safety hazards with high priority given to those that can significantly reduce roadway fatalities and serious injuries in emphasis areas.
Multidisciplinary approach	Must address a variety of factors—including the highway safety elements of engineering, education, enforcement, and emergency services—to both infrastructure and noninfrastructure emphasis areas.
Special requirements	States must include the definition of "high-risk rural roads" and include strategies to address older driver and pedestrian safety if there has been an increase in fatalities and serious injuries to those vulnerable users.
SHSP update	Must establish an update and evaluation cycle or schedule and update the document on a regular basis and no later than 5 years from the date of the previous approved version.
SHSP evaluation	Must include mechanisms for regularly tracking implementation and monitoring and must evaluate the SHSP based on current safety data and confirm the validity of the emphasis areas and strategies.
Approval of SHSP update	Process for updating the SHSP must be approved by the FHWA Division Office.

TABLE 5.6 Strategic Highway Safety Plan Requirements (*Ref. 45.*)

5.5   Safety Performance Management

A critical component of transportation performance management (TPM), which is discussed in Chap. 8, is safety performance management (Safety PM). As discussed throughout this chapter, agencies are challenged with optimizing their network and identifying performance measures across the broad range of operational conditions for the roadways. Safety is no exception. Safety PM supports the previously discussed HSIP in that it establishes performance measurement requirements for agencies in order to implement the HSIP. The key aspects of the requirements are to assess fatalities and serious injuries on public roads using five key performance measures reported as rolling 5-year averages:

- Total fatalities
- Rate of fatalities per 100 million VMT
- Total number of serious injuries
- Rate of serious injuries per 100 million
- Total number of non-motorized fatalities and serious injuries[46]

Through the Safety PM, agencies set performance targets for safety and use a variety of resources and strategies to report on an annual basis to what extent they have made significant progress toward reaching those targets. This program is another tool in the safety tool box that agencies utilize to reduce roadway fatalities.

5.6   Case Studies

The New York City Pedestrian Safety Study & Action Plan—New York, NY

In 2010, the New York City Department of Transportation (NYSDOT) funded a study to identify the causes, common factors, and geographic distribution of over 7,000 pedestrian crashes in New York City.[47] The study reflected on the United States Department of Transportation (USDOT) safety goal of reducing fatalities as well as the considerable costs of crashes and fatalities on public health, economic strength, equity, sustainability, and quality of life for the community. Motor vehicle crash fatalities in New York City are declining, but NYSDOT recognizes that one fatality is too many. The report focuses on vulnerable road users of pedestrians, bicyclists, and motorcyclists, which accounted for 71 percent of all New York City traffic fatalities.

Analysis of crash data from 2005 to 2009 indicated that the most problematic areas in terms of crash fatalities were citywide, but that crashes mostly occurred at intersections, though widely dispersed along high-crash corridors. Arterial streets accounted for approximately 60 percent of pedestrian fatalities yet only represent 15 percent of the road network in the city. Major causes of fatalities included driver inattention, failure to yield, crossing against the signal, left turns, speed, alcohol use, and lane changing. With respect to pedestrian fatalities, senior citizens and foreign-born residents were overrepresented, and areas with higher proportions of Hispanic or black residents experienced higher crash rates than other areas.

The region boasts a broad range of existing safety programs that work to address safety concerns for virtually every critical risk area, including pedestrians, bicyclists, seniors, children, speed, and driving while impaired. The study presented a series of action plans to supplement and to expand safety-related activities to strengthen ongoing efforts. The action plan included:

- Installation of countdown pedestrian signals at 1500 intersections
- Re-engineering of 60 miles of streets to enhance pedestrian safety
- Re-engineering of 20 intersections for pedestrian safety on major two-way streets in Manhattan
- Launching of a pilot program to test the safety performance of a neighborhood 20 miles per hour (mph) zone
- Implementation of a pilot program to improve visibility and left turns along major roadways in Manhattan

In addition to these efforts, the study emphasizes the importance of enforcement, education, outreach, marketing, interagency coordination, and policy and legislation as additional tools to improve safety in the city.[47]

Involving Tribal Governments in the Strategic highway Safety Plan Update Process—Washington

Washington State Department of Transportation (WSDOT) and the Washington Traffic Safety Commission (WTSC) first led the authoring of the Washington SHSP in 2000. That plan sets out goals and objectives for safety in the state, prioritizes the work that needs to be accomplished by the State and partnering agencies to achieve those benchmarks, and outlines countermeasures to help that happen.[48] What is unique about the Washington SHSP is the participation of the Tribal Government in updating and maintaining that document. American Indian and Alaska Native populations in the United States experience higher rates of transportation-related fatalities than the overall population. To that end, States and tribal governments work together to address this safety challenge, primarily through the SHSP process.

In Washington, the Centennial Accord establishes an environment in the State that fosters the collaboration between these entities to address the transportation safety-related challenge. The State of Washington has 29 federally recognized Tribes which are actively involved in the Washington SHSP update process through a variety of entities. These entities include the Washington Indian transportation Policy Advisory Committee; Tribal Transportation Planning Organizations; the Tribal Traffic Safety Advisory Board; and the Northwest Association of Tribal Enforcement Officers. The advantage of the Centennial Accord is that it sets out a protocol for interacting with the Tribes, and the boards and organizations mentioned previously offer the framework to ensure an ongoing dialogue between all of the stakeholder groups. The key challenges associated with the SHSP update process include the tendency to form silos, data sharing, and limited funding, all of which are not unusual with large organizations engaged in coordination effort. However, a number of benefits have been realized by both the Tribes and Washington State. These benefits include an increased awareness in the Tribes of the importance of addressing roadway safety; the Tribes taking ownership of the final SHSP plan and using it as a guide for their own transportation plans; an increase in awareness of Target Zero strategies among tribal planners, enforcement, and EMS; stronger relationships between the stakeholder groups; and a broader understanding of the State's roadway safety requirement and needs.[48]

5.7 Summary

As discussed throughout this chapter, safety is a critical issue facing transportation professionals at all levels. Fatalities and serious injuries are significant in the United States, affecting all segments of the population. A broad range of resources is available to practitioners to help address this challenge and reduce the likelihood of crashes. A comprehensive approach to safety and ensuring that safety is considered in all activities associated with planning, designing, operating, and maintaining the network so improve safety. The end result is a network that is as safe and efficient as possible and that enhances the livability and sustainability of the nation's communities.

Glossary of Acronyms

CMF—Crash Modification Factor

DOT—Department of Transportation

EMS—emergency medical services

FHWA—Federal Highway Administration

HRRR—High-Risk Rural Roads

HSIP—Highway Safety Improvement Program

HSM—Highway Safety Manual

LTAP—Local Technical Assistance Programs

MUTCD—Manual on Uniform Traffic Control Devices

NYSDOT—New York City Department of Transportation

RHCP—Railroad-Highway Crossings Program

RSA—Road Safety Audit

RSDP—Roadway Safety Data Program

Safety PM—safety performance management

SHSP—Strategic Highway Safety Plan

TCD—traffic control device

TPM—transportation performance management

TSMO—transportation systems management and operations

TTAP—Tribal Technical Assistance Program

VMT—vehicle miles traveled

WSDOT—Washington State Department of Transportation

Exercises

5.1 Write a paper (no more than 5 pages) describing three treatments that can be used to improve intersection safety for pedestrians and bicycles. Provide a description of each treatment and explain how in enhances safety for the intended user(s).

5.2 Write a paper (no more than 5 pages) describing two innovative intersection designs and describe how they function and address safety challenges as well as any challenges that may exist with the design.

5.3 Write a paper (no more than 5 pages) describing three improvements that can be made at conventional intersections to address safety challenges. Provide a description of each treatment and explain how it enhances safety.

5.4 Write a paper (no more than 5 pages) describing a safety-related problem common for rural roads and present three countermeasures that can work to improve safety for the rural roadway environment.

5.5 Write a paper (no more than 5 pages) describing a safety improvement that can address bicycling safety in the roadway environment. Present the challenge presented by the presence of bicycles and how the improvement helps overcome that challenge.

5.6 Write a paper (no more than 5 pages) discussing two State-level Roadway Departure Safety Implementation Plans. Compare and contrast the two plans and highlight the stakeholder groups that are likely to be involved in the plans.

5.7 Write a paper (no more than 5 pages) discussing two State-level Roadway Safety Data Programs. Compare and contrast the two plans and highlight any improvements you feel could be made to these documents.

5.8 Write a paper (no more than 5 pages) addressing traffic calming and how this approach works to manage speed in the roadway environment. Provide three specific examples of traffic calming that can be effective in reducing speed.

5.9 Write a paper (no more than 5 pages) addressing potential safety countermeasures or strategies to address distracted driving. Provide three unique examples of how state or local jurisdictions have implemented policies or laws to address this safety problem.

5.10 Write a paper (no more than 5 pages) discussing the unique safety challenges associated with one of the vulnerable populations noted in this chapter. Provide two detailed examples of how a transportation professional can work to address these challenges.

5.11 Write a paper (no more than 5 pages) comparing two different SHSP from two different states. Compare and contrast the documents and the elements included therein.

5.12 Write a paper (no more than 5 pages) addressing the unique challenges associated with road worker safety and work zones. Provide three examples of techniques, strategies, or countermeasures that are frequently used to ensure the safety or transportation personnel in work zones.

References

1. "Truck Parking." Federal Highway Administration, U.S. Department of Transportation, https://ops.fhwa.dot.gov/freight/infrastructure/truck_parking/ (accessed May 2018).
2. "Toward Zero Deaths," http://www.towardzerodeaths.org/ (accessed October 2017).
3. "Mission of the Office of Safety." Federal Highway Administration, U.S. Department of Transportation, https://safety.fhwa.dot.gov/about/ (accessed October 2017).
4. "Highway Safety Improvement Program (HSIP)." Federal Highway Administration, U.S. Department of Transportation, https://safety.fhwa.dot.gov/hsip/ (accessed March 2018).

5. "About the State Strategic Highway Safety Plan (SHSP)." Federal Highway Administration, U.S. Department of Transportation, https://safety.fhwa.dot.gov/shsp/about.cfm (accessed May 2018).

6. "Railway-Highway Crossings (Section 130) Program." Federal Highway Administration, U.S. Department of Transportation, https://safety.fhwa.dot.gov/hsip/xings/ (accessed May 2018).

7. "Traffic Safety Facts: Rural/Urban Comparison of Traffic Fatalities." DOT HS 812 393, National Highway Traffic Safety Administration, U.S. Department of Transportation, Washington, D.C., April 2017.

8. "Intersection Safety." Federal Highway Administration,U.S. Department of Transportation, https://safety.fhwa.dot.gov/intersection/ (accessed March 2018).

9. "Roadway Safety Data Dashboards." Federal Highway Administration, U.S. Department of Transportation, https://rspcb.safety.fhwa.dot.gov/Dashboard/Default.aspx (accessed March 2018).

10. "Roadway Safety Data Dashboards." Federal Highway Administration, U.S. Department of Transportation, https://rspcb.safety.fhwa.dot.gov/Dashboard/Default.aspx (accessed March 2018).

11. *Traffic Safety Facts—2014 Data: Rural/Urban Comparison.* Report DOT HS 812 301, National Highway Traffic Safety Administration, U.S. Department of Transportation, Washington, D.C., 2014, https://crashstats.nhtsa.dot.gov/Api/Public/Publication/812301 (accessed March 2018).

12. Atkinson, J., B. Chandler, V. Betkey, K. Weiss, K. Dixon, A. Giragosian, K. Donoughe, and C. O'Donnell. *Manual for Selecting Safety Improvements on High Risk Rural Roads.* Report FHWA-SA-14-075. SAIC for Federal Highway Administration, U.S. Department of Transportation, Washington, D.C., 2014.

13. *Highway Safety Manual.* American Association of State Highway and Transportation Officials, Washington, D.C., 2010.

14. "AASHTOWare Safety Analyst." American Association of State Highway and Transportation Officials, http://www.safetyanalyst.org/ (accessed March 2018).

15. "Crash Modification Factors Clearinghouse." Federal Highway Administration, U.S. Department of Transportation, http://www.cmfclearinghouse.org (accessed March 2018).

16. "Pedestrian & Bicycle Safety." Federal Highway Administration, U.S. Department of Transportation, https://safety.fhwa.dot.gov/ped_bike/ (accessed March 2018).

17. "Safe Transportation for Every Pedestrian." Federal Highway Administration, U.S. Department of Transportation, https://www.fhwa.dot.gov/innovation/everydaycounts/edc_4/step.cfm (accessed March 2018).

18. *Federal Highway Administration University Course on Bicycle and Pedestrian Transportation.*Report FHWA-HRT-05-109, Federal Highway Administration, U.S. Department of Transportation, Washington, D.C., 2006.

19. Nabors, D., R. Schneider, D. Leven, K. Lieberman, and C. Mitchell. *Pedestrian Safety Guide for Transit Agencies.* Report FHWA-SA-07-017, Federal Highway Administration, U.S. Department of Transportation, Washington, D.C., 2008.

20. "Roadway Departure Safety." Federal Highway Administration, U.S. Department of Transportation, https://safety.fhwa.dot.gov/roadway_dept/ (accessed March 2018).

21. *Proven Safety Countermeasures: Enhanced Delineation and Friction for Horizontal Curves.* Report FHWA-SA-17-058, Federal Highway Administration, U.S. Department of Transportation, Washington, D.C., 2017.

22. *Proven Safety Countermeasures: SafetyEdge$_{SM}$* Report FHWA-SA-17-062, Federal Highway Administration, U.S. Department of Transportation, Washington, D.C., 2017.

23. *Proven Safety Countermeasures: Median Barriers.* Report FHWA-SA-17-060, Federal Highway Administration, U.S. Department of Transportation, Washington, D.C., 2017.

24. Merritt, D.K., et al. *Evaluation of Pavement Safety Performance.* Report FHWA-HRT-14-065, Federal Highway Administration, U.S. Department of Transportation, Washington, D.C., 2015.

25. Albin, R., et al. *Lost-Cost Treatments for Horizontal Curve Safety 2016.* Report FHWA-SA-15-084. Federal Highway Administration, U.S. Department of Transportation, Washington, D.C., 2016.

26. "Roadway Safety Data Program." Federal Highway Administration, U.S. Department of Transportation, https://safety.fhwa.dot.gov/rsdp/ (accessed Marc 2018).

27. "Speed Management Safety." Federal Highway Administration, U.S. Department of Transportation, https://safety.fhwa.dot.gov/speedmgt/ (accessed March 2018).

28. *Manual on Uniform Traffic Control Devices,* 9th Edition. Federal Highway Administration, U.S. Department of Transportation, Washington, D.C., 2012.

29. "USLIMITS2." Federal Highway Administration, U.S. Department of Transportation, Washington, D.C., https://safety.fhwa.dot.gov/uslimits/ (accessed March 2018).

30. Forbes, G.J., et al. *Methods and Practices for Setting Speed Limits: An Informational Report.* Report FHWA-SA-12-004, Federal Highway Administration, U.S. Department of Transportation, Washington, D.C., 2012.

31. *Traffic Calming ePrimer.* Federal Highway Administration, U.S. Department of Transportation, Washington, D.C., https://safety.fhwa.dot.gov/speedmgt/traffic_calm.cfm (accessed March 2018).

32. *Proven Safety Countermeasures: Roundabouts.* Report FHWA-SA-17-055, U.S. Department of Transportation, Federal Highway Administration, Washington, D.C., 2017.

33. Goodwin, A., R. Foss, J. Sohn, and D. Mayhew. *Guidance for Implementation of the AASHTO Strategic Highway Safety Plan, Volume 19: A Guide for Reducing Collisions Involving Young Drivers.* NCHRP Report 500, Transportation Research Board, National Academy of Sciences, Washington, D.C., 2007.

34. Potts, I., J. Stutts, R. Pfefer, T. Neuman, K. Slack, and K. Hardy. *Guidance for Implementation of the AASHTO Strategic Highway Safety Plan, Volume 9: A Guide for Reducing Collisions Involving Older Drivers.* NCHRP Report 500, Transportation Research Board, National Academy of Sciences, Washington, D.C., 2004.

35. Potts, I., S. Garets, T. Smith, R. Pfefer, T. Neuman, K. Slack, K. Hardy. *Guidance for Implementation of the AASHTO Strategic Highway Safety Plan, Volume 22: A Guide for Reducing Collisions Involving Motorcycles.* NCHRP Report 500, Transportation Research Board, National Academy of Sciences, Washington, D.C., 2008.

36. *National Strategies for Advancing Child Pedestrian Safety.* Centers for Disease Control and Prevention and National Highway Traffic Safety Administration, Washington, D.C., 2001, https://safety.fhwa.dot.gov/ped_bike/legis_guide/nsacps102001/nsacps102001.pdf (accessed March 2018).

37. *FHWA Course on Bicycle and Pedestrian Transportation.* Federal Highway Administration, U.S. Department of Transportation, Washington, D.C., https://safety.fhwa.dot.gov/ped_bike/univcourse/pdf/swless124.pdf (accessed March 2018).

38. *Traffic Safety Facts – 2016 Data: Motorcycles.* Report DOT HS 812 301, National Highway Traffic Safety Administration, U.S. Department of Transportation, Washington, D.C., 2018, https://crashstats.nhtsa.dot.gov/Api/Public/ViewPublication/812492 (accessed May 2018).

39. Nicol, D., D. Heuer, S. Chrysler, J. Baron, M. Bloschock, K. Cota, P. Degges, et al. *Infrastructure Countermeasures to Mitigate Motorcyclist Crashes in Europe.* Report FHWA-PL-12-028. Federal Highway Administration, U.S. Department of Transportation, Washington, D.C., 2012.

40. *Countermeasures That Work: A Highway Safety Countermeasure Guide for State Highway Safety Offices,* 4th Edition. National Highway Traffic Safety Administration, U.S. Department of Transportation, Washington, D.C., 2009.

41. *Work Zone Safety: Everybody's Responsibility.* Report FHWA-HOP-18-044, Federal Highway Administration, U.S. Department of Transportation, Washington, D.C., 2018.

42. "National Work Zone Safety Information Clearinghouse," https://www.workzonesafety.org/ (accessed May 2018).

43. *Local and Rural Road Safety Briefing Sheets: Behavioral Safety Strategies for Drivers on Rural Roads.* Report FHWA-SA-14-082, U.S. Department of Transportation, Federal Highway Administration, Washington, D.C., 2014.

44. "Strategic Highway Safety Plan." Federal Highway Administration, U.S. Department of Transportation, Washington, D.C., https://safety.fhwa.dot.gov/shsp/ (accessed March 2018).

45. *SHSP Quick Reference Guide.* Report FHWA-SA-16-097, Federal Highway Administration, U.S. Department of Transportation, Washington, D.C., 2018.

46. "Safety Performance Management (Safety PM)." Federal Highway Administration, U.S. Department of Transportation, Washington D.C., https://safety.fhwa.dot.gov/hsip/spm/ (accessed May 2018).

47. *The New York City Pedestrian Safety Study & Action Plan.* New York City Department of Transportation, New York, NY, August 2010.

48. *Unique Accord in Washington State Helps State and Tribal Governments Work Proactively on Roadway Safety.* Noteworthy Practices Database, Federal Highway Administration, U.S. Department of Transportation, Washington, D.C., https://rspcb.safety.fhwa.dot.gov/noteworthy/html/shsp_tribal_wa.aspx?id=189 (accessed March 2018).

CHAPTER 6

Transportation Planning and Demand

6.1 Introduction

As discussed in Chap. 1, the surface roadway network is a critical element in the movement of people, goods, and services in a safe and efficient manner. As the population grows in the United States, the transportation profession must be able to plan of that growth and the resulting impact that population has on the transportation network. Anticipating that increase in travel demand is a complex undertaking that is closely interrelated with other elements such as operations, all of which directly impact the sustainability of the surface network. This chapter introduces the concept of regional transportation planning; discusses the elements of the travel demand model (trip generation, mode choice, destination choice, and route choice); the practice of forecasting for planning and operations purposes and travel demand management (TDM) and its integration with traffic management.

6.2 Transportation Planning

The purpose of transportation planning is for transportation professionals to make them able to estimate traffic patterns in the form of traffic volumes on various facilities. This information is useful in determining how to design the facility, how to operate the facility, and what improvements might be most useful in the long term to manage the demand for transportation. However, the overall planning process cannot be undertaken in a vacuum. Transportation professionals use a comprehensive planning process that incorporates a broad range of data and public input, which considers a breadth of issues and constraints along with past, present, and future trends. Specific issues and constraints include, but are not limited to land use, development, safety, security, financial resources, and environmental stewardship.[1]

The transportation planning process, as illustrated in Fig. 6.1, is a performance-driven process, cooperative in nature, that involves a broad range of transportation-related and agencies as well as stakeholder groups to represent the needs of the community.[2] Partners in the planning process include, but are not limited to:

- Metropolitan planning organizations (MPOs)
- State departments of transportation (DOTs)

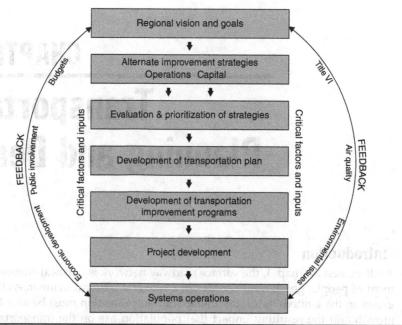

FIGURE 6.1   The transportation planning process. (*Ref. 2.*)

- Regional transportation planning organizations (RTPOs)
- Local transportation agencies
- Transit operators
- Community groups
- Environmental organizations
- Freight operators

The critical steps in this process provide context and establish a logical and stepwise framework for ensuring that the process incorporates all aspects of the community and addresses the need to ensure a sustainable transportation network that meets the needs of the citizens of the community. These steps are summarized below.[2]

- **Regional Vision and Goals:** Ensures that the vision, goals, and objectives for the community, its citizens, and its stakeholders are incorporated into the transportation planning process; serves as a guide against all actions can be measured.

- **Alternate Improvement Strategies:** Transportation planners and stakeholders use available data, planning tools, and analysis methods to generate both capital projects and operational alternatives and strategies for consideration.

- **Evaluation and Prioritization of Strategies:** All of the capital and operational strategies are evaluated against the regional vision, goals, and objectives and prioritized for advancement in the community.

- **Development of Transportation Plan:** The MPO works with regional partners and stakeholders to develop a long-range transportation plan for the metropolitan area. The long-range plan typically projects 20 years into the future and focuses on meeting the regional vision, goals, and objectives of a transportation network that accomplishes its purpose of the safe and efficient movement of people and goods.

- **Development of Transportation Improvement Programs:** Based on the long-range transportation plan, the MPO develops a transportation improvement program (TIP) that has a shorter horizon, typical 4 years, that sets out the specific projects and strategies to meet the goals and objective. The TIP is typically financially constrained and allocates the resources available to advance specific efforts.

- **Project Development:** Based on the TIP, the MPO works with the state, regional, and local transportation agencies to develop projects included in the TIP. A comprehensive project development process is followed to ensure appropriate implementation of capital and operational strategies.

- **Systems Operations:** Operating agencies monitor their systems and networks and assess their performance against a broad range of performance measures and benchmarks. They then evaluate the ongoing performance of the system and recommend dynamic actions to modify operations to enhance and improve system performance.

The transportation process is structured around critical factors and inputs and has a feedback process to ensure specific needs and issues are incorporated on an ongoing basis. The feedback loop is a mechanism for engaging the public and stakeholders to ensure that the goals and objectives for the community are incorporated into the process plans and resulting projects, as illustrated in Fig. 6.2.[2] The process is used to develop and prioritize alternatives for transportation investments; develop transportation plans and improvement programs to chart a path forward for making those investments; and supports project development and system operations.

FIGURE 6.2   Regional planning public meeting. (© *Jim Lyle, Texas A&M Transportation Institute [TTI].*)

Transportation planning activities take place across the spectrum of geographic conditions, from the corridor level up to the national and international levels, as shown in Fig. 6.3. Each level of analysis can build upon the other and can span everything from a fairly small, narrow scope geographically and/or temporally to broad geographic regions over long-term planning periods. For example, corridor or subarea planning can work to determine the effects of roads and road closures on traffic patterns in the planning area. Local planning efforts may examine the impacts of new developments on local area traffic. Long-term regional transportation planning can address the impacts of new roads and other major investments along with social and environmental implications of major transportation system investments. At the state level, statewide planning helps to establish a framework for making broad transportation investments across a state, and fosters collaboration and continuous process for that planning effort. Regardless of the scope of the planning effort, the involvement of stakeholder agencies and interest groups representing various segments of the community is vital to the overall success of the planning process. It helps gain buy-in from the community and recognizes that transportation is a vital component of the community's economic and social health and helps ensure that transportation projects meet the goals and objectives of the impacted area. The following sections provide information related to transportation planning and critical issues and trends transportation professionals address in the complex planning process.

Transportation planning activities

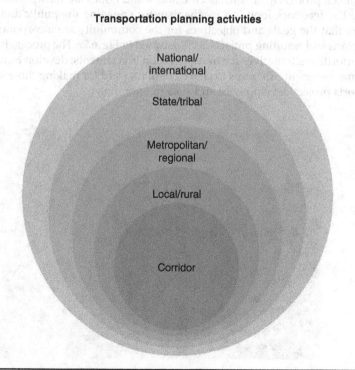

National/
international

State/tribal

Metropolitan/
regional

Local/rural

Corridor

Figure 6.3 Scope of transportation planning activities.

6.2.1 Key Planning Issues

The transportation planning process is complex and involves the consideration of numerous topics throughout the various steps. A number of the topics that transportation planners and operating agencies must consider are statutory in nature, the majority of which require the collaboration of various stakeholders representing all aspects of the community and are frequently required to receive funding from specific sources. They impact the overall transportation planning process in a variety of ways, some of which address issues that may be beyond the immediate area covered by the planning documents. A summary of statutory requirements that impact agencies involved in the planning process is provided in Table 6.1. Several of these topics are addressed in more detail in various chapters throughout this book.

Transportation professionals and agencies responsible for all levels of transportation planning are faced with other issues that impact their policy and planning efforts. While issues are not regulatory in nature and do not dictate activities or strategies, they

Statutory Requirement	Description
Air quality	The Clean Air Act (CAA) and Clean Air Act Amendments (CAAA) set out requirements for nonattainment areas (do not meet Federal air quality standards) and maintenance areas (violated Federal air quality standards at one time). Regulations require the development of a State Implementation Plan to improve air quality and require actions to reduce emissions from on-road mobile sources.
Congestion management process (CMP)	A CMP is required in a transportation management area (TMA) (any urban area greater than 200,000 in population[3]). The CMP includes information on system performance, provides alternative strategies for reducing travel demand and operational management strategies, and sets out an evaluation process to assess the impact of the strategies.
Transportation equity	The Civil Rights Act of 1964 along with other nondiscrimination statutes afford legal protection against discrimination by any agency, program, or activity that receives Federal assistance from the Department of Transportation. Additional Federal Executive orders also direct Federal agencies to address environmental justice issues in minority populations, low-income populations, and with persons with limited English proficiency.
Financial planning and programming	Transportation agencies have access to funding from a broad range of Federal, state, local, and private sources, most of which have specific eligibility requirements and require the development of financial planning documents (i.e., Statewide Transportation Improvement Program, Transportation Improvement Program, Long-Range Statewide Transportation Plan) and financial programming in order to receive funds.
Performance-based planning: programming measures and targets	Recent Federal transportation legislation (MAP-21[4] and FAST Act[5]) requires states and MPOs to establish performance measures in various areas, including congestion, emissions, fatalities and injuries, and freight movement on the Interstate system and the National Highway System (NHS) and set performance targets.

TABLE 6.1 Statutory Requirements Impacting the Transportation Planning Process (*Ref. 2.*)

Statutory Requirement	Description
Planning data and tools: models, GIS, and visualization	Transportation planning agencies and state DOTs have the ability to understand the potential impact of projects and programs on the transportation network, the human environment, and the natural environment through the use of travel forecasting models, land use models, air quality emissions models, data visualization techniques, and geographic information system (GIS) mapping.
Public involvement	Agencies are responsible for actively involving the public and other stakeholder groups in an open, cooperative, and collaborative process to gather input on needs, issues, and concerns in developing transportation projects, resulting in better-informed decisions and a mutual understanding and trust between the public and the implementing agencies.
Safety	MAP-21[4] requires states and MPOs to develop safety-related performance measures, targets, and plans, including Strategic Highway Safety Plans and a State Highway Safety Improvement Program to support safety-related performance targets that align with safety performance measures prepared by United States Department of Transportation (USDOT). Public transportation operators must prepare Public Transportation Agency Safety Plans.
Security	Due to the vulnerability of the transportation system and its role in emergency evacuations, Federal law requires that transportation planners consider security during all transportation planning and programming activities.
Transportation asset management	MPOs are required to develop a risk-based asset management plan for the NHS to improve or preserve the condition of the assets and the performance of the system. Public transportation providers are also required to develop a Transit Asset Management plan and coordinate them with states and MPOs. Asset management helps agencies consider the life-cycle cost of managing their assets and how they prioritize investments.
Transportation systems management and operations (TSMO)	Agencies are required to consider TSMO in the metropolitan and statewide transportation planning process and include appropriate strategies to optimize the performance of the existing transportation network through the reduction of congestion and an emphasis on mobility and safety.

TABLE 6.1 Statutory Requirements Impacting the Transportation Planning Process (*Ref. 2.*) (*Continued*)

reflect emerging trends and concerns associated with transportation safety and mobility. Emerging policy and planning considerations facing transportation planners and operations agencies are described in Table 6.2. Some of these and other related topics are discussed in detail later in this chapter.

6.2.2 Land Use and Transportation

As noted previously, there is a direct link between land use and transportation. The role of the transportation professional is to understand the relationship between the two and to coordinate the investment in the transportation network within the planning context. What is important to note regarding the integration of land use and transportation is that the integration effort is an ongoing process. At each step throughout the planning process shown in Fig. 6.1, agencies have ample opportunities to consider how

Consideration	Description
Climate change	Agencies and their stakeholders are working to address climate change through the implementation of strategies related to mitigation to reduce greenhouse gas (GHG) emissions; adaptation of planning, design, construction, operation, and maintenance of the infrastructure in response to climate concerns; development of sustainable transportation systems; and reducing energy use in all sectors of the transportation industry.
Freight movement	Agencies are incorporating freight movement issues into planning activities to foster the efficient movement of freight; to include freight movement as a system performance measure; to develop freight-oriented data collection and modeling; and to work with advisory committees to identify freight network bottlenecks that need to be addressed.
Land use and transportation	Agencies recognize the direct relationship between land use and transportation and regularly review statewide plans to ensure they contain the most current information on forecasted demographics, transportation, and land-use data to ensure that the transportation system can accommodate population and economic growth and that transportation and land use are better coordinated to mitigate or prevent congestion.
Planning and environment linkages	Agencies work to incorporate sustainability into the transportation sector through relationship building with stakeholder agencies responsible for land-use management, natural resources, environmental protection, conservation, and historic preservation; identify areas with environmental issues and work to limit the impact or avoid these areas; and adopt efficiencies and flexibility in processes.
Scenario planning	Agencies undertake scenario planning to examine alternative transportation policies, plans, and programs to determine how they will impact their jurisdiction from both a qualitative and quantitative perspective and how those impacts compare to regional goals and objectives—including benefits, disbenefits, and trade-offs—to determine how to invest in the transportation infrastructure.
Travel model improvement program (TMIP)	Agencies can access services and products developed by FHWA as part of the TMIP to assess the most appropriate analysis, modeling, and simulation tools, techniques, and resources to support planning-related efforts and strategic transportation investments.

TABLE 6.2   Other Policy and Planning Considerations (*Ref. 2.*)

land use and transportation intersect. The involvement of stakeholder groups and partnering agencies throughout the process helps ensure that decisions reflect the relationship between land use and transportation and work to meet the overall needs of the community. Examples of how this integration can be accomplished throughout various steps in the planning process are provided in Table 6.3. Some of these implementation topics are discussed in more detail in this chapter.

6.2.3   Livability

Community livability is an important issue transportation professionals are incorporating into the overall planning process and when developing transportation plans and projects. Livability reflects the ideals of a community, incorporating a range of aspects, both

Integration Approaches	Implementation Examples for Communities
Planning activities and programs	Development management and urban design
	Transportation demand management
Project development and programming	Project prioritization and funding strategies
	Roadway design guidelines and standards
Stakeholder engagement and visioning	Public involvement
	Visioning and scenario planning
Analytical tools	Gis and technical analysis
Emerging topics	Linking planning to the environmental review process
	Linking planning and public health

TABLE 6.3 Tools and Practices to Integrate Transportation and Land Use (*Ref. 6.*)

qualitative and quantitative in nature, that include quality of life, environmental sustainability, increased transportation and housing choices, affordability, and economic vitality.[7] In today's reality of limited resources, transportation professionals are challenged with making investments that benefit the community in impactful ways and which enhance the effective delivery of transportation services and provide options for its citizens to live a meaningful life. As noted previously, transportation professionals cannot operate in a silo when it comes to planning and project development. Every decision they make has an impact on numerous elements of the community framework, and working with community leaders helps ensure that those decisions work to improve the quality of life for all.

The idea of community livability is not new. Over the past three decades, it has become a common theme in community development and involves partnerships with agencies, businesses, and the public to achieve goals and objectives. Similar terms that have overlapping goals and objectives with livability and which strive to meet similar objectives include sustainability, smart growth, active transportation, complete streets, transit-oriented development, and others. The common theme around all of these terms is the desire for a better place to live. The general principles of livability with respect to transportation and its role in advancing livability are provided in Table 6.4. As evidenced by these principles, nearly every aspect of transportation has a direct impact on or is a contributor to community livability. The interrelationship between transportation and these principles is a key driver behind more effective transportation planning and programming.

Specific examples of transportation-related efforts and specific projects that enhance liability include, but are not limited to:

- Rail transit and transit-oriented development
- Corridor-focused bus rapid transit
- Regional transportation and land use planning
- Rural roadways
- Multimodal bridges
- Statewide corridor planning
- Right-sizing and road diets

Livability Principle	Description
Provide more transportation choices	Develop safe, reliable, and economical transportation choices to decrease transportation costs, reduce GHG emissions and dependence on foreign oil, improve air quality, and promote public health.
Promote equitable, affordable housing	Expand housing choices for people of all ages, incomes, races, and ethnicities that are efficient and which increase mobility and lower the costs of both housing and transportation.
Enhance economic competitiveness	Provide reliable and timely access to employment centers, educational opportunities, community services, and other needs to enhance economic competitiveness of citizens and the business community.
Support existing communities	Increase community revitalization and sustainability by targeting Federal funding toward projects, strategies, and public works investments such as transit-oriented, mixed-use development.
Coordinated and leverage federal policies and investment	Coordinate and leverage Federal funding and policies through collaboration across all levels of government to increase accountability and promote smart and sustainable growth.
Value communities and neighborhoods	Work with community leaders and stakeholder groups to invest in healthy, safe, and walkable neighborhoods to enhance the value of communities of all sizes.

TABLE 6.4 Principles of Livability (*Ref. 7.*)

These examples illustrate how livability can be incorporated into the transportation infrastructure throughout the entire planning and project development process. Effective strategies for getting started along the path of enhancing livability include engaging community residents and stakeholders, selecting a place or project that matters to the community, welcoming partners and stakeholders into the collaborative process, and working to pool and leverage funding to optimize the benefits of those resources.[7]

6.2.4 Planning for Operations

Planning for operations is a broad multimodal planning practice that involves regional collaboration and coordination with respect to transportation operations, management, and operations considerations within the context of the transportation planning process.[8] Transportation professionals and agencies at the state, regional, and local levels involved in transportation planning and investment processes work to identify ways in which various regional operational initiatives and strategies can be incorporated into these processes through collaboration and coordination. A unique aspect of this objectives-driven, performance-based approach is that it helps transportation operations projects compete on an equal playing field for funding with capacity projects in a region. Additional information related to planning for operations is provided in Chap. 8.

6.2.5 Congestion Management Process

The congestion management process (CMP) builds upon the opportunities for regional cooperation and collaboration to identify strategies to increase capacity through effective planning, modeling, and environmental reviews. A CMP is required for metropolitan areas of 200,000+ populations as intended for agencies to identify and mitigate congestion-related problems through the prioritization of investments.[9] The CMP is an objective-driven performance-based structured process for analyzing congestion issues. A critical component in the metropolitan planning process is it involves a broad range of partners and stakeholders and increases collaboration and coordination, much like other processes and approaches discussed throughout this chapter. It represents another tool that agencies have at their disposal to help ensure more effective allocation of resources to optimize the transportation infrastructure investment. The actions that are part of the CMP are illustrated in Fig. 6.4 and describe the stepwise process for agencies developing a CMP for their jurisdiction. It is important to note that the process is cyclical in nature, illustrating the idea that this process is not static and will likely be part of a continuous improvement process for the agency. This approach helps ensure that the

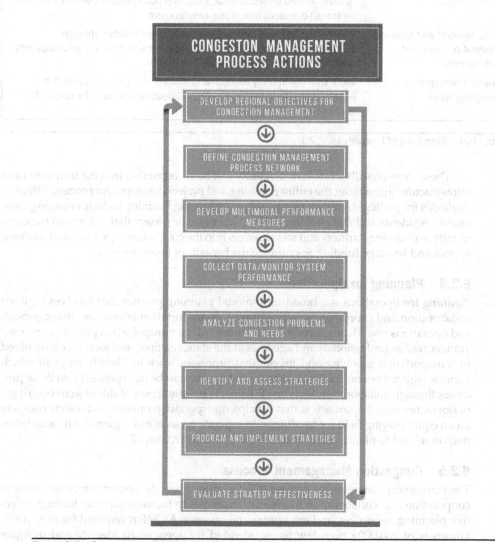

FIGURE 6.4 Congestion management process actions.

needs of the region are incorporated into the CMP as they evolve, and that the process is likely to be fluid with each agency adapting the process to the overall planning initiatives and processes in place. Each region's CMP will be unique to the local needs, goals, and objectives and the characteristics that drive the planning process.

Within the context of transportation planning and livability, the CMP should reflect the overall regional goals and objectives emphasized in the overall planning process. For example, the CMP might address all modes of transportation, including an emphasis on TDM and TSMO strategies. Much like the overall transportation planning process, the CMP incorporates the collection of data and monitors the ongoing system performance. Practitioners analyze congestion problems and needs to identify and assess potential operational strategies that might address those projects within the overall regional goals and objectives. Strategies are selected and implemented, with ongoing evaluation of those strategies taking place to determine to what extent they address congestion challenges and require modification, if necessary to enhance results.

6.3 Travel Demand Modeling

A critical and fundamental activity in the transportation planning process is to anticipate the travel demand on the transportation network. Understanding this demand allows the transportation professional to predict the number and type of trips that can be expected on the network. This information can then be used to plan for system improvements. A trip is considered the basic unit of travel behavior, which involves the movement from a single origin to a single destination; for a particular purpose; at a specific time of the day; by a specific mode; and along a particular route. Transportation demand analysis explains that traveler behavior in economic terms based on the concept of utility. Utility functions, within the transportation context, express an individual's perspective of the usefulness or comparison of one choice among many. The utility function, which is an abstract model of individual behavior, is the fundamental framework for a travel demand model.

To be useful, a travel demand model should predict the behavior of a group of the travelers on the transportation network. Most demand models used by transportation professionals structure choices made by travelers into a basic sequence of discrete choices. The basic travel demand model, commonly known as the "four-step" process, is illustrated in Fig. 6.5. This diagram illustrates a simplified process that involves many more activities related to the overall travel demand modeling exercise, but which all provide inputs and refinement to these steps. Additionally, this process is centered on the trip made by the traveler, and though the process is shown as being serial in nature, it is recognized that travelers may not make each of these decisions one at a time, in this particular order, or independent of other trips.[10]

In this basic travel demand model, the selection of a particular mode for a trip is dependent upon the time of day and the trip destination. Other approaches to categorizing trips by purpose or other descriptor include:

- Work trips versus non-work trips
- Peak versus off-peak trips
- Weekday versus weekend trips

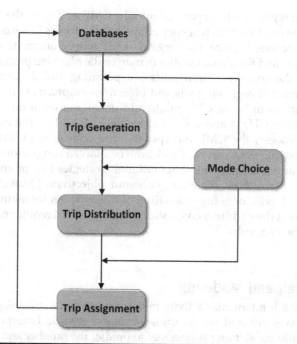

FIGURE 6.5 Basic travel demand model.

For each combination of trip purpose and time of day, transportation planners typically use models that analyze the overall number of trips made (trip generation); the origins and destinations of the trips (trip distribution); and mode used to make each trip (mode choice); and the route followed to complete the trip (traffic assignment). These are the discrete steps in the travel demand model shown in Fig. 6.5.

A travel demand model requires information and specific data to effectively predict demand on the system. This data typically include socioeconomic data and land-use information for the region as well as information about the transportation network. The data reflect the nature of the population and the business environment that influences trips on the transportation network. Examples of the type of data needed for travel demand modeling are provided in Table 6.5. The transportation planner needs to gather these data on an ongoing basis as it establishes the framework for the travel demand model. Periodic updates and validity checks need to be performed to ensure that the data are current and represent the latest information about the region, resulting in the best predictions for demand on the system.

The transportation professional typically works to structure the population into homogenous groups and to quantify utility functions for representative individuals. Two types of groupings are typically used: the average characteristics in geographic zones and market segments present in all zones. The overall goal for the use of these data are to predict the number of trips made between origins and destinations within the region.

The following sections provide a general and simplified process for calculating travel demand on a transportation network. The intent is to illustrate the process and to gain an appreciation for the complexities associated with modeling to predict future trips and be able to plan for those trips in an effective and meaningful way. A variety of models exist that are used by planners for a variety of planning efforts, many of which are very complex

Data Category	Type	Sources
Socioeconomic data and transportation zones	Population and households	Decennial U.S. Census
		American Community Survey (ACS)
		ACS Public Use Microdata Samples
		Local area population data
	Employment	Quarterly census of employment and wages
		State employment commissions
		Current population survey
		Market research listings
		Longitudinal employer-household dynamics
		Local area employment data
	Special sources	Census transportation planning products
		Aerial photography
		Other sources such as school district data
Network data	Highway networks	Highway network attributes
		Facility type and area type
		Link speeds
		Link capacity
		Typical highway network database attributes
	Transit networks	Transit line files
		Access links
		Travel times and fares
Validation data	Model validation plan	
	Example model validation tests	

TABLE 6.5   Data Needed for Modeling (*Ref. 10.*)

and integrate vast amounts of data. The analysis of these models is beyond the scope of this text, but it is important to realize that the fundamentals discussed in this chapter set the stage for those models and their overall assessment of demand.

6.3.1   Trip Generation

Trip generation models are intended to predict the number of trips produced and attracted by a traffic analysis zone for a typical weekday. A traffic analysis zone is typically some geographic unit in size in the region about which the transportation planner has the aforementioned information. Trips are typically divided into home-based trips and non-home-based trips. Trips made by system users are normally stratified by purpose for each trip type, such as a trip that is initiated at home and ends at the traveler's place of employment. Trips are then broken down by the number produced in a particular zone or area and assumed to depend on the size of the zone and characteristics of the population residing or working in that zone.

Figure 6.6 illustrates home-based trips where the trip either begins or ends at a home in a zone. For home-based trips where the trip begins at the home, the home represents a production and the non-home end represents the attraction. For home-based

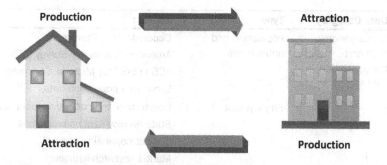

Figure 6.6   Home-based trip production and attraction.

trips where the trip begins at the non-home end, the non-home end represents the production and the home represents the attraction. Home-based trips are a function of the population in the zone: the more homes in the zone, the higher the trip production.

Figure 6.7 illustrates non-home-based trips where the trip begins and ends at some place other than a home in a zone. These are trips that take place in and around a community but are only partially dependent on the number of households in a zone. They also depend on the number of attractions in a zone and the nature of those attractions. For non-home-based trips, the production end of the trip is the origin, and the attraction end of the trip is the destination.

The most common form of a trip generation model is a cross-classification model where a matrix of number of households and household characteristics are established. The characteristics can include such factors as the number of adults, number of children, number of vehicles, and income level of the households. The cross-classification model for trips generated in a zone, or trip productions, is illustrated as follows:

$$P_i^p = \sum_k P \text{ rate}_{pk} * h_{ik}$$

where P_i^p = the number of trip ends produced for purpose p in zone i
$P \text{ rate}_{pk}$ = the production trip rate for purpose p per household for category k
h_{ik} = the number of households in category k in zone i[10]

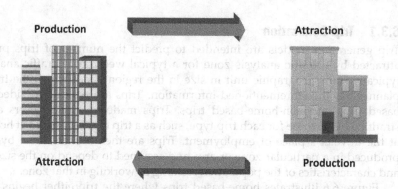

Figure 6.7   Non-home-based trip production and attraction.

The model for trips attracted to a zone is illustrated as follows:

$$A_i^p = \sum_k A \text{ rate}_{pk} * v_{ik}$$

where A_i^p = attraction of trip ends for purpose p in zone i
$A \text{ rate}_{pk}$ = rate of attraction trip ends for a purpose p per unit of variable k
v_{ik} = value of variable k in zone i[10]

The development of a trip generation model is based upon estimates of household travel behavior, which can be obtained through such means as travel surveys, such as the National Household Travel Survey (NHTS),[11] which is considered the authoritative source on national travel behavior with respect to daily non-commercial travel by all modes in the United States. A variety of factors are considered when predicting trip productions and attractions. Factors such as population, the number of employed individuals in particular zones, and availability of an automobile greatly influence the number of trips generated in a community. Additionally, the income levels of the population and the diversity of occupations in a zone play into trip production and attraction. However, specific indicators related to the population are not the only factors influencing trips. The nature and size of land use in a zone impact trip attractions. Features such as the amount of developed land in a zone, the total employment numbers in the zone, as well as the floor space and nature of the business influence trips.

When using a cross-classification model, the planner typically uses trip tables for a zone, which categorize the number of trips taken by such factors as household size or vehicle ownership. Those trip generation rates are then multiplied by the number of corresponding households with the same size and vehicle ownership and tabulated to determine the total number of trips produced by that zone.

Example Problem 6.1. Calculate the number of home-based work trips produced in the zone with the household data shown in Table 6.6 and the trip rates for the zone shown in Table 6.7.
For households with auto ownership 0, calculate the following:

$$P_i^p = \sum_k P \text{ rate}_{pk} * h_{ik} =$$

$$P_{i1}^{hbw} = (0.3)(25) + (0.7)(15) + (0.9)(10) + (1.0)(0) + (1.2)(0)$$

$$P_{i1}^{hbw} = (7.5) + (10.5) + (9) + (0) + (0) = 27$$

Repeat for each auto ownership row and complete Table 6.8.

Autos	Household Size (Persons)					
	1	2	3	4	5+	Total
0	25	15	10	0	0	50
1	70	110	65	20	5	270
2	0	160	210	105	75	550
3+	0	10	35	70	100	215
Total	95	295	320	200	180	1090

TABLE 6.6 Example Number of Households by Household Size and Autos, Zone 1

Autos	Household Size (Persons)					
	1	**2**	**3**	**4**	**5+**	**Average**
0	0.3	0.7	0.9	1.0	1.2	**0.82**
1	0.7	0.9	1.4	1.6	1.9	**1.3**
2	0.8	1.4	2.0	2.2	2.2	**1.72**
3+	0.9	1.4	2.5	2.8	3.2	**2.16**
Average	**0.675**	**1.1**	**1.7**	**1.9**	**2.125**	**1.5**

TABLE **6.7**   Example Home-Based Work Trip Rates Based on Household Size by Number of Autos, Zone 1

Autos	Household Size (Persons)					
	1	**2**	**3**	**4**	**5+**	**Total**
0	7.5	10.5	9	0	0	**27**
1	49	99	91	32	9.5	**280.5**
2	0	224	420	231	165	**1040**
3+	0	14	87.5	196	320	**617.5**
Total	**56.5**	**347.5**	**607.5**	**459**	**494.5**	**1965**

TABLE **6.8**   Example Number of Home-Based Work Trips, Zone 1

Example Problem 6.2.   Calculate the number of home-based nonwork trips produced in the zone with the household data shown in Table 6.6 and the trip rates for the zone in Table 6.9.
For households with auto ownership 0, calculate the following:

$$P_i^p = \sum_k P\,\text{rate}_{pk} * h_{ik} =$$

$$P_{i1}^{hbmw} = (1.1)(25) + (3.2)(15) + (5.2)(10) + (7.9)(0) + (10.2)(0)$$

$$P_{i1}^{hbmw} = (27.5) + (48) + (52) + (0) + (0) = 127.5$$

Repeat for each auto ownership row and complete Table 6.10.

Autos	Household Size (Persons)					
	1	**2**	**3**	**4**	**5+**	**Average**
0	1.1	3.2	5.2	7.9	10.2	**5.52**
1	1.7	3.7	6.5	9.5	10.2	**6.32**
2	2.1	3.4	7.1	9.5	12.0	**6.82**
3+	1.9	3.5	7.0	9.8	14.5	**7.34**
Average	**1.7**	**3.45**	**6.45**	**9.175**	**11.725**	**6.5**

TABLE **6.9**   Example Home-Based Nonwork Trip Rates Based on Household Size by Number of Autos, Zone 1

Autos	Household Size (Persons)					
	1	**2**	**3**	**4**	**5+**	**Total**
0	27.5	48	52	0	0	**127.5**
1	119	407	422.5	190	51	**1189.5**
2	0	544	1491	997.5	900	**3932.5**
3+	0	35	245	686	1450	**2416**
Total	**146.5**	**1034**	**2210.5**	**1873.5**	**2401**	**7665.5 ≈ 7666**

TABLE 6.10 Example Number of Home-Based Nonwork Trips, Zone 1

Example Problem 6.3. Calculate the number of non-home-based trips produced in the zone with the household data shown in Table 6.6 and the trip rates for the zone shown in Table 6.11.

For households with auto ownership 0, calculate the following:

$$P_i^p = \sum_k P \, \text{rate}_{pk} * h_{ik} =$$

$$P_{i1}^{nhb} = (0.8)(25) + (1.5)(15) + (1.9)(10) + (3.5)(0) + (4.1)(0)$$

$$P_{i1}^{nhb} = (20) + (22.5) + (19) + (0) + (0) = 127.5$$

Repeat for each auto ownership row and complete Table 6.12.

Trip attractions for a zone are determined in a similar manner as trip productions and are function of various factors in a zone, such as household size, school enrollment, the number of workers in a zone, and the type of employment in the zone, and the size of employment locations.

Autos	Household Size (Persons)					
	1	**2**	**3**	**4**	**5+**	**Average**
0	0.8	1.5	1.9	3.5	4.1	**2.36**
1	1.5	2.4	3.5	4.1	4.1	**3.12**
2	1.7	2.6	3.8	5.7	5.5	**3.86**
3+	1.7	2.8	4.6	5.8	7.0	**4.38**
Average	**1.425**	**2.325**	**3.45**	**4.775**	**5.175**	**3.43**

TABLE 6.11 Example Non-home-Based Trip Rates Based on Household Size by Number of Autos, Zone 1

Autos	Household Size (Persons)					
	1	**2**	**3**	**4**	**5+**	**Total**
0	20	22.5	19	0	0	**61.5**
1	105	264	227.5	82	20.5	**699**
2	0	448	966	609	525	**2548**
3+	0	28	161	406	700	**1295**
Total	**125**	**762.5**	**1373.5**	**1097**	**1245.5**	**4603.5 ≈ 4604**

TABLE 6.12 Example Number of Nonhome-Based Trips, Zone 1

Zone	Households (HH)	School Enrollment (SCE)	Basic Employees (BE)	Retail Employees (RE)	Service Employees (SE)	Attractions (A)
1	7000	1100	780	250	320	**13,361**
2	2800	200	3450	50	1500	**7750**
3	4800	450	710	60	80	**7685**
4	4200	500	3500	850	520	**14,757**
5	8200	2100	1010	70	450	**15,176**
6	3500	350	2800	320	670	**9480**
7	2100	120	1000	10	30	**3325**
Total	**32,600**	**4820**	**13,250**	**1610**	**3570**	**71,534**

TABLE 6.13 Household Information, City A

Example Problem 6.4. Calculate the number of attractions for each zone in City A based on the following trip attraction model:

$$A = 1.3 * HH + 1.4 * SCE + 0.3 * BE + 7.9 * RE + 1.6 * SE$$

For each zone, calculate the number of attractions:

$$A = 1.3 * (7000) + 1.4 * (1100) + 0.3 * (780) + 7.9 * (250) + 1.6 * (320) =$$

$$A = 9100 + 1540 + 234 + 1975 + 512 = 13,361 \text{ attractions}$$

Repeat for each auto ownership row and complete Table 6.13.

The variations and combinations of land use and size are staggering, all of which have unique trip generation characteristics. The Institute of Transportation Engineers (ITE) produces the *Trip Generation Manual*, which is in its 10th edition and which contains over 3000 pages on trip generation statistics for a broad range of land uses.[12] For example, the manual contains land use descriptions and plots for all land use/time period/independent variable combination for such land uses as:

- Residential
- Lodging
- Recreational
- Port/terminal
- Industrial
- Institutional
- Medical office
- Retail
- Services

Additionally, the manual includes guidance on the appropriate technique for estimating both person and vehicular trip generation rates; for mixed-use developments and local trip generation rates; and for pass-by trip and truck trip generation information.[12] Trip generation data is also stratified by general site location (i.e., rural, suburban, urban), geography, development size, and other factors that provide a wealth of information on the nature of trip generation.

6.3.2 Trip Distribution

The second step in the four-step travel demand modeling process, trip distribution is intended to determine how the trips produced in a zone get distributed among other traffic analysis zones. Trip distribution is a function of the number of trips produced and attracted in the zones as well as other factors that might limit the attractiveness of a particular zone. These factors may include travel time or cost. The most common trip distribution model used in the four-step model is the gravity model. This model calculates the trips between zones based on the productions and attractions for each zone and the factors impacting the travel between each pair of zones. The gravity model based on attractions is shown below:

$$T_{ij}^p = \frac{A_j^p (P_i F_{ij})}{\sum_i P_j F_{ij}}$$

and

$$F_{ij} = C_{ij}^{-\alpha}$$

A gravity model based on productions is shown below:

$$T_{ij}^p = \frac{P_i^p (A_j F_{ij})}{\sum_i A_j F_{ij}}$$

where T_{ij}^p = number of trips produced in zone i and attracted to zone j
 P_i^p = production of trip ends for purpose p in zone i
 A_j^p = attraction of trip ends for purpose p in zone j
 F_{ij} = impedance of travel from zone i to zone j, often a specific function of the travel time or generalized cost of travel between two zones
 C_{ij} = generalized cost function for travel from zone i to zone j
 α = model parameter to be determined by calibration

Example Problem 6.5. Calculate the trip distribution matrix for City A based on the travel times provided in Fig. 6.8 and assuming a trip impedance shown below:

$$F_{ij} = \frac{1}{C_{ij}}$$

where C_{ij} represents the travel time between zones. Use the trip generation information provided in Table 6.14.

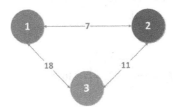

Figure 6.8 City A zones with travel times between zones.

Zone	Productions	Attractions
1	750	640
2	600	820
3	850	740
Total	2200	2200

TABLE 6.14   Projected Trip Generation for City A

Determine the zone-to-zone travel time in minutes.

Origin Zone	Destination Zone		
	1	**2**	**3**
1	1	7	18
2	7	1	11
3	18	11	1

Determine the zone-to-zone travel time impedance.

Origin Zone	Destination Zone		
	1	**2**	**3**
1	1/1	1/7	1/18
2	1/7	1/1	1/11
3	1/18	1/11	1/1

Estimate the number of trips from Zone 1 to all other zones.

$$\sum A_i F_{ij} = A_{11}F_{11} + A_{12}F_{12} + A_{13}F_{13} = 640\left(\frac{1}{1}\right) + 820\left(\frac{1}{7}\right) + 740\left(\frac{1}{18}\right) = 798$$

$$T_{1j} = P_1\left(\frac{A_i F_{ij}}{\sum A_i F_{ij}}\right)$$

$$T_{11} = 750\left[\frac{640\left(\frac{1}{1}\right)}{798}\right] = 601.50$$

$$T_{12} = 750\left[\frac{820\left(\frac{1}{7}\right)}{798}\right] = 110.09$$

$$T_{13} = 750 \left[\frac{740 \left(\frac{1}{18} \right)}{798} \right] = 38.64$$

$$\sum A_2 F_{ij} = A_{21} F_{21} + A_{22} F_{22} + A_{23} F_{23} = 640 \left(\frac{1}{7} \right) + 820 \left(\frac{1}{1} \right) + 740 \left(\frac{1}{11} \right) = 979$$

$$T_{2j} = P_2 \left(\frac{A_i F_{ij}}{\sum A_i F_{ij}} \right)$$

$$T_{21} = 600 \left[\frac{640 \left(\frac{1}{7} \right)}{979} \right] = 56.0$$

$$T_{22} = 600 \left[\frac{820 \left(\frac{1}{1} \right)}{979} \right] = 502.6$$

$$T_{23} = 600 \left[\frac{740 \left(\frac{1}{11} \right)}{979} \right] = 41.2$$

$$\sum A_3 F_{ij} = A_{31} F_{31} + A_{32} F_{32} + A_{33} F_{33} = 640 \left(\frac{1}{18} \right) + 820 \left(\frac{1}{11} \right) + 740 \left(\frac{1}{1} \right) = 850$$

$$T_{3j} = P_3 \left(\frac{A_i F_{ij}}{\sum A_i F_{ij}} \right)$$

$$T_{31} = 850 \left[\frac{640 \left(\frac{1}{18} \right)}{850} \right] = 35.6$$

$$T_{32} = 850 \left[\frac{820 \left(\frac{1}{11} \right)}{850} \right] = 74.5$$

$$T_{33} = 850 \left[\frac{740 \left(\frac{1}{1} \right)}{850} \right] = 740$$

Initial gravity model trip table.

Origin Zone	Destination Zone				
	1	**2**	**3**	**Total**	
1	601.5	110.1	38.6	**750.2 ≈ 750**	Productions
2	56.0	502.6	41.2	**599.8 ≈ 600**	
3	35.6	74.5	740.0	**850.1 ≈ 850**	
Total	**693.1**	**687.2**	**819.8**	**2200**	
	Attractions				

In this example, the productions are equal to those in the original trip generation table. However, the attractions do not match up with the original ones in the trip generation table. They can be modified using the following equation:

$$T'_{ij} = \frac{A_j}{\sum T_{ij}}$$

This process will yield productions that do not equal the originals as well. The next step is to modify them using the following equation:

$$T'_{ij} = \frac{P_i}{\sum T_{ij}}$$

The planner can repeat these calculations until the productions and attractions converge to match those in the original trip generation table.

6.3.3 Mode Choice

The third step in the four-step travel demand modeling process is mode choice. From a transportation perspective, this step is important as planners can use it to determine how and when facilities need to be constructed and to work to leverage modal options to the traveling public. The basic mode choice model incorporates those modes available to system users, typically classified as auto, transit, and nonmotorized modes. The modal choice models consider various factors, including the level of service for each mode; traveler characteristics, such as vehicle availability, household income, age, gender, and worker student status; and regional characteristics, such as development density.[10]

Mode choice models are typically based on a utility function that expresses the utility that an individual traveler derives from a particular goods or service, in this case a mode of travel. A typical utility function is:

$$u_m = \beta_m + \sum_j a_j z_{mj} + \varepsilon$$

where u_m = utility of mode m
β_m = mode-specific parameter
a_j = parameters of the model to be determined by calibration
z_{mj} = set of travel characteristics of mode m, such as time or money costs
ε = stochastic term with zero mean

The most common model for mode choice is the logit model:

$$p_m = \frac{e^{u_m}}{\sum_{m'} e^{u_{m'}}}$$

where p_m = probability that mode m is chosen
e = base of natural logarithms
m' = index over all modes included in the choice set

Example Problem 6.6. Calculate the mode split for a market segment of 750 individuals in a travel analysis zone and the additional data provided in the table below. A multinomial logit mode choice model calibrated for this market segment is as follows:

$$u = \beta_m - 0.35C - 0.03T$$

where T = travel time
C = out-of-pocket expense

Mode	β_m	T	C
Auto	2.15	14 min	$3.75
Rail	0.35	25 min	$2.50
Bus	0.05	30 min	$1.95

Determine the utility function for each mode.

$$u_{auto} = 2.15 - (0.35)(3.75) - (0.03)(15) = 0.3875$$
$$u_{rail} = 0.35 - (0.35)(2.50) - (0.03)(25) = -1.275$$
$$u_{bus} = 0.05 - (0.35)(1.95) - (0.03)(30) = -1.5325$$

Determine the probability of each mode.

$$\sum_{m'} e^{u_{m'}} = e^{0.3875} + e^{-1.275} + e^{-1.5325} = 1.473 + 0.279 + 0.216 = 1.969$$

$$p_{auto} = \frac{1.473}{1.969} = 0.748$$

$$p_{rail} = \frac{0.279}{1.969} = 0.142$$

$$p_{bus} = \frac{0.216}{1.969} = 0.110$$

Calculate the number of trips by mode.

$$T_{auto} = 0.748(750) = 561$$

$$T_{auto} = 0.142(750) = 106$$

$$T_{auto} = 0.110(750) = 82$$

$$561 + 106 + 82 = 749 \approx 750$$

6.3.4 Trip Assignment

Trip assignment, which is the last step in the four-step travel demand model, determines which trips between zones take place on specific links in the network. The processes associated with trip assignment have become synonymous with computer modeling and algorithms, though most of them reflect the basic conceptual formula as shown below:

$$V_a = \sum_{ij} t_{ij} * P_{ija}$$

where V_a = the volume of vehicles on link a
  t_{ij} = the number of vehicles trips from origin i to destination j
  P_{ija} = the probability of using link a on the path from origin i to destination j[10]

These variables and the assignment of trips to links involve numerous factors which include, but are not limited to:

- Congestion flow travel time on a link
- Free-flow travel time on link
- Capacity of a link per unit of time
- Actual travel time on a link
- Length of a link in units of distance
- Per vehicle toll on a link in monetary units

The concept of dynamic traffic assignment (DTA) is a modeling approach used by transportation professionals to analyze the complex elements of the transportation system. This approach captures the relationships between dynamic route choice behaviors and the characteristics of the network. Research over the past four decades has generated a number of models that incorporate traveler behavior assumptions, model formulations, and solution algorithms for both equilibrium-based and non-equilibrium based models.[13] Information that influences these models includes, but is not limited to:

- Route choice from the perspective of the traveler
- Routing policy from the perspective of the transportation system
- System mobility objectives, such as user optimal, system optimal, or local optimal
- Assumptions about traveler behavior, such as reactive, repeated learning, or decisions based on limited information
- The availability of information to the traveler, such as pre-trip information or en route information

The study of DTA models is beyond the scope of this textbook, but understanding the overall purpose of these models and their role in the travel demand analysis process is of interest to transportation professionals.

6.4 Analysis, Modeling, and Simulation

Analysis, modeling, and simulation (AMS) are needed to help various agencies and stakeholders evaluate operational strategies at the planning, design, and operational stages. They are an integral part of the travel demand analysis process and its integration with operations. Through the use of various tools and assets, traffic flow is managed and driver behavior is influenced in real time to achieve operational objectives. The AMS strategy involves the creation of a model to analyze the supply and demand during a specified time period along with a predictive component to forecast travel conditions in the future. The analysis framework of AMS consists of the components listed below.

- **Scenario manager**—creates multiple scenarios for the analyst to choose from (e.g., lane closure due to incidents, varying traffic patterns). The scenario generator provides the necessary demand and supply updates to the network simulator, which in turn replicates the real world in a simulation-based modeling environment.

- **Data**—collect historical and real-time data from multiple sources/modes and create the necessary inputs for analysis in a virtual environment using simulation.

- **Model-based environment**—creates a virtual simulated world that not only monitors the system but predicts future performance and evaluates the impacts of various dynamic actions.

- **Analysis and decision**—allows system's managers to make decisions and select appropriate strategies based on measures of effectiveness collected from network simulators. For real-time operations, a decision support system (DSS) should be used to evaluate and propose the best active traffic management (ATM) strategies.

Simulation-based tools of transportation systems and mobility management, using real-time and historical data, should be incorporated into the system analysis, which can be conducted both before and after implementing ATM strategies. Some of the functions of the system should include the evaluation and/or design of the traffic flows, determination of the most reliable mode of operation of supply and demand objects, and interaction between the objects and their impact on the entire system.

Traffic analysis tools can be generally grouped into the following categories as shown in Table 6.15.

Each of the categories above has certain capabilities and limitations with regard to types of scenarios and facilities that can be modeled by a tool, the phase of the project (planning, design, operations/construction) during which the tool needs to be used, and the geographic scope of the study area (isolated locations, segments, corridors/small networks, region).

6.5 Travel Demand Management

The majority of this chapter focuses on how to predict the demand on the transportation network based on a variety of factors. One important element that impacts travel demand analysis is the concept of TDM. This approach is an effort to

Traffic Analysis Tool Type	Description
Sketch-planning tools	Evaluate alternatives or projects without performing a detailed traffic analysis and are appropriate for high-level analysis.
Travel demand models	Predict future travel demand based on existing conditions and projections of socioeconomic characteristics.
Analytical/deterministic *Highway Capacity Manual* (HCM)-based tools	Evaluate the performance of isolated or small-scale facilities and are based on the *Highway Capacity Manual* methodologies and procedures.
Real-time datasets	Serve as the basis to analyze existing operations and estimate the effect of changes.
Macroscopic simulation tools	Simulate traffic on a section-by-section basis and are based on deterministic relationships of traffic network parameters (speed, flow, density).
Mesoscopic simulation tools	Combine capabilities of both microscopic and macroscopic simulation models and consider the individual vehicle as the traffic flow unit, whose movement is governed by the average speed on a link.
Microscopic simulation tools	Rely on car-following and lane-changing theories and simulate the movement of individual vehicles.
Traffic signal optimization tools	Develop optimal signal phasing and timing plans for isolated signal intersections, arterial streets, and signal networks.
Ramp metering optimization tools	Update the cycle of the metering rate and the location of the downstream detector station.

TABLE 6.15   Types of Traffic Analysis Tools Used for Transportation Planning

influence the demand on the transportation network by offering travel choices to system users. This high-level policy effort advances strategies that work to reduce congestion and optimize the existing network.[14] Those strategies are frequently included as specific components of transportation projects in the TIP for a region. In general, TDM supports the broader concept of TSMO, which is addressed in Chap. 8. TDM has the potential to influence decisions made by travelers at every stage of the trip chain using a broad range of strategies that offer choices at each stage, as illustrated in Fig. 6.9.

TDM presents opportunities for agencies to promote sustainability for the transportation network. Specific opportunities include, but are not limited to:

- Reducing the need for new or wider roads
- Making personal travel decisions more efficient
- Maximizing the return on infrastructure spending
- Making the most of current transportation assets
- Providing a versatile and dynamic management tool for various audiences

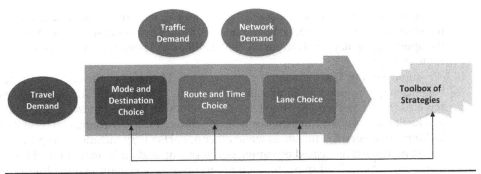

FIGURE 6.9 Travel demand management concept. (*Ref. 15.*)

- Offering initiatives that have multimodal benefits
- Working at the scale of individuals but impacting the entire community[14]

Specific examples of TDM strategies that agencies could implement, some by working to regional stakeholders, include:

- Flextime
- Alternative work schedule
- Compressed work week
- Telecommuting
- Ride sharing (carpooling)
- Vanpooling
- Bicycling
- Walking
- Park-and-ride lots
- Car sharing
- Traditional transit
- Express bus service
- Installing/increasing intelligent transportation system
- Ramp metering
- Traffic calming
- Linked trips
- Preferential parking for rideshare/carpools/vanpools
- Subsidized transit by employers
- Mandatory TDM measures for large employers
- Transit-oriented development
- Guaranteed ride home programs for transit riders

As evidenced by this list, most of these strategies require the cooperation with other regional agencies and direct engagement with the business community. Additionally, the operating agency needs to ensure that facilities and resources are in place to support these strategies.

Implementing TDM strategies can have varied benefits in the community. Specific benefits might include travel impacts, such as mode shift and a reduction in vehicle miles traveled. Traffic and network impacts might include an increase in travel time reliability, a reduction in delay, and an increase in person throughput. Environmental benefits might include a reduction in emissions, while other impacts might include an improvement in goods movement, increased economic development, and an increase in livability in the community. As with all transportation programs, it is important that the transportation agency have a clear set of goals and objectives associated with TDM, and know what performance measures it will use to determine to what extent they are achieving them.

6.6   Case Studies

The following are case studies illustrating examples of transportation planning across a variety of institutional levels.

I-485 Interchange Analysis—Charlotte, NC

The Mecklenburg-Union MPO in the Charlotte, North Carolina, metropolitan area conducted a comprehensive study starting in 1998 to assess potential approaches to mitigate the impacts of construction on the I-495 beltway around greater Charlotte.[16] The 65-mile beltway with 35 interchanges was intended to accommodate the regional growth and increased traffic in the Charlotte region. However, concerns over the potential negative impact on local communities in the interchange areas prompted the study 10 years into the construction schedule. The land use and transportation plan study focused on the following issues within a one-mile radius of each interchange:

- Congestion at the interchange areas
- Compatibility between the development and the existing communities
- Noise pollution
- Existence of pedestrian and bicycle connections

Through a thorough analysis of the plans and extensive public engagement, the Mecklenburg-Union MPO provided recommendations related to land use and transportation improvements to better link the transportation, land use, and enhance livability in the Charlotte area. Recommendations, in addition to the removal of some interchanges, included:

- Accommodation of bicycle and pedestrian traffic on roadways and bridges to enhance connectivity
- Provision of internal connectivity between developments near individual interchanges
- Inclusion of pedestrian-focused streetscape improvements to better integrate the facility into local communities

- Addition of access improvements, service roads, and subdivision processes to reduce the occurrence of landlocked parcels
- Passage of local ordinances to help mitigate the noise and visual impacts of the beltway facility
- Addition of lighting improvements at ramps and other locations to support safety along the beltway[16]

The recommendations focused on improving the livability of the communities in the Charlotte region by improving multimodal connectivity and accessibility, which were innovative approaches at the time. Lessons learned from this comprehensive activity to directly integrate transportation and land use decisions focusing on livability included:

- Coordinating land use and transportation planning lays the groundwork for innovation in the region and inclusion of multimodal options in projects.
- Adopting regional approaches to interchange area planning yields many benefits, including increased accessibility, a reduction in traffic congestion, and preservation of bicycle and pedestrian access to increase travel options.
- Using the interchange development process enabled the MPO to balance many needs in the region by supporting market dynamics and helping meet community goals and mitigate impacts of transportation projects.
- Delayed construction presents challenges to coordinated planning.[16]

Congestion Management Process—Atlanta Regional Council, Atlanta, GA

The Atlanta Regional Commission (ARC), which is the MPO for the Atlanta metropolitan area, utilizes a CMP model that is closely linked with the goals and objectives in the regional metropolitan transportation plan (MTP) for the region and integrated with most planning activities of local agencies.[17] The ARC recognizes the following five elements, which are a variation on some of the steps in a typical CMP:

- Monitor and evaluate performance.
- Identify causes.
- Identify and evaluate alternative strategies.
- Provide information supporting implementation.
- Evaluation effectiveness of implementation.

This CMP process is not formal in the region, but the ARC incorporates these concepts throughout the planning-related activities and studies that are undertaken by the ARC and its member agencies. The ARC continually refines the process, incorporating a variety of mobility-related data elements to help determine success with respect to congestion management.

One particular element of note in the ARC CMP is related to the identification and evaluation of alternative strategies. Congestion management strategies are prioritized based on a weighting distribution of related the anticipated benefits and congestion-related improvements expected from each strategy. The weighting distribution across congestion performance metrics is as follows:

- Delay (20 percent)
- Connectivity (20 percent)
- Safety (20 percent)
- Freight friendly (10 percent)
- Economic growth (10 percent)
- Environment (20 percent)[17]

The ARC CMP has been in place for more than a decade, and ARC updates it on a regular basis, investigating new and innovative approaches to incorporating data, analyzing trends, and utilizing visualization techniques to illustrate congestion levels and potential benefits of CMP-related strategies. Over time, ARC has learned that the greatest challenge to implementing strategies identified in the CMP is conducting before-after strategies to assess the impacts of those strategies.[17] Scarcity of resources and the timeline for implementation contributes to this difficulty. Additionally, ARC continues to make the connection between the need for TSMO strategies at the regional level, and helping the regional partners understand their importance. The formation of a committee comprised of operators and planners from the regional operational agencies has helped establish a collaborative process for identifying goals, policies, strategies, and opportunities for TSMO strategies to address congestion in the region.

6.7 Summary

The concepts of transportation planning and travel demand are interrelated and directly connected to community issues such as land use, livability, and congestion management. Anticipating that increase in travel demand is a complex undertaking that is closely interrelated with other elements such as operations, all of which directly impact the sustainability of the surface network. The transportation professional has a broad range of options to determine travel demand as well as to influence that demand to foster livability in the community and the optimization of the transportation network. There is no single solution to addressing transportation demand, but operating agencies need to work closely with stakeholder partners to determine the best approach and options for the community at large to meet regional goals and objectives.

Glossary of Acronyms

ACS—American Community Survey

AMS—analysis, modeling, and simulation

ARC—Atlanta Regional Commission

ATM—active traffic management

CAA—Clean Air Act

CAAA—Clean Air Act Amendments of 1990

CMP—congestion management process

DOT—department of transportation

DTA—dynamic traffic assignment

GIS—geographic information system

LRSTP—Long-Range Statewide Transportation Plan

MAP-21—Moving Ahead for Progress in the 21st Century Act

MPO—metropolitan planning organization

MTP—metropolitan transportation plan

NHS—National Highway System

NHTS—National Household Travel Survey

RTPO—regional transportation planning organizations

STIP—Statewide Transportation Improvement Program

TAM—Transit Asset Management

TDM—travel demand management

TIP—Transportation Improvement Program

TMA—transportation management area

TMIP—Travel Model Improvement Program

TSMO—transportation system management and operations

USDOT—United States Department of Transportation

Exercises

6.1   Write a paper (no more than five pages) on the connection between land use and transportation. Provide three real-world examples of how regional agencies have recognized the importance of this relationship in their regional planning activities.

6.2   Write a paper (no more than five pages) comparing three CMP case studies for different metropolitan areas. Compare and contrast the case studies and identify lessons learned that other agencies might benefit from implementation.

6.3   Calculate the number of home-based work trips produced in a travel analysis zone with the household data shown in the table below and the trip rates for the zone shown using the cross-classification model.

| Autos | Household Size (Persons) | | | | | |
	1	2	3	4	5+	Total
0	20	20	15	5	0	
1	65	120	60	20	15	
2	5	140	190	105	60	
3+	0	15	30	70	90	
Total						

Number of Households by Household Size and Autos

Autos	Household Size (Persons)					
	1	**2**	**3**	**4**	**5+**	**Average**
0	0.8	1.5	1.9	3.5	4.1	
1	1.5	2.4	3.5	4.1	4.1	
2	1.7	2.6	3.8	5.7	5.5	
3+	1.7	2.8	4.6	5.8	7.0	
Average						

Home-Based Trip Rates

6.4 Calculate the number of attractions for each zone based on the following trip attraction model:

$$A = 1.2 * HH + 1.1 * SCE + 0.4 * BE + 6.8 * RE + 1.5 * SE$$

Zone	Households (HH)	School Enrollment (SCE)	Basic Employees (BE)	Retail Employees (RE)	Service Employees (SE)	Attractions (A)
1	6000	1100	780	760	300	
2	2900	200	600	180	840	
3	4500	450	600	80	900	
4	5100	500	2800	630	430	
5	9800	2100	2050	500	690	
6	3800	350	1100	320	340	
7	2800	120	920	20	60	
Total						

6.5 Calculate the number of nonhome-based work trips produced in a travel analysis zone with the household data shown in the table below and the trip rates for the zone shown.

Autos	Household Size (Persons)					
	1	**2**	**3**	**4**	**5+**	**Total**
0	10	35	0	0	0	
1	60	220	70	20	15	
2	5	180	230	100	45	
3+	0	10	35	70	85	
Total						

Number of Households by Household Size and Autos, Zone 1

Autos	Household Size (Persons)					Average
	1	**2**	**3**	**4**	**5+**	
0	0.7	1.5	1.8	3.2	4.1	
1	1.3	2.4	3.2	4.5	4.8	
2	1.7	2.6	4.1	5.9	6.0	
3+	1.5	2.8	4.6	6.1	7.5	
Average						

Nonhome-Based Trip Rates

6.6 Calculate the trip distribution matrix for City A based on the travel times provided in the table below and assuming a trip impedance shown below and using the gravity model:

$$F_{ij} = \frac{1}{C_{ij}}$$

where C_{ij} represents the travel time between zones. Use the trip generation information provided.

Origin Zone	Destination Zone			
	1	**2**	**3**	**4**
1	1	3	7	11
2	3	1	8	4
3	7	8	1	9
4	11	4	9	1

Zone	Productions	Attractions
1	500	450
2	760	820
3	490	520
4	910	870
Total	2660	2660

6.7 Calculate the mode split for a market segment of 1250 individuals in a travel analysis zone and the additional data provided in the table below. A multinomial logit mode choice model calibrated for this market segment is as follows:

$$u = \beta_m - 0.30C - 0.025T$$

where T = travel time
        C = out-of-pocket expense

Mode	β_m	T	C
Auto	2.25	17 min	$3.60
Rail	0.42	25 min	$2.45
Bus	0.04	28 min	$2.10

6.8   Write a paper (no more than five pages) providing a case study of an agency TDM program. Describe the program, the engaged partners, specific elements, and strategies that are implemented to manage demand.

6.9   Write a paper (no more than five pages) describing how a CMP would specifically incorporate environmental-related performance measures into the document. Provide three examples of CMPs for regions that incorporate such measures.

6.10   Write a paper (no more than five pages) providing a case study of a regional MPO that has incorporated livability into its regional planning process. Describe specific performance measures incorporated into the plan that reflect livability for the community.

6.11   Write a paper (no more than five pages) providing a case study of a comprehensive TDM program in a region that addresses the need to manage demand on the transportation network. Provide examples of performance measures and how the TDM program is incorporated into a regional planning process.

References

1. "Planning." Federal Highway Administration, U.S. Department of Transportation, Washington, D.C., https://www.fhwa.dot.gov/planning/ (accessed March 2018).
2. *The Transportation Planning Process: Key Issues, 2017 Update.* Report FHWA-HEP-18-005, Federal Highway Administration, U.S. Department of Transportation, Washington, D.C., 2018.
3. "Designation of Transportation Management Areas," United States Federal Register, https://www.federalregister.gov/documents/2012/07/18/2012-17514/designation-of-transportation-management-areas (accessed March 2018).
4. "Moving Ahead for Progress in the 21st Century Act." Federal Highway Administration, U.S. Department of Transportation, https://www.fhwa.dot.gov/map21/ (accessed March 2018).
5. "Fixing America's Surface Transportation (FAST) Act." Federal Highway Administration, U.S. Department of Transportation, https://www.fhwa.dot.gov/fastact/ (accessed January 2017).
6. "Tools and Practices for Land Use Integration." Federal Highway Administration, U.S. Department of Transportation, Washington, D.C., https://www.fhwa.dot.gov/planning/processes/land_use/land_use_tools/index.cfm (accessed March 2018).
7. *Livability in Transportation Guidebook: Planning Approaches that Promote Livability.* Report FHWA-HEP-10-028. ICF International for Federal Highway Administration, Federal Transit Administration, U.S. Department of Transportation, Washington, D.C., 2010.
8. "Planning for Operations." Federal Highway Administration, U.S. Department of Transportation, https://ops.fhwa.dot.gov/plan4ops/ (accessed June 2017).
9. Grant, M., B. Bowen, M. Day, R. Winick, J. Bauer, A. Chavis, and S. Trainor. *Congestion Management Process: A Guidebook.* Report FHWA-HEP-11-011, ICF International, Inc. for Federal Highway Administration, U.S. Department of Transportation, Washington, D.C., 2011.
10. *NCHRP Report 716, Travel Demand Forecasting: Parameters and Techniques.* NCHRP Report 716, National Cooperative Highway Research Program, Transportation Research Board, National Academy of Sciences, Washington, D.C., 2012.

11. *National Household Travel Survey.* Federal Highway Administration, U.S. Department of Transportation, Washington, D.C., https://nhts.ornl.gov/ (accessed March 2018).

12. *Trip Generation Manual*, 10th Edition, Institute of Transportation Engineers, Washington, D.C., 2018.

13. Sloboden, J., J. Lewis, and V. Alexiadis. *Traffic Analysis Toolbox Volume XIV: Guidebook on the Utilization of Dynamic Traffic Assignment in Modeling.* FHWA-HOP-13-015. Cambridge Systematics, Inc., for Federal Highway Administration, U.S. Department of Transportation, Washington, D.C., 2012.

14. Gopalakrishna, D., E. Schreffler, D. Vary, D. Friedenfeld, B. Kuhn, C. Dusza, R. Klein, et al. *Integrating Demand Management into the Transportation Planning Process: A Desk Reference.* Report FHWA-HOP-12-035, Battelle for Federal Highway Administration, U.S. Department of Transportation, Washington, D.C., 2012.

15. *Integrating Active Traffic and Travel Demand Management: A Holistic Approach to Congestion Management.* Report FHWA-PL-11-11. Federal Highway Administration, U.S. Department of Transportation, Washington, D.C., 2011.

16. "Charlotte I-485 Interchange Land Use and Transportation Analysis." Federal Highway Administration, U.S. Department of Transportation, Washington, D.C., https://www.fhwa.dot.gov/planning/processes/land_use/case_studies/charlotte_nc/index.cfm (accessed March 2018).

17. *Congestion Management Process: A Case Study—Atlanta Regional Commission.* Federal Highway Administration, Federal Transit Administration, U.S. Department of Transportation, Washington, D.C., 2010, https://www.fhwa.dot.gov/planning/congestion_management_process/case_studies/arc.pdf (accessed March 2018).

CHAPTER **7**

Transportation Systems Management and Operations

7.1 Introduction

As discussed in Chap. 1, the United States has grappled for over a century with the challenge of providing convenient and safe transportation options to its citizens. In the rapidly evolving landscape of transportation, the national policy on providing mobility has shifted from construction to the wholesale operations and maintenance of a system that is safer, more efficient, and sustainable. The 2015 Fixing America's Surface Transportation Act (FAST Act) represents an emphasis on sustainability with its programs to improve safety, to maintain the condition of the transportation system, to reduce congestion and improve efficiency and freight movement, to protect the environment, and to further reduce delays in project delivery.[1] Today, the overall national transportation policy agenda focuses on maintaining and expanding the national transportation system and fostering a sound financial base for that system to create jobs and ensure its long-term reliability. This reliability includes public safety and national security, environmental quality, sustainability, and the incorporation of technologies to advance that sustainability for the safe and efficient method of transporting people, goods, and services across the country.

Transportation systems management and operations (TSMO) has emerged as the modern approach to addressing mobility and safety issues by capitalizing on the infrastructure investment through optimization. It includes the guiding principles of active, integrated, and performance-driven management and operations (Fig. 7.1). Key descriptors associated with TSMO include dynamic, predictive, proactive, performance driven, continuous monitoring, and supply and demand oriented. The overall objective of TSMO for an agency is to extract as much capacity and operational efficiency as possible out of its existing network and to optimize its investment in mobility. Throughout the active management cycle of TSMO, agencies monitor their systems and networks and assess their performance against a broad range of performance measures and benchmarks. They then evaluate the ongoing performance of the system and recommend dynamic actions to modify operations to enhance and improve system performance. An agency then implements those dynamic actions and continues monitoring to

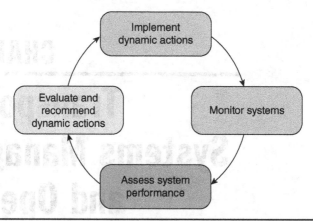

FIGURE 7.1   The active management cycle. (*Ref. 2.*)

determine if the actions affected the desired improvement. TSMO differs from traditional management in that the actions address immediate and near-term needs in system operations rather than longer-term expansion. Efficient management and operations can benefit all users of a network and possibly delay the need to expand capacity, particularly when resources to do so are limited.

TSMO represents new challenges to state Departments of Transportation (DOTs) and other agencies. From the beginning of the era of the automobile, DOTs and other operating agencies focused on building, expanding, and improving the transportation infrastructure to meet growing demand. However, over the past few decades, the emphasis has shifted to TSMO, which has generated a growing need for advanced technologies to facilitate efficient operations as well as a highly proficient workforce that can provide both technical and managerial expertise within the TSMO framework.

Transportation professionals must be prepared to face the challenge of operating and maintaining a complex system within the context of TSMO. This chapter provides a discussion on TSMO and the overall optimization of the existing infrastructure, including the types of congestion; how agencies can organize and ensure capabilities related to TSMO; engaging in planning for operations to include funding and finance; designing systems for long-term operations; examples of how agencies apply TSMO to meet regional objectives; how performance measurement and monitoring support TSMO; and case studies related to TSMO.

7.2   Types of Congestion

Congestion within the transportation context is quite simply the inability to move freely within the transportation network. Travelers recognize congestion when roads are filled with all manner of vehicles, travel speeds are much slower than normal, and they cannot get to their destination in a timely fashion. Congestion occurs across all segments of the transportation system and at all times of the day, causing frustration for every user. As illustrated in Fig. 7.2, it occurs when the facility is unable to meet the demand, occurs for a whole host of reasons.

FIGURE 7.2   Traffic congestion along I-81, Salem, VA. (© *D. Allen Covey, Virginia Department of Transportation [VDOT].*)

Congestion falls into two broad categories of recurring congestion and non-recurring congestion, as shown in Fig. 7.3 and Table 7.1. Recurring congestion typically occurs during peak travel periods and occurs because the capacity of the network simply cannot accommodate the number of vehicles attempting to use it at a particular moment in time.[3] About half of the congestion experienced by travelers in the United

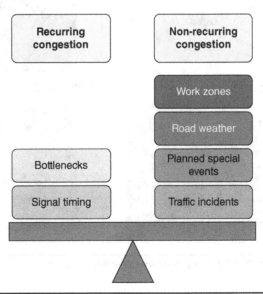

FIGURE 7.3   Recurring versus non-recurring congestion.

TABLE 7.1   Causes of Recurring and Non-Recurring Congestion

States is a result of daily recurring congestion. Agencies can use TSMO strategies to manage this congestion by working to affect the number of vehicles placing a demand on the network (i.e., travel demand management [TDM]) or by managing the demand once it reaches the network with operational strategies. The concept of TDM is covered in Chap. 6.

Non-recurring congestion is a result of any unplanned or temporary disruption on a facility that impacts its ability to provide the capacity needed to meet demand.[4] The name non-recurring illustrates the randomness, unscheduled, or atypical nature of these events. Non-recurring disruptions include incidents such as crashes or disabled vehicles, work zones, weather events, or planned special events. Approximately half of congestion experienced by system users is a result of non-recurring congestion. As with recurring congestion, operating agencies can utilize TSMO strategies to manage non-recurring congestion and reduce the duration and magnitude of the disruption to help get travelers on their way.

For the majority of the time in many locales across the country, travelers experience free movement on the transportation system whenever they choose to take a trip. Capacity easily meets the demand and travelers experience few delays. In other regions of the country, congestion is commonplace and the "rush" hour extends through major portions of the day. In both circumstances, expending large sums of money and resources expanding capacity simply to meet demand during peak periods or during random non-recurring congestion events is not practical. TSMO helps manage congestion when agencies need added capacity during those timeframes and represents an effective use of limited resources. The following sections provide a brief overview of each type of congestion, which are the target of TSMO strategies.

7.2.1 Bottlenecks

According to Federal Highway Administration (FHWA), a transportation-related bottleneck—the first type of recurring congestion—can be defined as a segment of roadway that frequently experiences reduced speeds and increased delays as a result of recurring congestion.[5] As shown in Fig. 7.4, this congestion often occurs in one direction, such as in the peak period direction on a freeway or at a merge point of ramps with the main lanes. In many of these circumstances, the traffic on the facility is imbalanced with more heading in one direction, such as from the suburbs into downtown. While this scenario is not a bottleneck, it does present one of the challenges with managing recurring congestion. If more lanes were in the peak period direction, the congestion would be mitigated. However, the same problem would occur in the opposite direction in the opposite peak, from downtown to the suburbs. Some TSMO strategies discussed later in this chapter can help address this imbalance.

One physical reason for a bottleneck is the narrowing of a facility that reduces capacity, such as a lane drop or exclusive exit on a freeway. In this situation, the traffic flow is restricted, creating a reduction in speed at the point of reduced capacity. However, other factors can create a bottleneck that do not physically reduce capacity but which generate the effect of a bottleneck in terms of what a driver experiences. For example, sun glare, the presence of a significant vertical incline, or weaving areas can create conditions that cause drivers to slow down or create turbulence in the traffic flow. All of these scenarios can be managed through TSMO solutions discussed in this chapter.

Figure 7.4   Congestion on I-95, Richmond, VA. (© D. Allen Covey, VDOT.)

7.2.2   Signal Timing

As discussed in Chap. 4, traffic signals assign right-of-way to different movements at an intersection to avoid conflicts. Traffic signals are, by nature, a cause of recurring congestion because traffic must periodically stop at a traffic signal to allow cross-traffic to pass through an intersection. The more complex the intersection and the more diverse the users of that intersection (e.g., passenger cars, pedestrians, bicycles, transit vehicles, rail and emergency vehicles, freight), the more challenges presented to the transportation professional developing a signal timing plan for an intersection, corridor, or network. As shown in Fig. 7.5, congestion frequently occurs on surface streets when traffic volumes are high. TSMO, and a traffic signal operations program in particular, can be effective at reducing the impact of signals on congestion.

7.2.3   Work Zones

A frequent cause of non-recurrent congestion is a work zone. Since maintenance of the transportation network is essential to mobility and safety, transportation agencies must schedule construction, maintenance, and rehabilitation projects on specific facilities. This work, whether during the day (see Fig. 7.6) or at night (Fig. 7.7) often causes congestion. Decreased speeds and increased delay occur for a number of reasons. Frequently, posted speeds are dropped through work zones to enhance safety. The presence of atypical roadway conditions and the presence of workers increase the workload for drivers, increasing the need for unique work zone traffic control. Additionally, work zones typically involve a reduction in capacity to accommodate the construction activity, thereby creating a bottleneck on the facility. TSMO strategies that address work zones and their unique challenges can improve congested conditions and improve safety and mobility for the traveling public.

FIGURE 7.5 Congestion in downtown Austin, TX. (© *Jim Lyle, TTI.*)

FIGURE 7.6 Work Zone, I-35, Waco, TX. (© *Jim Lyle, TTI.*)

7.2.4 Road Weather

Unfortunately, weather events impact mobility and safety on roadways. This form of non-recurring congestion can frequently cause havoc for travelers and pose operational challenges for transportation agencies. Examples of weather events or conditions transportation agencies must address include high winds, all forms of precipitation, fog, and flooding. These weather events can impact transportation facilities with respect to

FIGURE 7.7   Nighttime Work Zone, I-81, Virginia. (© D. Allen Covey, VDOT.)

reduced travel speeds, increased speed variance, increased travel time delay, increased accident risk, and reduced capacity.[6] Many weather events are short-lived, such as fog during a morning commute as illustrated in Fig. 7.8. For fog events, transportation agencies may need to provide travel advisories to drivers, reduce speeds, or limit access to a facility when visibility is extremely. Other weather events such as blizzards (see Fig. 7.9) have longer durations and require ongoing and more complex response on the part of

FIGURE 7.8   Fog conditions on I-95, Richmond, VA. (© D. Allen Covey, VDOT.)

Figure 7.9 Blizzard conditions on I-95, Woodbridge, VA. (© *Trevor Wrayton, VDOT.*)

operating agencies and their stakeholder partners. In the case of a snow event, an agency may need to provide comprehensive and broad traveler information and weather advisories, undertake road treatment strategies, reduce speed limits, limit access, or coordinate responses with partnering agencies—both during the event and afterwards—to mitigate the impact of the snow event on mobility as soon as possible. Other weather-related events can have longer-lasting ramifications. Bridge washouts, landslides, avalanches, or widespread flooding require can be much more complicated to manage and possibly long-term mitigation is that roadway facilities are damaged or destroyed by the event. TSMO programs that address road weather management can enable transportation managers to make informed decisions and to work with their regional partners to minimize the disruption of weather events.

7.3   Planned Special Events

Another form of non-recurring congestion results from planned special events. Unlike congestion that results from recurring or non-recurring sources, congestion from planned special events impacts not only regular traffic on the transportation network, but everyone attending the event across all modes. Thousands of events take place across the country each year, all of which impact travelers in some manner. Collectively, hundreds of thousands of individuals descend on communities and venues for these special events. In many cases, nearby transportation facilities become oversaturated with traffic, and mobility is limited, as shown in Fig. 7.10. These events can impact both urban and rural locations, frequently overwhelming the traditional responsibilities of local operating agencies. Additionally, transportation agencies have to work with their partner stakeholders (e.g., transit, law enforcement, first responders, etc.) to manage the resulting congestion. Effective planning and coordination across all regional partners can help to ensure the safety and mobility of everyone impacted by the event.

FIGURE 7.10   Traffic management during College Game Day, Texas A&M University, College Station, TX. (© *Tim Lomax, TTI.*)

7.3.1   Traffic Incidents

Traffic incidents have a major impact on congestion across the country on all levels of transportation facilities. The size of incidents can range from a stalled vehicle on a shoulder to a major overturned truck that blocks an entire roadway (see Fig. 7.11). As with planned special events, transportation agencies need to partner with a broad range

FIGURE 7.11   Overturned truck blocking a facility. (© *Tom Saunders, VDOT.*)

of stakeholders to ensure traffic incident management is effective. These partners include, but are not limited to, law enforcement, fire and rescue, emergency medical services, public safety communications, towing and recovery companies, hazard materials contractors, and the media.[7] Comprehensive traffic incident management (TIM) programs, which are a critical part of TSMO, help reduce delay and improve the overall reliability of the transportation network.

7.4 Planning for Operations

A fundamental step in ensuring that agencies have the resources necessary to advance TSMO within their jurisdictions is to engage in the broad practice of multimodal planning known as planning for operations, which supports TSMO. The key aspect of this approach involves regional collaboration and coordination with respect to transportation operations, management and operations considerations within the context of the transportation planning process, and linkages between these collaboration and planning efforts.[8] Planning for operations provides the foundation for incorporating TSMO in various ways. Transportation professionals and agencies at the state, regional, and local levels involved in transportation planning and investment processes work to identify ways in which various regional TSMO initiatives and strategies can be incorporated into these processes through collaboration and coordination. They recognize that TSMO is not a single "project" or a set of projects shoehorned into the planning process but rather a key element in planning and programming as a viable path toward optimizing system operations.

Planning for operations is an objectives-driven, performance-based approach that helps ensure transportation operations is on equal footing with capacity projects in a region. Key elements of this approach are illustrated in Fig. 7.12. The need and justification for TSMO in a region emerges from the requirements to meet the regionally agreed-upon goals and objectives in the planning process. Once an agency identifies and agrees to goals and objectives, TSMO and its supporting strategies can become customizable to local priorities and constraints under which a transportation network or specific corridor may operate.

The next step in planning for operations is to incorporate TSMO into the regional and statewide planning, programming, and funding activities. These activities range

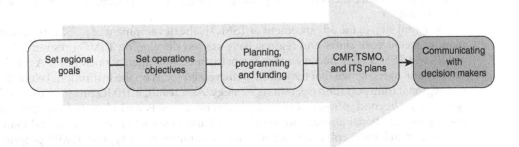

Figure 7.12 Integrating TSMO into planning for operations. (*Ref. 5.*)

from long-range strategic planning to more focused near-term planning at the state, county, district, regional, or corridor level. Ideally, TSMO is a programmatic effort that can be represented or articulated as a priority as part of a long-term investment plan, such as a long-range transportation plan (LRTP), or as part of a near-term transportation improvement program (TIP), TSMO plan, or an intelligent transportation systems (ITS) strategic plan. Metropolitan regions and MPOs are responsible for maintaining LRTPs for their respective jurisdictions. Covering a long time horizon, these documents establish the vision for the region's transportation system and identify current and future needs based on a region's population projects and travel demand. Metropolitan planning organizations (MPOs) typically update these documents every 5 years, and transportation projects seeking federal funding must be included in the LRTP. TIPs are regional documents that are updated yearly to reflect priority projects within the LRTP. TIP projects include all major transportation projects planned to receive funding, whether federal, state, or local, over a period of a number of years as defined by the agencies. Any large regional project that supports TSMO should be included in the LRTP and TIP. Incorporating TSMO into these documents ensures that they are recognized as a priority through the planning process and are considered strong candidates for project selection of funds.

As discussed in Chap. 6, another approach to planning for operations is through the congestion management process (CMP). The CMP builds upon the opportunities for regional cooperation and collaboration to identify strategies to increase capacity through effective planning, modeling, and environmental reviews. The CMP is a required process for urban areas to identify and mitigate congestion-related problems. TSMO and TSMO-related projects can greatly influence the CMP and associated reporting. Various agencies across the country have incorporated TSMO as part of their CMP and have found the CMP to be a helpful tool in prioritizing investments to address significant congestion issues. Although a CMP is a requirement for metropolitan areas of 200,000+ populations, there is some flexibility in how regions can develop their respective CMPs.

ITS strategic plans and TSMO program plans offer two other mechanisms to promote planning for operations. Both of these plans can incorporate ITS deployments and technology options that might help alleviate congestion or improve safety on a transportation network. They are relevant within the TSMO context because technology frequently enables effective TSMO. For example, ITS strategic plans (and deployment plans) are typically developed on a regional or statewide level, and might include (or reference) a regional or statewide ITS architecture. These plans typically include mobility or safety goals and objectives, transportation issues that could be addressed through TSMO, performance measures and performance goals, and priorities for deployment and integration.

A critical step in the advancement of TSMO is the development of a TSMO program plan. In recent year, states and regions have started developing TSMO program plans as ITS and TSMO have become more mainstreamed into agency operations. Agencies have begun to recognize that they need an increased focus on the institutional elements of a regional transportation operations strategy. As a result, a TSMO program plan will typically go beyond infrastructure and deployment needs and identify how agencies and regions can better address project planning, lifecycle costing, operations and maintenance, institutional collaboration, and other parameters. A typical TSMO program plan incorporates three elements: strategic, programmatic, and tactical. The strategic element outlines the business case for TSMO and establishes a vision, mission, goals and objectives for a TSMO program. The programmatic element of a TSMO program plan outlines an organizational structure that supports TSMO, and identifies the related business processes, staffing, and workforce needs for an agency intent on advancing TSMO within their organization. Finally, a TSMO program plan's tactical element includes such specifics as TSMO projects, services, and policies related to the implementation of the program plan.[9]

Finally, operating agencies need to effectively communicate with relevant decision makers the importance of operations and to gain their support. Gaining buy-in for collaborative operations and TSMO programs and projects is critical to successful implementation.[10] Decision makers can include a broad range of stakeholders, including MPO board members, state and local DOTs, transit agencies, state legislators, county and local elected officials, or other groups or individuals who help make transportation investment decisions or set transportation priorities and policies. Understanding what is important to these stakeholders helps an agency craft the message and establishes a dialogue with them to provide clear information about the benefits of TSMO for the traveling public and the region as a whole.

7.5 Organizing for Operations

If a transportation agency seeks to establish TSMO as a central part of its mission and institutional structure, it must incorporate TSMO within the fabric and structure of its organization. The foundation for establishing an organizational structure that supports TSMO lies in the operations capability improvement process.[11] The operations capability improvement process if based on the capability maturity model (CMM), which originated in the information technology industry.[12] The concept of a CMM for transportation operations emerged from the Strategic Highway Research Program 2 (SHRP2) reliability projects L01[13] and L06[14] which promoted a process-driven approach to improve TSMO. The projects focused on the role of institutions and the necessary business processes to improve management of programs and projects. The notion of the CMM within the context of transportation operations follows three principles for effectiveness:

1. *Process matters:* Projects fail or do not achieve desired functionality for a variety of reasons unrelated to the technology.

2. *Prioritizing the right actions is important:* Is an agency ready, how do they know, and what should they do next.

3. *Focus on the weakest link:* What is holding the agency back in becoming a leader in a particular area.[15]

In 2011, SHRP2 released the results of a study that focused on integrating business processes to improve travel time reliability (TTR), a key performance measurement that agencies across the country are using as a significant benchmark for their systems.[16,17] The focus was on processes that have a direct impact on transportation network reliability in which operational functions and TSMO as a whole are an integral part of the day-to-day business of the agency. The specific operational areas that have the greatest influence on reliability, as discussed previously, were identified as:

1. Incident management

2. Work zone management

3. Planned special event management

4. Road weather management

5. Traffic control and traffic operations[12]

By examining their business processes and identifying gaps and opportunities for improvement, transportation agencies can develop action plans to improve TSMO in their region and implement and institutionalize specific business processes to help them reach TSMO goals and objectives.[13]

A related SHRP2 study focused on institutional architectures to advance operational strategies.[18, 19] The objective was to conduct an assessment of how agencies should be organized to ensure they have TSMO programs that improve network and TTR. The study, conducted in three segments, identified the more effective transportation agencies in terms of reducing non-recurring congestion, determined the technical and business process features that agencies use to support operations, and identified institutional characteristics that seem essential in the development, support, and sustainment of these business processes.[14] The key outcome of the research was to recommend adapting the CMM to fit the transportation service context, which was developed in a companion guidance document focusing on support for strategies to address both recurring and non-recurring congestion.

The American Association of State Highway Transportation Officials (AASHTO) supported the conversion of that SHRP2 L01 and L06 research into a web-based tool for user-friendly and easy access to the results and to foster seamless updates to the content so that users have the most current guidance available.[8] The resulting AASHTO TSMO CMM targets the entire gamut of systems operations and management at a state or regional context. The framework can be applied at various levels of transportation operations and management depending on the specific needs of the agency or region. The target audience for the tool is transportation agency managers, policy makers, and other managers of systems operations related activities to help them identify the current agency capability associated with operations and management of the roadway system and identify actions to improve capabilities to enhance system performance.[8] Table 7.2 presents the organizational dimensions and subdimensions of capability for transportation agencies and their activities included in the AASHTO TSMO CMM.

Furthermore, the levels of capability in the AASHTO TSMO CMM are shown in Table 7.3.

In 2013, FHWA developed a series of six business process frameworks, also noted as capability maturity frameworks (CMFs), based on the AASHTO TSMO CMM.[20] The intent of the effort was for the CMFs to elaborate on, and be consistent with, the AASHTO TSMO CMM, but which provide more focused assessment and suggested actions in each of the following operations program areas related to recurring and non-recurring congestion:

1. Traffic management[21]

2. Traffic incident management[22]

3. Planned special events[23]

4. Work zone management[24]

5. Road weather management[25]

6. Traffic signal management[26]

Dimension	Sub-Dimensions
Business processes	Planning Scoping Programming/budgeting Project development/procurement
Systems and technology	Regional architectures Project systems engineering/testing and validation Standards/interoperability
Performance measurement	Measures definition Data acquisition Measures utilization
Culture	Technical understanding Leadership/championship Outreach Program status/authorities
Organization/workforce	Program status Organizational structure Recruitment and retention Staff development
Collaboration	Public safety agency collaboration Local government/MPO/RTPA cooperation Outsourcing/PPP

TABLE 7.2 AASHTO TSMO CMM Guidance Dimensions (*Ref. 8.*)

CMM Level	Characteristics of Capability Maturity Level
1	Activities and relationships ad hoc Informal Champion driven Mostly outside mainstream DOT activities
2	Basic strategy applications understood Key support requirements identified Key capacities under development Limited internal accountability Uneven alignment with external partners
3	Standardized strategy applications implemented TSMO technical and business processes development and documented Integration into DOT Partnerships aligned
4	TSMO a full, sustainable core DOT program priority Established on the basis of continuous improvement Top level management status Formal partnerships

TABLE 7.3 AASHTO TSMO CMM Guidance Levels of Capability (*Ref. 8.*)

Each of these CMFs is an interactive online support tool that can help transportation agencies identify their current capability with respect to TSMO and traffic management for specific types of congestion and to identify actions to improve that capability to better manage the complex transportation mobility challenges in their region.

Broadly, the frameworks assess an agency's capability to efficiently manage the movement of traffic on streets and highways and include corridor management approaches.[27] The capability levels and the actions are focused and defined from a traffic manager's perspective. The actions may require other agencies to be the responsible party, which is intended to foster multiagency collaboration and dialogue about traffic management at the regional level. The use of these CMFs can help an agency organize for operations and ensure they are ready for the challenge of TSMO within their organization.

7.6   Designing for Operations

As with planning for operation, designing for operations considers the overall management and operations of a transportation network during design and development. Likewise, it involves the consideration of regional and statewide operational objectives and performance measures by designers and operators as they consider how to design a transportation facility for optimal operation.[28] Performance-based practical design (PBPD) is an approach to decision making that helps transportation agencies better manage their infrastructure investments by considering TSMO. The process helps ensure that agencies meet their system-level needs and performance priorities within the context of limited resources.[29] Related to context-sensitive solutions, PBPD allows agencies to use a variety of operational and safety analysis tools to evaluate and compare the performance of various alternatives or projects. The end result is the efficient use of resources, the faster deployment of operational strategies, and the potential postponement or reduction in the need for capacity improvements.[25] Additionally, PBPD focuses on performance improvements that benefit both a particular project and the overall transportation system. It allows an agency to analyze each element of a project in terms of value, need, and urgency to help maximize the return on the investment, which is the overall objective TSMO approaches and TSMO-related projects.

7.7   Benefits and Costs of Operations

In order for an agency to determine whether a TSMO strategy is appropriate for addressing its regional operational challenges, they need to understand the costs and benefits of different strategies. This assessment of strategies should consider all of the costs associated with a strategy—from design and construction to operations and maintenance—and weigh those costs against the benefits that can be realized by the operating agency and the traveling public. As discussed previously, operational strategies can promote changes within the transportation network in a variety of ways. Typical changes might include, but are not limited to, volumes and speed; the number, severity, and duration of incidents and crashes; route choice, mode choice, and trip frequency by system users; and the overall procedures of operating agencies.[30] Typical measures of effectiveness (MOEs) that related to the benefits of TSMO strategies include, but are not limited to, user travel time savings and operating costs; crashes; emissions; travel time reliability; induced travel; as well as livability and customer satisfaction.

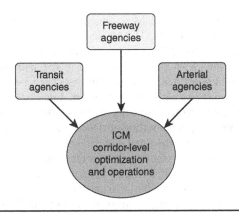

FIGURE 7.13 Integrated corridor management. (*Ref. 33.*)

7.8 TSMO in Action

Various operational strategies fall under the overall concept of TSMO. Two broad initiatives that represent TSMO in action are integrated corridor management (ICM) and active transportation and demand management (ATDM). ICM represents a collection of proactive approaches and strategies to address congestion and TTR issues using multimodal solutions within specific travel corridors.[31] As presented in Fig. 7.13, multimodal operating agencies partner together to manage a corridor as a single system rather than the more traditional approach of managing individual transportation networks (e.g., freeways, arterials, transit).[32] Within the ICM context, these agencies advance their respective system management and operations capabilities via active management. They collaborate and cooperate to integrate their systems, share data and information, and provide coordinated, multimodal responses to optimize operations across an entire corridor and better manage congestion.

ATDM, as defined by the FHWA, is the dynamic management, control, and influence of every aspect of the entire transportation trip chain.[2] It incorporates three major categories of strategies to impact the trip chain. These categories are active demand management (ADM), ATM, and active parking management (APM). Figure 7.14 provides an

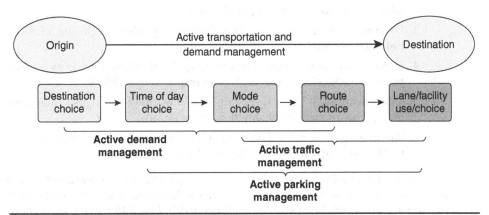

FIGURE 7.14 ATDM and the trip chain. (*Ref. 28.*)

overview of the influence of ATDM on the various steps within the trip chain and illustrates how the components of ATDM often overlap in terms of influence and can be implemented together to optimize system performance. Additionally, an agency can implement these strategies across a geographical spectrum from the regional scale to the corridor, facility, or site level, as well as at intersections between different levels of facilities, such as between freeways and arterials (i.e., intersections).

ADM is the ability to dynamically influence travel behavior and manage system demand in real time using information and technology.[34] ADM influences the initial stages of the trip chain to maximize the available choices for travelers with respect to destination, time of day, mode, and even route for a select trip. It includes strategies such as dynamic ridesharing, on-demand transit, dynamic pricing and incentives, comparative multimodal travel times, and predictive traveler information.

APM is the dynamic management of parking facilities to optimize the use of those facilities while influencing travel behavior.[35] This concept includes strategies such as dynamically priced parking, dynamic parking reservations, dynamic wayfinding, and dynamic overflow transit parking. The objective of APM is to provide technology-supported information and resources to travelers to influence their behavior related to parking. Parking information offered by APM can influence trip timing choices, mode choice, and parking facility choice at the end of the trip.[31] The strategies help optimize the use of parking facilities and also have a positive impact on localized traffic flow by ensuring travelers have parking and limit their circulation searching for spots.

ATM involves dynamically and proactively managing congestion on an entire facility based on real-time or pre-planned traffic conditions.[36] It focuses on trip reliability and works to maximize the effectiveness and efficiency of a facility while increasing throughput and enhancing safety. ATM strategies rely on the use of integrated systems with new technology, including comprehensive sensor systems, real-time data collection and analysis, and automated dynamic deployment to optimize system performance quickly and, in some cases, without the delay that occurs when operators must deploy operational strategies manually. Several strategies typically included as ATM strategies in the United States include, but are not limited to, the following:

1. Adaptive ramp metering—The deployment of traffic signals on ramps to dynamically control the entrance of vehicles onto a limited access facility.

2. Dynamic lane reversal—The dynamic reversal of on or all lanes on a facility to allocate the capacity of congested roads.

3. Dynamic lane use control—The dynamic opening or closing of individual traffic lanes based on prevailing conditions.

4. Dynamic shoulder lanes—The opening of a shoulder for use as a travel lane based on congestion levels and/or in response to incidents.

5. Queue warning—The real-time display of warning messages to alert motorists that queues or significant slowdowns are ahead.

6. Variable speed limits—The adjustment of speed limits based on real-time traffic, roadway, and/or weather conditions.[37]

The concept of ATM in the United States emerged from widespread experience with these strategies overseas. For example, the Netherlands was one of the first countries to utilize variable speed limits (VSLs), as illustrated in Fig. 7.15.[38] Experience shows that

FIGURE 7.15 Variable speed limits in the Netherlands. (© *Beverly Kuhn, TTI.*)

when compliance with the reduced speeds is high, the traffic stream experiences a reduced severity of shockwaves upstream of a bottleneck. The concept is that a slower, more consistent flow is less likely to break down into congested flow, therefore improving travel times. The speed limit is changed automatically by using the information from the loops in a computer algorithm. By gradually reducing the speed as volumes are predicted to increase, this strategy allows a slight increase in capacity. The Road Directorate of the Danish Ministry of Transport and Energy decided to deploy VSLs as part of work zone traffic management strategies for the multiyear widening of the M3 (see Fig. 7.16).

FIGURE 7.16 Variable speed limits in a work zone in Copenhagen, Denmark. (© *Beverly Kuhn, TTI.*)

The Road Directorate noted that incidents on the motorway did not increase during the reconstruction project as a result of this work zone ATM application while the existing two lanes were maintained at a narrower-than-normal width and no entrance ramps, exit ramps, or bridges were closed.[38]

The following sections provide a brief overview of each of these strategies. Transportation operating agencies have utilized some of these strategies for a number of years, with many of them becoming more prevalent as technology evolves and as the need for effective TSMO strategies grows.

7.8.1 Adaptive Ramp Metering

Adaptive ramp metering is the strategy of controlling the rate at which traffic is allowed to enter a freeway facility dynamically adjusted based on current (or predicted) operating conditions of both the freeway *and* the ramps.[39] An adaptive ramp metering system balances freeway demands and queue growth over multiple ramps in an attempt to maintain smooth flow on the freeway for as long as possible, delaying the onset of congestion (see Fig. 7.17). By facilitating a more uniform rate of vehicles entering the traffic stream, vehicles enter at a decontrolled rate rather than in large groups, which can create a bottleneck at the merge point of the main lane and the ramp and increase delay on both facilities. Agencies can utilize traffic detection systems and advanced control algorithms to change metering strategies as congestion builds and dissipates.

7.8.2 Dynamic Lane Reversal

Dynamic lane reversal is the practice of dynamically allocating the capacity of congested roads, to allow capacity to better match traffic demand throughout the day.[39] Agencies can implement dynamic lane reversal on both freeways (see Fig. 7.18) and

FIGURE 7.17 Adaptive ramp metering on I-45, Houston, TX. (© *TTI*.)

Figure 7.18 Dynamic reversible lane on I-30, Dallas, TX. (© *TTI*.)

Figure 7.19 Dynamic lane reversal on FM 157, Arlington, TX. (© *TTI*.)

arterial facilities (see Fig. 7.19), and this strategy is most applicable on facilities with a directional imbalance in excess of 65/35 with primary through traffic and predictable congestion patterns. Moreover, agencies can utilize this strategy during emergencies to enable emergency personnel to respond to incidents on a facility with limited access.[37]

7.8.3 Dynamic Lane Use Control/Dynamic Shoulder Use
Dynamic lane use control is the process of dynamically closing or opening individual traffic lanes as warranted and providing advance warning of closures (typically

FIGURE 7.20 Dynamic lane use control on a freeway. (© *Jim Lyle, TTI.*)

through dynamic lane control signs) to safely merge traffic into adjoining lanes.[39] The goal of the strategy is to direct traffic into appropriate lanes based on conditions. Dynamic lane use control, as illustrated in Fig. 7.20, can be effective at meeting variable demand or in managing traffic flow around incidents or for special events. Dynamic lane use control allows agencies to change lane assignments to meet different traffic demands, as illustrated in Fig. 7.21. In arterial applications, an approach with heavy left-turn movements in the morning peak time can operate with dual left-turn lanes during that peak period but can allow a through movement in the second left-turn lane once the left-turn demand has abated (see Fig. 7.19).

Dynamic shoulder use is a variation of dynamic lane use control that involves opening the shoulder as a travel lane(s) based on recurring congestion levels during peak periods and in response to incidents or other conditions as warranted during both peak and non-peak periods.[39] Typical applications for dynamic shoulder use are for managed lanes (for transit vehicles or high-occupancy vehicle [HOV] only) or for all vehicles. Both applications offer potential improved travel time and trip reliability for users.

7.8.4 Queue Warning

Queue warning is the practice of providing real-time display of warning messages, typically on dynamic message signs (DMS) and/or possibly coupled with flashing lights) along a roadway to alert motorists that queues or significant slowdowns are ahead, thus reducing rear-end crashes and improving safety.[39] Figure 7.22 shows an example of a queue warning system in operation at the beginning of a major work zone on I-35 in Waco, Texas. The objective of a queue warning system is to alert drivers to the possibility of stopped traffic so that they do not come upon the end of a queue unawares. They are cognizant of the potential conditions and are more likely to slow down their speed in order to be prepared to stop. Queue warning is often deployed with VSLs.

FIGURE 7.21   Dynamic lane use control at an intersection. (© *Jim Lyle, TTI.*)

FIGURE 7.22   Queue warning work zone application on I-35, Waco, TX. (© *TTI.*)

7.8.5   Variable Speed Limits

VSLs involve the adjustment of speed limits based on real-time traffic, roadway, and/or weather conditions.[39] Either regulatory or as recommended speed advisories, VSLs can be applied to an entire roadway segment or individual lanes. These are also known as dynamic speed limits, variable advisory speeds, and speed harmonization.

FIGURE 7.23   Variable speed limits on I-5, Seattle, WA. (© *Beverly Kuhn, TTI.*)

Figure 7.23 shows an example of VSLs as deployed in Seattle, Washington. In this application, Washington State Department of Transportation (WSDOT) installed the VSL along with dynamic lane use control, DMS, and enforceable VSL signage to alert drivers of delays and to direct drivers out of incident-blocked lanes.[40] The left lane, which is an HOV lane, has a higher speed limit as it provides an added benefit to those HOV users in the lane when the VSL is active.

7.9   Managed Lanes

One TSMO operational strategy that has been used for several decades in the United States in one form or another is managed lanes. As agencies have struggled to optimize the capacity of their congested corridors, they have frequently implemented managed lanes as a lane management strategy, similar to those discussed as ATM strategies. Specifically, managed lanes are intended to help an agency regulate demand, separate traffic streams to reduce friction, and to optimize the available capacity.[41] Examples of managed lanes facilities include, but are not limited to: HOV lanes, value priced lanes, high-occupancy toll (HOT) lanes, or exclusive use lanes. The concept is to use one or a combination of operational strategies to control how the managed lanes are utilized by roadway traffic. Access to the facility can be regulated through pricing, vehicle eligibility, or physical access. Figure 7.24 pictures the entrance to the HOV lane on US 290 in Houston, Texas, which runs down the center of the freeway. Access is limited to vehicles with three or more passengers between 6:45 and 8:00 AM and to vehicles with two or more passengers at all other times the lane is open. This particular HOV lane is reversible, offering a reliable travel alternative along the corridor in the peak direction to eligible vehicles.

Figure 7.24   HOV lane entrance on US 290, Houston, TX. (© *Jim Lyle, TTI*.)

7.10   Real-Time Traveler Information

One of the most powerful TSMO tools an agency can utilize to help optimize system performance is traveler information. A well-informed driver is prepared for the road ahead, and can make decisions about their trip based on information provided to them through a variety of mechanisms and media. As discussed throughout this chapter, information is a critical component of virtually every TSMO strategy. As illustrated in Figs. 7.25 and 7.26, drivers can benefit from real-time and site-specific information about work zones, anticipated travel times, weather events, delays, queues, and much more. The more current that information is, the more valuable it is to the traveler. A comprehensive TSMO program plan will incorporate strategic real-time traveler information system that targets key corridors and specific system users. The system offers a breadth of information relative to a variety of trip routes and modes to enable travelers to make the best decisions to meet their personal needs about when, where, and how to take a trip.

7.11   Performance Measurement and Performance Monitoring

As discussed previously, TSMO is intended to extract as much capacity and operational efficiency as possible out of its existing network and to optimize its investment in mobility. To fully understand how TSMO impacts their system, an agency needs to establish comprehensive performance measurement and performance monitoring programs. Through these programs, an agency can track progress on meeting regional goals and objectives, identify needs, and deficiencies in system performance, evaluate the effects of implemented projects, document accomplishments, and communicate effectively with decision makers and stakeholders.[42]

Figure 7.25 Construction message on DMS. (© *Jim Lyle, TTI.*)

Figure 7.26 Travel time information on DMS, Austin, TX. (© *TTI.*)

Performance measurement is defined by FHWA as the "use of statistical evidence to determine progress toward specific defined organizational objectives."[43] From an operational perspective, performance measurement allows an agency to measure its progress toward meeting its TSMO goals and objectives with both quantitative and qualitative data. Typical goals for a transportation system are safety, mobility, and productivity. An agency can use a variety of performance measures for different uses related to TSMO, including but not limited to:

1. Evaluate current operations, make immediate decisions on modifying TSMO-related operations, and guide agency activities related to TSMO.
2. Assess overall system performance resulting from TSMO programs or strategies and factors that may indicate adjustments needed to TSMO-related operations.
3. Assess the overall administration of a TSMO program or strategy.
4. Determine costs and benefits of TSMO.

Major issues that an agency should consider when looking at performance measures and a performance measurement program include, but are not limited to:

1. Costs associated with data collection
2. Assuring appropriate comparisons to other operations
3. Data quality, completeness, and timeliness
4. Extrapolating data from partial coverage of the network
5. Matching performance measures to their purposes
6. Understanding extraneous influences in the data and external factors
7. Using performance measures in the allocation of funding
8. Liability for action (or lack thereof) based on measurement results
9. Responsibility for measures for which there may be limited control
10. Establishing benchmarks and targets for performance
11. Identifying good multimodal measures[33]

The first step in the performance measurement process for TSMO is to define the mission and outcome-related goals of the transportation network. These goals should be developed with the involvement of key stakeholders, and should be aligned with activities, core processes, and resources so that an agency can achieve them.[33] These are the regional goals and objectives that an agency is likely to use in its TSMO program and as part of critical regional and statewide planning documents such as the LRTP.

The second step in the performance measurement process is the measurement task. At this stage, an agency develops a set of performance measures tied to the goals and objectives for the organization and TSMO and of a reasonable number so as to keep the program cost-effective. It is essential that the performance measures demonstrate results in a meaningful way for the agency. Once an agency determines which performance measures to use, they go about collecting the appropriate data or acquiring it from third-party entities if appropriate, ensuring that the data is sufficiently complete, accurate, and consistent for documenting performance. They then analyze and report the data in a way that is useful to the agency, system users, and decision makers.[33]

The third step in performance measurement is the use of the data. An agency can analyze the data collected and use it in a variety of ways to advance TSMO and overall organizational advancement. They can use the system performance information to manage their organization to achieve regional performance goals and objectives; demonstrate how TSMO program performance has been effective and/or improved through implementation; package the information in a digestible format to inform key stakeholders, decision makers, and the traveling public; and use the information internally or with policy makers to allocate resources for future programs and projects.[33] Performance measurement data are extremely valuable, and agencies should take advantage of being able to craft the story of their region's improvements as a result of TSMO.

The final critical practice associated with performance measurement is the management of an agency's transportation network based on performance. An agency can use performance measurement as the guiding force in a TSMO program and to reinforce the importance of such a program to the agency and the traveling public. It ensures that decisions are made based on critical, relevant, and quality data with decision makers being held accountable for the results of their actions. An agency can also use such a program to help build expertise in strategic planning, overall performance measurement efforts within the organization, and leverage that information when making decisions. As such, it also helps ensure that performance-based management becomes part of the overall culture and daily activities of an agency.[33]

7.12 Transportation Management Centers

The transportation management center (TMC) is an important element of a broad TSMO program for operating agencies. It functions as the central operating point for a region, bringing together different elements of the transportation system to facilitate the effective management of the network. All available data about the transportation network, such as sensor data and camera feeds, comes into the TMC operating system. Depending on the complexity and size of the network, that information is likely to include the freeway network, the surface streets and traffic signal systems, transit services, and emergency services (see Fig. 7.27). The data are used to monitor the real-time

FIGURE 7.27   TransGuide TMC, San Antonio, TX. (© *Jim Lyle, TTI.*)

operations of the network and to initiate control strategies to improve performance. For example, a TMC would be the central hub for an ICM initiative. It supports the effective management of the transportation network in response to both recurring and non-recurring congestion. Frequently, TMCs are staffed with personnel from a variety of stakeholder agencies to foster real-time coordination. Agency personnel also use that data to calculate performance measures to drive both operational enhancements and to benchmark performance.

TMCs are not a new innovation. Early versions of TMCs have been in operation for decades. One aspect of TMCs that has remained consistent since their inception is the use of technology to monitor and operate the network. As technology has advanced, the capabilities of TMCs have expanded to handle the new data generated by that technology and to manage technology-driven operational strategies or to enhance traditional strategies. Recent advancements in wireless communications, the broad use of social media, and the emergence of third-party data providers have had the most recent impact on TMC operations and functionality to support TSMO.[44] Emerging trends related to operations that TMC managers are working on consider include, but are not limited to:

1. A nimble service-oriented program mindset and organizational structure
2. ATDM concept and toolkit
3. Accommodating toll and other pricing operations
4. Performance monitoring and management
5. Automation tools and related tools to increase efficiency
6. Involvement of third parties in data and traveler information
7. Mobile communications and wireless networks
8. Social media for traveler information and crowd sourcing[34]

TMC managers across the country from regions of all sizes continue to assess technologies and strategies that correspond to many of these trends and how they can enhance their current operations and help optimize the efficiency of their transportation network.

As discussed previously, recurring congestion is only one aspect of operations that impact the safety and mobility of the network. TMCs play a significant role in managing non-recurring congestion because they have ready access to monitoring and other data sources and the capability to respond quickly to unplanned events on the network. For example, TMCs regularly manage the impact of incidents on the network as well as any planned special events and work zones. When capacity is impacted by these events, the TMC deploys operational responses to mitigate the impact of these events, including the dissemination of traveler information. This role is particularly important with respect to emergency operations.[45] Specifically, the TMC can provide specific support activities that enable emergency response. These activities include, but are not limited to:

1. Planning for anticipated emergency events
2. Detection, verification, and monitoring of roadway conditions
3. Assessment of transportation network damage and related capacity
4. Identification and management of public safety lifeline routes
5. Development and implementation of traffic control strategies to support emergency response and evaluation

6. Management of detours and evacuation routes
7. Dispatching of maintenance and support vehicles
8. Coordination with local agencies
9. Development of event-specific operational strategies to address response phases
10. Provision of public information and traveler alerts
11. Stabilization of traffic demand in the impacted area
12. Delivery of post-event debriefings[35]

All of these activities support emergency operations and the incident command, regardless of whether the emergency is a significant weather event, such as a hurricane, or a national security incident, and emphasize the importance of cooperation with first responders to ensure the safety of the traveling public and the swift and safe response to the emergency.

Most large urban areas in the United States have TMCs that managed the network from a single facility. Many of these centers have been in place for many years, and have evolved over time to incorporate a broad range of data sources and activities along with the frequent co-location of partnering agencies. However, the costs associated with such a facility can be prohibitive to agencies in today's reality of limited resources. Thus, a virtual traffic management center (VTMC) may be a viable option for agencies considering the construction of a new TMC; considering the merging of two or more TMCs; responsible for the monitoring of rural facilities; or needing to enhance current operations.[46] A VTMC is accomplished by utilizing computers or a computer network to accomplish the broad range of TMC operations and functionality absent in a single physical structure to house the TMC operations. The advantages and disadvantages of VTMCs are described in Table 7.4. Overall, while establishing a VTMC can be complex and require

Advantages of VTMCs	Disadvantages of Virtual TMCs
1. Capital cost savings realized by eliminating the need for a large facility.	7. Requires broader staff capabilities since they work independently.
2. Recurring cost savings realized by eliminating hardware and software maintenance contracts.	8. Requires expanded and/or revised training programs for operators to ensure they can handle all required tasks.
3. Computer and software technologies allow operations from any location.	9. Network security systems and policies need to be extended due to the reliance on connectivity.
4. Staff are able to work from anywhere.	10. Existing agency agreements to share and operate facilities and systems may be impacted by the virtual model.
5. Security of staff is enhanced through a dispersed structure.	11. Computer software and system integration costs are higher because of the complex integration required.
6. Multiagency operations are facilitated by the virtual structure.	12. Some agencies may prefer a command and control center.

TABLE 7.4 Advantages and Disadvantages of Virtual TMCs (*Ref. 36.*)

more integration and security systems, it can be a viable pathway for many regions, helping them enhance their TSMO activities within the reality of limited resources.

7.13   Case Studies

The following are case studies illustrating examples of state and local agencies implementing TSMO-related programs and projects to improve the management and operations of their transportation systems within their jurisdictions.

TSMO Program Plan—Iowa

The Iowa Department of Transportation (IDOT) has a TSMO plan[47] for the state, which includes a TSMO Strategic Plan[48] and a TSMO Program Plan.[49] Launched in 2016, the IDOT TSMO program focuses on improving operations in Iowa by helping IDOT prioritize projects and operations strategies; deploy technology and strategies to achieve improved mobility, safety, delay, and information access; focus on performance; focus on customer service and outreach, and invest strategically in its transportation system.

The core elements of the IDOT TSMO Program Plan target programmatic, deployment, and strategic improvements in operations. Programmatic elements target IDOT's business structure and capability, working to ensure that IDOT has the organizational ability to undertake TSMO as a long-term strategic program. Deployment elements target IDOT's decision-making efforts related to investment priorities and resource management so that the agency optimizes its infrastructure, which is at the heart of TSMO. Strategic elements target helping IDOT make the business case for TSMO by establishing an organizational culture for TSMO and putting TSMO in the geo-political context to benefit all the traveling public across the state.

The IDOT TSMO Strategic Plan sets out the challenge facing Iowa with respect to TSMO and why it matters to the state DOT, primarily as a result of the cost of congestion. It provides the strategic direction for the TSMO program, including the state's vision, mission, and strategic goals and objectives for the program, as shown in Table 7.5. These strategic goals are safety, reliability, efficiency, convenience, coordination, and integration, all of which benefit the state and the citizens of Iowa.

Strategic Goal	Strategic Objective
Safety	Reduce crash frequency and severity
Reliability	Improve transportation system reliability, increase resiliency, and increase capacity in critical corridors
Efficiency	Minimize delay and maximize system efficiency
Convenience	Facilitate easy access to mobility choices for travelers
Coordination	Engage all disciplines within the DOT and stakeholder partners to proactively operate the transportation system
Integration	Incorporate TSMO strategies through the agency's planning, design, construction, maintenance, and operations activities

TABLE 7.5   IDOT TSMO Strategic Goals and Objectives (*Ref. 47.*)

   The IDOT TSMO Program Plan is a companion document to the TSMO Strategic Plan and provides structure for the comprehensive TSMO Program. Elements included in the program plan are:

   1. Program objectives
   2. TSMO integration with current plans and programs
   3. Leadership and organization
   4. Business processes and resources
   5. Performance management and decision support assessment
   6. 5-year TSMO Program

The 5-year TSMO Program includes, among other elements, a 5-year list of activities that deliver TSMO strategic goals and objectives and a 5-year budget plan for the program.[39]

   The final component of the Iowa TSMO Program Plan is TSMO Service Layer Plans. These plans, which are based on the overall program objectives, provide detailed recommendations and actions for eight service areas provided by IDOT. The service layers are defined in Table 7.6. IDOT is committed to TSMO and recognizes that it

Service Layer	Definition
Traffic management center	The around-the-clock hub of DOT traffic coordination activities throughout the state; the traffic management center recently relocated from Ames to a newly remodeled facility in the Iowa Motor Vehicle Division Building in Ankeny.
ITS and communications	Fixed and mobile traffic detectors, non-enforcement traffic cameras, dynamic message signs, highway advisory radio, and supporting communications infrastructure
Traveler information	Traveler Information tools that help publicly broadcast planned and prevailing traffic conditions, such as Iowa 511 and various social media
Traffic incident management	The coordination of how IDOT and its partners respond to routine highway traffic incidents
Emergency transportation operations	The coordination of how IDOT and its partners respond to large-scale incidents (not necessarily highway related), such as flooding, tornado, epidemics, etc.
Work zone management	The planning and deployment of various strategies to maintain traffic flow and safety through highway work zones
Active transportation and demand management	Innovative strategies to maximize available capacity of roadways, such as ramp metering, variable speed limits, lane control signing, and time-of-day shoulder use
Connected and autonomous vehicles	An emerging technology that considers the challenges and opportunities of vehicle-to-vehicle, vehicle-to-infrastructure, and autonomous vehicles to improve vehicle safety and efficiency; IDOT's primary role is an information service provider.

TABLE 7.6   IDOT TSMO Service Layer Definitions (*Ref. 38.*)

complements the investments made in infrastructure by enhancing system management and traffic operations, building upon the existing people, processes, and systems to help the department realize the full capacity of the existing transportation system.

Integrated Corridor Management—Dallas

The Dallas Area Rapid Transit (DART) led a coalition of state and regional agencies in the deployment of ICM on US-75 in the Dallas region. The demonstration project, which was funded by the U.S. Department of Transportation (USDOT), was a component-based corridor management system that enabled the sharing of internal and external information among partner agencies.[50] Information was shared data related to incidents, construction, special event, transit, parking, and traffic flow. That data were then used to provide operational planning and evaluation through a decision support system (DSS) deployed as part of the project.

US 75 is a corridor in the Dallas area that carries over 330,000 vehicles a day on the main lanes through the center of Dallas and includes concurrent-flow, HOV lanes in the freeway median that are operated by the Texas Department of Transportation (TxDOT). The corridor also contains a light-rail line that serves the communities along the corridor and connects with downtown and a regional commuter line that extends to Fort Worth. A number of arterials form a grid pattern along US-75.

The stakeholders involved in the project included TxDOT Dallas District and Traffic Operations Division, DART, the City of Dallas, the City of Richardson, the City of Plano, the Town of Highland Park, the City of University Park, North Central Texas Council of Governments, and North Texas Tollway Authority. The purpose of the system, which included three major subsystems, provided the following integrated features for the region:

1. An integrated platform for coordinated response by the stakeholders to incidents, construction, and special events in the corridor.

2. An information exchange tool based on center-to-center standards and the Traffic Management Data Dictionary (TMDD).

3. A data fusion engine for the corridor to feed information to the regional 511 systems.

4. A DSS real-time information on incidents, construction, special events, transportation network status, and device status throughout the corridor.

5. A response plan coordination tool for multiple agencies to coordinate actions in responding to incidents within the corridor.[41]

A diagram illustrating the DSS for the Dallas ICM is displayed in Fig. 7.28. The benefits of such a system, which forms the backbone of the ICM system, include improved TTR for commuters, enhanced decision-making support for operating agencies, a return on investment for the project, and less pollution from idling vehicles in congested traffic.[41]

Over the initial 18 months of operation, the Dallas ICM system provided expected benefits to the stakeholder agencies and the traveling public using the corridor. It provided system operators with comprehensive information related to operating conditions in the corridor across all modes. Response plans were coordinated when incidents occurred and improved over time as the data matured and agencies became more familiar with the DSS and operational processes. After the initial phase of the project,

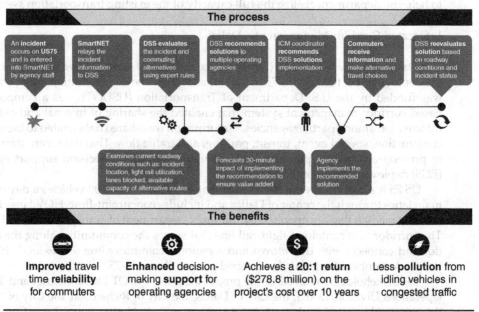

Integrated corridor management (ICM) decision support system (DSS)
Alternatives for agencies, options for commuters when incidents occur on US75

The process

| An incident occurs on **US75** and is entered into SmartNET by agency staff | **SmartNET** relays the incident information to DSS | **DSS evaluates** the incident and commuting alternatives using expert rules | **DSS recommends solutions** to multiple operating agencies | ICM coordinator **recommends DSS solutions** implementation | **Commuters receive information** and make alternative travel choices | **DSS reevaluates solution** based on roadway conditions and incident status |

Examines current roadway conditions such as: incident location, light rail utilization, lanes blocked, available capacity of alternative routes

Forecasts 30-minute impact of implementing the recommendation to ensure value added

Agency implements the recommended solution

The benefits

| **Improved** travel time **reliability** for commuters | **Enhanced** decision-making **support** for operating agencies | Achieves a **20:1 return** ($278.8 million) on the project's cost over 10 years | Less **pollution** from idling vehicles in congested traffic |

Figure 7.28   Dallas ICM decision support process. *(Ref. 41.)*

the partner agencies agreed to continue to support the ICM, and other agencies in the region asked to become part of the stakeholder group through the integration of their specific data into the ICM and 511 systems.

Active Traffic Management—Virginia

One of the newest ATM installations in the country is the Virginia Department of Transportation (VDOT) system along I-66 from U.S. 29 in Centreville to the Capital Beltway (I-495) in suburban Washington, D.C. Completed in September 2015, this project was constructed to improve safety and operations along I-66 by better managing the existing roadway capacity.[51] The deployment included the following ATM strategies:

1. **Advisory variable speed limits (AVSLs).** The posted speed limits displayed on signs over each lane change based on current traffic or roadway conditions detected along the facility. The intent of the strategy is to encourage more uniform speed distributions and provide advance warning of slowed traffic. The speed limits are advisory rather than regulatory.

2. **Queue warning systems (QWS).** Drivers receive advanced notice of congested conditions along the facility. Messages are displayed on DMS that work with AVSLs to alert drivers to slow or stopped traffic.

3. **Lane use control signs (LUCSs).** Electronic signs mounted over each travel lane on an overhead gantry display indications to alert drivers to blocked lanes.

4. **Hard shoulder running (HSR).** The shoulder is opened or closed dynamically for travel depending on roadway conditions. The intent of the strategy is to temporarily increase capacity on the facility when it is needed most.

Technologies installed as part of the system include overhead sign gantries, shoulder and lane control signs, shoulder monitoring system, speed limit displays, incident and queue detection, and additional traffic cameras.

The new ATM system along I-66 replaced an older ATM system along the corridor that included temporary shoulder use and HOV lanes. The older system operated along 6.5 miles of the corridor and allowed general-purpose traffic to use the rightmost shoulders only during peak periods Monday to Friday (eastbound, 5:30–11:00 AM; westbound, 2:00–8:00 PM). The installation was a result of the adaptation of leftmost general purpose lane to HOV-2 lane concurrent with opening of shoulder lane (eastbound, 5:30–9:00 AM; westbound, 3:00–7:00 PM). Advance signage and traffic control signaling provided travelers with information of the operations, including large signs alerting drivers to nine emergency refuge areas. The shoulder was also opened to all traffic during traffic incidents and construction.[52]

An evaluation of the ATM deployment along I-66 was conducted to determine the impact of the system on operations and safety on the facility.[42] MOEs used to evaluate the system included ATM utilization rate, average travel time, TTR, and total travel time delay along the corridor. These are all TSMO-related MOEs that VDOT can use to illustrate the impacts of the strategies. A preliminary before-and-after study utilizing safety and operations data yielded positive results. Benefits included a 2% to 6% improvement in weekday travel times during midday in the off-peak direction; 10% improvement in average travel times and TTR during weekend peak periods; and promising safety benefits. Furthermore, a benefit–cost ratio of 1.54 using weekend operational improvements only indicated that the I-66 ATM deployment was a cost-effective application of ATM in terms of operations and safety.

Performance Measurement—Minnesota

The Minnesota Department of Transportation (MnDOT) has had a performance management system in place since 2009 that guides the major products, services, and priorities of the department.[53] The measures are used by the department to evaluate and improve the transportation system to meet its 50-year vision for transportation in the state. The system is structured around performance measures and targets that are set through a policy that lays out a uniform process for adopting, revising, and retiring them.[54] The measures assess progress toward meeting statewide goals and objectives, guide investment in the statewide highway system or modal system, and assess the impact of the products and services provided by MnDOT to its customers, that is, the traveling public.

MnDOT prepares an annual performance report that serves as a benchmark for the performance measure system. It provides a scorecard on the following performance measures:

1. Public trust

2. Civil rights: Workforce and small business participation

3. Traveler safety

4. Pavement condition

5. Bridge condition

6. Twin Cities freeway congestion

7. Snow and ice control

8. Freight mode share

9. Air transportation

10. Twin Cities transit ridership

11. Greater Minnesota transit ridership

12. Bicycle use

13. Pedestrian accessibility

14. Fuel use

The most recent annual report was released in 2015[55] and makes the connection between statewide goals, objectives, and performance measures for transportation and those at the national level set forth in MAP-21 and the FAST Act. The document presents detailed information on these performance measures and highlights both performance gains and challenges faced by the agency. Features of the performance measurement scorecard include clear indications of whether the results for a particular measure are good (green), need improvement (yellow), or are poor (red). Special designations are also made for those measures that are the primary responsibility of MnDOT. Trend graphs are provided as well to indicate how the measure has changed over the past 5 years, with the target marked numerically as well as on each graph by a yellow horizontal line. The format of the scorecard can be used in a variety of ways by the department, including communicating with stakeholder groups and guiding capital investments and annual operational budgets for the agency.

7.14 Summary

As discussed in this chapter, TSMO is the modern approach to addressing mobility and safety issues by capitalizing on the infrastructure investment through optimization. Through active, integrated, and performance-driven management and operations, TSMO enables transportation agencies to extract as much capacity and operational efficiency as possible out of its existing network and to optimize its investment in mobility. It differs from traditional management in that the actions address immediate and near-term needs in system operations rather than longer-term expansion. Efficient management and operations can benefit all users of a network and possibly delay the need to expand capacity, particularly when resources to do so are limited. As described in this chapter, an agency considering TSMO is effective when an agency considers operations across all of its organizational activities. Establishing a TSMO program ensures an agency factors TSMO into the planning, organizational, design, and operational services it undertakes, with performance measurement and performance serving as the foundation of a performance-based management of its infrastructure investment.

Glossary of Acronyms

AASHTO—American Association of State Highway Transportation Officials

ADM—active demand management

APM—active parking management

ATDM—active transportation and demand management

ATM—active traffic management

AVSL—advisory variable speed limit

CMF—capability maturity framework

CMM—capability maturity model

CMP—congestion management process

DART—Dallas Area Rapid Transit

DMS—dynamic message sign

DOT—Department of Transportation

DSS—decision support system

FAST Act—Fixing America's Surface Transportation Act

FHWA—Federal Highway Administration

HOV—high-occupancy vehicle

HSR—hard shoulder running

ICM—integrated corridor management

IDOT—Iowa Department of Transportation

ITS—intelligent transportation systems

LRTP—long-range transportation plan

LUCS—lane use control signal

MnDOT—Minnesota Department of Transportation

MOE—measure of effectiveness

PBPD—Performance-based practical design

QWS—queue warning system

SHRP2—Strategic Highway Research Program 2

TDM—travel demand management

TIM—traffic incident management

TIP—Transportation Improvement Program

TMC—transportation management center

TMDD—traffic management data dictionary

TSMO—transportation systems management and operations

TTI—Texas A&M Transportation Institute

TTR—travel time reliability

TxDOT—Texas Department of Transportation

USDOT—United States Department of Transportation

VDOT—Virginia Department of Transportation

VTMC—virtual traffic management center

WSDOT—Washington State Department of Transportation

Exercises

7.1 Write a paper (no more than 10 pages) on the importance of TSMO in today's transportation profession and how it is different from traditional capital improvement projects. Provide at least three examples of regional or statewide TSMO programs and the specific goals, objectives, and strategies are included therein.

7.2 Write a case study paper (no more than 10 pages) on the implementation of an ATDM strategy or combination of strategies, presenting the overall goals and objectives of the strategy, key implementation issues, impacts of the implementation, and lessons learned by the implementing agency(ies).

7.3 Write a paper (no more than 10 pages) providing a critical discussion on the difference between performance measurement and performance monitoring. Provide information on appropriate performance measures for TSMO-related projects and how an agency might use those measures for daily operations or longer-term planning.

7.4 Write a paper (no more than 5 pages) discussing the important functions that are typically performed in a transportation management center. Explain some of the benefits to having a TMC. Explain some of the factors agencies need to consider when establishing a TMC.

References

1. "Fixing America's Surface Transportation (FAST) Act." Federal Highway Administration, U.S. Department of Transportation, https://www.fhwa.dot.gov/fastact/ (accessed January 2017).
2. Federal Highway Administration (FHWA), *ATDM Program Brief: An Introduction to Active Transportation and Demand Management*, Report FHWA-HOP-12-032, FHWA, Washington, D.C., June 2012.
3. "Reducing Recurring Congestion." Federal Highway Administration, U.S. Department of Transportation, https://ops.fhwa.dot.gov/program_areas/reduce-recur-cong.htm (accessed June 2017).
4. "Reducing Non-Recurring Congestion." Federal Highway Administration, U.S. Department of Transportation, https://ops.fhwa.dot.gov/program_areas/reduce-non-cong.htm (accessed June 2017).
5. "Traffic Bottlenecks." Federal Highway Administration, U.S. Department of Transportation, https://ops.fhwa.dot.gov/bn/lbr.htm#g2 (accessed May 2018).
6. "How Do Weather Events Impacts Roads?" Federal Highway Administration, U.S. Department of Transportation, https://ops.fhwa.dot.gov/weather/q1_roadimpact.htm (accessed May 2018).

7. "Traffic Incident Management." Federal Highway Administration, U.S. Department of Transportation, https://ops.fhwa.dot.gov/eto_tim_pse/about/tim.htm (accessed May 2018).

8. "Planning for Operations." Federal Highway Administration, U.S. Department of Transportation, https://ops.fhwa.dot.gov/plan4ops/ (accessed June 2017).

9. "Transportation Systems Management and Operations (TSMO) Plans." Federal Highway Administration, U.S. Department of Transportation, https://ops.fhwa .dot.gov/plan4ops/focus_areas/integrating/transportation_sys.htm (accessed May 2018).

10. "Communicating with Decisionmakers." Federal Highway Administration, U.S. Department of Transportation, https://ops.fhwa.dot.gov/plan4ops/focus_areas/ integrating/communicating_d.htm (accessed June 2017).

11. "Organizing for Operations." Federal Highway Administration, U.S. Department of Transportation, https://ops.fhwa.dot.gov/plan4ops/focus_areas/organizing_ for_op.htm (accessed June 2017).

12. "Transportation Systems Management & Operations." American Association of State Highway and Transportation Officials, Washington, D.C., http://www .aashtotsmoguidance.org (accessed July 2016).

13. "SHRP2 L01, Integrating Business Processes to Improve Reliability." Transportation Research Board, National Academy of Sciences, Engineering and Medicine, http:// apps.trb.org/cmsfeed/TRBNetProjectDisplay.asp?ProjectID=2177 (accessed June 2016).

14. "SHRP L06—Institutional Architectures to Advance Operational Strategies." Transportation Research Board, National Academy of Sciences, Engineering and Medicine, http://apps.trb.org/cmsfeed/TRBNetProjectDisplay .asp?ProjectID=2180 (accessed June 2017).

15. *Traffic Management Capability Maturity Framework Factsheet*, U.S. Department of Transportation, Federal Highway Administration, Washington, D.C., February 2016.

16. Kimley-Horn and Associates, Inc., with PB Consult, *Integrating Business Processes to Improve Travel Time Reliability*, Report S2-L01-RR-1, Transportation Research Board, Washington, D.C., 2011, http://onlinepubs.trb.org/onlinepubs/shrp2/SHRP2_ S2-L01-RR-1.pdf (accessed July 2016).

17. Kimley-Horn and Associates, Inc., with PB Consult, *Guide to Integrating Business Processes to Improve Travel Time Reliability*, Report S2-L01-RR-2, 2011, Transportation Research Board, Washington, D.C., http://onlinepubs.trb.org/onlinepubs/shrp2/ SHRP2_S2-L01-RR-2.pdf (accessed July 2016).

18. Parsons Brinckerhoff with Delcan, Philip J. Tarnoff, George Mason University School of Public Policy, and Housman and Associates, Institutional Architectures to Improve Systems Operations and Management, Report S2-L06-RR-1, 2012, Transportation Research Board, Washington, D.C., http://onlinepubs.trb.org/onlinepubs/shrp2/ SHRP2_S2-L06-RR-1.pdf (accessed July 2016).

19. Parsons Brinckerhoff with Delcan, George Mason University School of Public Policy, and Housman and Associates, *Guide to Improving Capability for Systems Operations and Management*, Report S2-L06-RR-2, 2012, Transportation Research Board, Washington, D.C., http://onlinepubs.trb.org/onlinepubs/shrp2/SHRP2_ S2-L06-RR-2.pdf (accessed July 2016).

20. "Welcome to Business Process Frameworks for Transportation Operations." Federal Highway Administration, U.S. Department of Transportation, https://ops.fhwa .dot.gov/tsmoframeworktool/index.htm (accessed June 2017).

21. "Traffic Management Capability Maturity Framework Tool." https://ops.fhwa.dot. gov/tsmoframeworktool/available_frameworks/traffic.htm (accessed May 2018).

22. "Traffic Incident Management Capability Maturity Framework." https://ops. fhwa.dot.gov/tsmoframeworktool/available_frameworks/traffic_incident .htm (accessed May 2018).

23. "Planned Special Events Capability Maturity Framework Tool." https://ops. fhwa.dot.gov/tsmoframeworktool/available_frameworks/planned_events.htm (accessed May 2018).

24. "Work Zone Management Capability Maturity Framework Tool." https://ops.fhwa. dot.gov/tsmoframeworktool/available_frameworks/work_zone.htm (accessed May 2018).

25. "Road Weather Management Capability Maturity Framework Tool." https://ops .fhwa.dot.gov/tsmoframeworktool/available_frameworks/road_weather.htm (accessed May 2018).

26. "Traffic Signal Management Capability Maturity Framework Tool." https://ops .fhwa.dot.gov/tsmoframeworktool/available_frameworks/traffic_signal.htm (accessed May 2018).

27. Federal Highway Administration (FHWA). *Capability Maturity Frameworks for Transportation Systems Management and Operations (TSM&O) Program Areas.* Report FHWA-HOP-16-031. U.S. Department of Transportation, February 2016.

28. "Designing for Operations." Federal Highway Administration, U.S. Department of Transportation, https://ops.fhwa.dot.gov/plan4ops/designing_ops.htm (accessed June 2017).

29. *Fact Sheet: #1: Performance-Based Practical Design.* Federal Highway Administration,U.S. Department of Transportation, https://www.fhwa.dot.gov/ design/pbpd/documents/pbpd_fs01.pdf (accessed June 2017).

30. Sallman, D., E. Flanigan, K. Jeannotte, C. Hedden, and D. Morallos. *Operations Benefit-Cost Analysis Desk Reference.* Report FHWA-HOP-12-028, Federal Highway Administration, U.S. Department of Transportation, Washington, D.C., 2012.

31. Gonzalez, P., D. Hardesty, G. Hatcher, M. Mercer, and M. Waisley, *Integrated Corridor Management: Implementation Guide and Lessons Learned,* Report FHWA-JPO-12-075, U.S. Department of Transportation, ITS Joint Program Office, Washington, D.C., 2012.

32. "Knowledge and Technology Transfer (KTT) for ATDM-Related Programs." Federal Highway Administration, http://ops.fhwa.dot.gov/atdm/knowledge/ kttrelprograms.htm (accessed June 11, 2015).

33. Federal Highway Administration (FHWA), *Webinar #4—Organizing for ATM: Applying the Traffic Management Capability Maturity Framework,* PowerPoint Presentation, Office of Operations, Washington, D.C., 2015.

34. Federal Highway Administration (FHWA), *ATDM Program Brief: Active Demand Management,* Report FHWA-HOP-13-002, FHWA, Washington, D.C., October 2012.

35. Federal Highway Administration (FHWA), *ATDM Program Brief: Active Parking Management,* Report FHWA-HOP-12-033, FHWA, Washington, D.C., 2012.

36. Federal Highway Administration (FHWA), *ATDM Program Brief: Active Traffic Management,* Report FHWA-HOP-13-003, FHWA, Washington, D.C., October 2012.

37. Kuhn, B., K. Balke, T. Lomax, J. Shelton, P. Songchitruksa, I. Tsapakis, M. Waisley, et al. *Planning and Evaluating Active Traffic Management Strategies.* NCHRP 03-114 Draft Final Guidebook. Unpublished. 2016.

38. Mirshahi, M., J. Obenberger, C. Fuhs, C. Howard, R. Krammes, B. Kuhn, R. Mayhew, et al. *Active Traffic Management: The Next Step in Congestion Management*, Report FHWA-PL-07-012, American Trade Initiatives for Federal Highway Administration, Alexandria, VA, 2007.

39. "Active Transportation and Demand Management." Federal Highway Administration, http://ops.fhwa.dot.gov/atdm/index.htm (accessed June 9, 2014).

40. Battelle, *Seattle/Lake Washington Corridor Urban Partnership Agreement—National Evaluation: Interim Technical Memorandum on Early Results,* Columbus, OH, Battelle, 2012.

41. *Managed Lanes: A Primer.* Report FHWA-HOP-05-031, Federal Highway Administration, U.S. Department of Transportation, Washington, D.C., 2008.

42. "Performance Measures and System Monitoring." Federal Highway Administration, U.S. Department of Transportation, https://ops.fhwa.dot.gov/plan4ops/focus_areas/analysis_p_measure/sys_monitoring.htm (accessed June 2017).

43. "Performance Measurement Fundamentals." Federal Highway Administration, U.S. Department of Transportation, https://ops.fhwa.dot.gov/perf_measurement/fundamentals/index.htm (accessed June 2017).

44. Mizuta, A., K. Swindler, L. Jacobson, and S. Kuciemba. *Impacts of Technology Advancements on Transportation Management Center Operations.* FHWA-HOP-13-008. Parsons Brinckerhoff for Federal Highway Administration, U.S. Department of Transportation, Washington, D.C., 2013.

45. Krechmer, D., A. Samano III, P. Beer, N. Boyd, and B. Boyce. *Role of Transportation Management Centers in Emergency Operations Guidebook.* Report FHWA-HOP-12-050. Cambridge Systematics, Inc., Fortress, Inc., and Mixon-Hill for Federal Highway Administration, U.S. Department of Transportation, Washington, D.C., 2012.

46. Lukasik, D., M. Castellanos, A. Chandler, E. Hubbard, R. Jagannathan, and T. Malone. *Guidelines for Virtual Transportation Management Center Development.* Report FHWA-HOP-14-016. Leidos Corp. for Federal Highway Administration, U.S. Department of Transportation, Washington, D.C., 2014.

47. "Transportation Systems Management & Operations (TSMO)." Iowa Department of Transportation, https://www.iowadot.gov/tsmo/home (accessed June 2017).

48. *Iowa Transportation Systems Management and Operations (TSMO) Strategic Plan, Version 1.0.* Iowa Department of Transportation, Office of Operations, https://www.iowadot.gov/TSMO/TSMO-Strategic-Plan.pdf (accessed June 2017).

49. *Iowa Transportation Systems Management and Operations (TSMO) Program Plan, Version 1.0.* Iowa Department of Transportation, Office of Operations, https://www.iowadot.gov/TSMO/TSMO-Program-Plan.pdf (accessed June 2017).

50. Miller, K., F. Bouattoura, R. Macias, C. Poe, M. Le, and T. Plesko. *Final Report: Dallas Integrated Corridor Management (ICM) Demonstration Project.* Dallas Area Rapid Transit for U.S. Department of Transportation, ITS Joint Program Office. Report FHWA-JPO-16-234, August 2015.

51. Chun, P., M. Fontaine. *Evaluation of the Impact of the I-66 Active Traffic Management System.* Report VTRC 17-R5, Virginia Transportation Research Council, Charlottesville, VA, 2016.

52. Kuhn, B. *Efficient Use of Highway Capacity Summary*. Report FHWA-HOP-10-023. Texas Transportation Institute for U.S. Department of Transportation, FHWA, 2010.

53. "Performance Measures." Minnesota Department of Transportation, http://www.dot.state.mn.us/measures/index.html (accessed June 2017).

54. "Performance Measure & Target Adoption." Minnesota Department of Transportation, MnDOT Policies, http://www.dot.state.mn.us/policy/admin/ad006.html (accessed June 2017).

55. *Annual Minnesota Transportation Performance Report, 2015*. Minnesota Department of Transportation, St. Paul, Minnesota, October 2016, http://www.dot.state.mn.us/measures/pdf/12-2%20publicationsmall.pdf (accessed June 2017).

CHAPTER 8

Emerging Transportation Topics

8.1 Introduction

The transportation profession has always been challenged with providing mobility to system users in a safe and efficient manner. As technology evolves, the ability to meet that challenge also evolves. The transportation professional needs to be ready to adapt to the changing urban form and take advantage of technology and societal trends to meet the demands of the future. This chapter discusses emerging topics related to transportation that are currently impacting and will likely continue to impact the future of the infrastructure and the broader transportation profession. These topics include:

- The current state of the infrastructure and the need for investment.
- Ensuring livability and sustainability of the system.
- Transportation system resiliency.
- The profession's commitment to improving roadway safety.
- How disruptive technology will affect the transportation industry and profession.
- The impact connected and automated vehicles will have on operations and infrastructure elements.
- The interrelationship between transportation and smart cities.
- Highway automation and the profession's response to the new demands on the infrastructure.

These emerging issues are interrelated and present the transportation professional with the challenges they will be facing when they enter the workforce. Furthermore, these topics are likely to evolve over time with the rapid advancement of technology. The following sections address these topics in an effort to illustrate the ever-changing landscape of transportation how a variety of topics, technologies, and issues will shape that landscape into the future.

8.2   State of the Transportation Infrastructure

One of the most critical challenges facing the transportation profession today is the current state of the infrastructure. As discussed in this chapter and throughout this textbook, the surface transportation network is the backbone of the United States. It is interrelated with the economic vitality of the country, providing the network for the delivery of goods and services to every corner of the nation. It provides jobs, mobility, and contributes to the quality of life of its citizens, whether they live in the urban core or in a small town. Failure to invest in that infrastructure can have a longstanding impact on the overall ability for the United States to remain an economic world leader and to ensure a sustainable life for generations to come.

The American Society of Civil Engineers (ASCE) estimates that the United States currently only invests about half of the resources needed to keep the infrastructure in working order.[1] That investment covers all sectors of the nation's infrastructure, including surface transportation, waste and wastewater, electricity, airports, and inland waterways and marine ports. For surface transportation, approximately $941 billion of infrastructure investment has been allocated through 2025 out of the nearly $1.1 trillion needed to meet the growing demand. This lagging investment impacts a broad range of elements of the economic fabric of the country, from businesses to the individual family. For example, roads and bridges that are not in good repair translate into increased travel times for everyday commuters, and inadequate water distribution and an aging electric grid translate into higher costs for goods and services.[1] Those higher costs mean the loss of jobs and families paying more for necessities, which mean less disposable income. Less disposable income translates into realities such as fewer vacations, a lack of savings for college, and may even keep home ownership out of reach for many Americans. The most recent Infrastructure Report Card by ASCE highlights three critical areas of the surface transportation network: bridges, roads, and transit.[2] Each of these components of the network is in various states of disrepair and requires significant investment to meet the funding gap and secure a strong economic future for the United States. Additionally, leadership at all levels of government focused on planning and preparing for the future can help ensure the capacity of the surface transportation system meets the demand in a way that benefits all users and remains sustainable for the long term.

8.2.1   Bridges

The transportation network in the United States contains over 600,000 bridges. These bridges are vital links in the transportation system, spanning rivers, lakes, canyons, interchanges, and other features to provide a seamless system (see Fig. 8.1). However, approximately 40 percent of the bridges currently in use are more than 50 years old. While these facilities were likely the state-of-the-art at the time, they have likely gone beyond their expected life span for providing safe and efficient service. As illustrated in Fig. 8.2, over 56,000 of the bridges in the United States were structurally deficient, meaning they are in need of significant maintenance, rehabilitation, or replacement.[2] While not unsafe for travel, the condition of the load-carrying elements of these bridges has suffered from age, deterioration, and damage. They still provide upward of 188 million trips to travelers each day, making them a priority for investment. Even though the bridges are still in service, their reduced condition can impact their ability to provide effective service to system users. For example, if they cannot handle vehicles over a specific weight or speed, operating agencies implement load restrictions on the bridge.

FIGURE 8.1   I-35 Bridge, Waco, TX. (© *Jim Lyle, Texas A&M Transportation Institute [TTI].*)

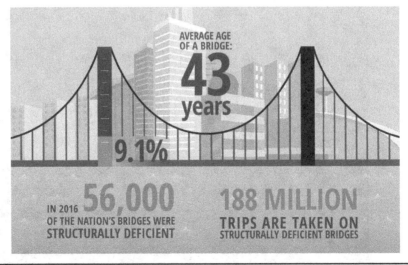

FIGURE 8.2   Current state of bridges in the United States. The American Society of Civil Engineers 2017 Infrastructure Report Card. (*Ref. 2.*)

Thus, some larger vehicles can no longer use the bridge, thereby increasing their travel time as they see alternative routes that are not load-restricted.[2] In addition to structurally deficient bridges, some bridges are functionally obsolete. Increased travel demand has put a strain on many bridges on the network that are older and which do not meet such minimum standards as lane width and shoulder width. In 2016, more than one in eight bridges in the United States were functionally obsolete, creating further delays, decreasing economic productivity and quality of life for system users.[2]

Over the past decade, operating agencies and the transportation profession in general have made inroads into reducing the number of structurally deficient bridges on the network. Bridge maintenance, rehabilitation, and replacement have been a priority for agencies. Innovative technologies, materials, construction techniques, and funding mechanisms have helped increase the rate at which agencies at all governmental levels address the bridge challenge. However, there is still room for improvement. Consistent and adequate levels of funding continue to be a challenge for agencies, and bridge owners need to develop comprehensive approaches to ongoing maintenance and rehabilitation throughout the life span of the bridges on the network.[2]

8.2.2   Roads

The second component of the surface transportation network that suffers from inadequacy is the roadway system. The United States has over 4 million miles of public roads across the country, with Texas (~314,000 mi), California (~175,000 mi), and Illinois (~145,000 mi) rounding out the top three states with total miles owned by a State highway agency, county, town, township, municipality, federal agency, or other jurisdiction.[3] Many of these roadways suffer from both congestion and poor conditions, which drastically affect the economic vitality of the country and cost travelers in many ways. For example, only a fraction of those roadways are urban interstates (~18,000 mi) such as the one shown in Fig. 8.3, but those interstates account for much of the congestion

FIGURE 8.3   I-35, Waco, TX. (© *Jim Lyle, TTI.*)

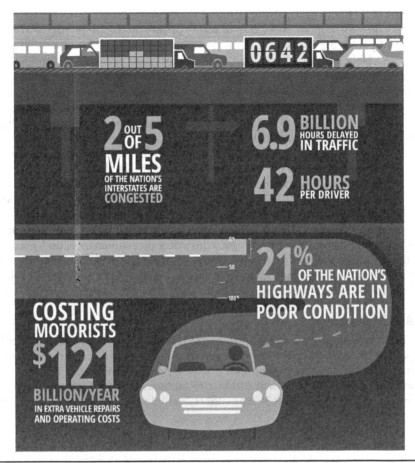

FIGURE 8.4   Current state of roadways in the United States. The American Society of Civil Engineers 2017 Infrastructure Report Card. (*Ref. 2.*)

travelers experience each day. As illustrated in Fig. 8.4, two of every 5 miles of urban interstates experience congestion on a daily basis, causing drivers to waste nearly 7 billion hours sitting in traffic each year.[2] This problem is pervasive in most of the nation's top 100 metropolitan areas. Population growth and the resulting demand on the network during peak travel periods and beyond far exceeds the network's available capacity. The delay and resulting wasted fuel translates into a dollar amount of nearly $1,000 per person, or a nationwide total of over $160 billion each year.[4]

The actual physical condition of the roadway network in the United States also struggles to meet the challenge of providing efficient transport to system users. Approximately 21 percent of the network has poor pavement conditions in need of repair. This reality means additional costs to the vehicle owner in terms of higher operating costs and more vehicle repairs, with estimates topping $121 billion each year.[2] As noted previously, highway spending over the past few decades has not kept pace with the growing demand placed on the aging network. A backlog of over $800 million needed for highway repairs continues to put a strain on the network, affecting travelers and consumers more every day in terms of lost productivity, higher costs, and more out-of-pocket expenses.

A viable path to addressing this roadway challenge is more funding for highway projects to meet the growing demand. Estimated benefit–cost numbers for highway spending top 5:1 with lower vehicle operating and maintenance costs, reduced delay, improved safety, reduced overall network maintenance costs, and reduced vehicle emissions.[2] As discussed earlier, the availability of funding continues to be a challenge, with agencies and policy-makers continuing to explore alternative funding avenues to ensure a reliable and long-term funding stream for ongoing transportation needs. The current funding model of motor fuel taxes and the Highway Trust Fund continues to lose viability as vehicle fuel economy improves, the number of hybrid and electric vehicles increase in the vehicle fleet, and as vehicle ownership changes with the emergence of mobility-on-demand services. Innovative funding concepts, such mileage-based user fees, may have the potential to solve the long-term transportation funding challenge. Additionally, innovation in design, construction, maintenance, and management can help improve the roadway network by ensuring the system is optimized for performance. Funding and policies to support these innovations are critical to the successful implementation of these approaches to maintaining the complex roadway network.

8.2.3 Transit

The third component of the surface transportation network that struggles to keep pace with growth is the transit system. As the population in metropolitan areas increases, so does the demand on the transportation network. For many Americans in large urban areas, transit offers a reliable and cost-effective alternative to commuting alone (see Fig. 8.5). For others, vehicle ownership is either impractical or

FIGURE 8.5 Dallas area rapid transit rail station. (© *Jim Lyle, TTI.*)

FIGURE 8.6 Current state of transit in the United States. The American Society of Civil Engineers 2017 Infrastructure Report Card.

financially impossible, making transit a primary means of transportation. When transit funding does not keep pace with demand, problems arise as they do with bridges and roads. As demonstrated in Fig. 8.6, transit providers have seen an increase in ridership over the past 20 years, and new lines are added each year to try and meet this demand. However, as with the surface network, transit funding is inadequate to handle maintenance needs and to expand in areas that need accessibility to transit, with a backlog of projects needed to maintain the current system in a state of good repair topping 90 billion.[2]

Accessibility to a reliable public transit option continues to be a challenge in some urban areas. Despite 81 percent of the nation's population living in urban areas, only 51 percent of them have the option of traveling to the grocery store using public transit.[2] This limited accessibility to transit puts a strain on an individual's quality of life as they have difficulty meeting their basic needs if they do not own a personal vehicle. Traditionally, transit agencies have received funding from various sources for both operating and capital expenses: federal, state, local, fares, and other directly generated funds. When funding needs outpace demand, agencies tend to focus on maintaining and improving existing service rather than expansion.[2] Innovation and increased resources can help transit agencies meet demands while providing flexible and cost-effective service to the most passengers. Strategies such as expanding service to meet the first mile-last mile challenge for riders, apps to provide real-time traveler information to system users, conversion so sustainable vehicles, and other working collaboratively with other regional partners offer potential solutions that can be successful with adequate funding.

8.3   Livability and Sustainability

In recent years, the concepts of livability and sustainability have emerged as focal points in the dialogue surrounding transportation. As defined by Merriam-Webster, livability refers to "suitability for human living"[5] while sustainability refers to ". . . a lifestyle involving the use of sustainable methods sustainable society."[6] Within the transportation context, livability and sustainability are becoming important barometers for how federal, state, and local transportation agencies invest in the infrastructure and how the public as a whole views mobility. Transportation has a broad impact on society, and that impact needs to be considered across a broad range of topics and social aspects of livability and sustainability. These topics include, but are not limited to:

- Management and operations
- Safety
- Environment
- Health
- Land use
- Economic development
- Freight
- Housing
- Rural livability

Transportation is intertwined with all of these elements of society, and the transportation professional needs to have a broad understanding of the impacts their decisions have on the overall quality of life and the long-term success of their customer, that is, the traveling public.

In response to the increasing awareness of livability and sustainability in society, the U.S. Department of Transportation (USDOT) has established a series of principles that are intended to guide investment in the transportation infrastructure. These principles are:

- To provide more transportation choices to travelers
- To expand housing choices that are location-efficient and energy-efficient
- To improve the economic competitiveness of neighborhoods in communities
- To target federal funding toward existing communities
- To align federal policies and funding
- To enhance the unique characteristics of all communities[7]

Gone are the days when the transportation agency might divide communities with highways and eliminate innercity neighborhoods for the sake of the suburban commuter. The future considers existing communities, the need to ensure long-term viability of those communities, and the desire to enable citizens to live, work, and achieve a quality of life for themselves and their families.

The USDOT and transportation profession as a whole recognizes that this challenge cannot be met in a vacuum. One example of how it is working to address this challenge is the interagency partnership for sustainability communities it formed, which is led by three federal agencies: the U.S. Department of Housing and Urban Development (USHUD), the USDOT, and the Environmental Protection Agency (EPA).[8] The partnership's interagency collaboration works to remove barriers, increase flexibility, and identify ways to more efficiently invest taxpayer dollars to improve local communities. This partnership recognizes the links between housing, transportation, livability, and sustainability. Since the partnership began, over 1000 communities across the United States have benefited from over $4 billion in the form of grants, technical assistance, and ongoing federal programs to benefit their citizens and help improve their quality of life.[9] Working through regional offices through each of the agencies, the partnership provides a wealth of resources and tools to community leaders and citizens across the spectrum of sustainability topics, including but not limited to, partnerships, clean air and water, community planning, economic development, energy efficiency, equity and environmental justice, housing choices, performance measures and data, rural communities, and transportation choices. The partnership also provides information on case studies covering these topics to illustrate how local communities have tackled an issue to address sustainability for their citizens.[4] This partnership, which works to collaboratively help communities address a wealth of challenges, is one of several federal partnerships that focus on interagency collaboration to foster prosperous communities. Similar partnerships include, but are not limited to, the Strong Cities, Strong Communities Initiative,[10] and the Urban Waters Federal Partnership.[11]

As discussed in Chap. 7, transportation systems management and operations (TSMO) is a contemporary modern approach to optimizing the infrastructure investment while providing the safe, efficient, and effective movement of people, goods, and services across town or across the country. This responsibility is a considerable challenge given the complexity of the surface transportation system.[12] Given the overall goals and objectives of TSMO, it is clearly a powerful tool to support livability and sustainability of the transportation infrastructure. Aimed at improving the travel experience, TSMO focuses on improving the efficiency and safety of all transportation modes, enhancing the overall network for all system users. Specifically, TSMO improves livability by reducing congestion and fuel waste through efficient operations, and saves agencies money by reducing the need to expand capacity. It also makes walking, biking, and transit more attractive (see Fig. 8.7) and safer for all travelers, including children, seniors, and persons with disabilities, and coordinates incidents, emergencies, and events so that travel returns to normal faster and the traveling public is impacted less.[13] In short, TSMO strategies improve the interface between the transportation network and the communities it serves, impacting the lives of its citizens in a variety of ways that reach beyond transportation. Effects of TSMO strategies include mobility and accessibility, safety, reliability, community life, economic vitality, and environmental quality.[14]

Transportation safety is an integral component of a livable and sustainable community. To ensure that the transportation system provides safe mobility for the traveling public, the transportation professional needs to accommodate all modes, not just automobiles and trucks. As communities strive to provide mobility options for all travelers, including pedestrians, cyclists, and travelers with disabilities, it is important to design a transportation system that these users can navigate safely. Road networks that are safer for all users not only support livability for citizens but help provide access to jobs and services, reduce congestion, and can invigorate investment

FIGURE 8.7 Multimodal transportation options. (© *Jim Lyle, TTI.*)

in neighborhoods and businesses in the community.[15] A growing trend in the safety arena is the concept of complete streets. These facilities are designed and operated such that all system users (i.e., pedestrians, bicyclists, motorists, transit riders, etc.) have safe and efficient access to the facility. Complete streets incorporate such features as sidewalks, raised medians, better bus stop placement, and traffic calming to improve safety (see Fig. 8.8).[7] They also provide connectivity for the community and

FIGURE 8.8 Complete streets elements. (© *Jim Lyle, TTI.*)

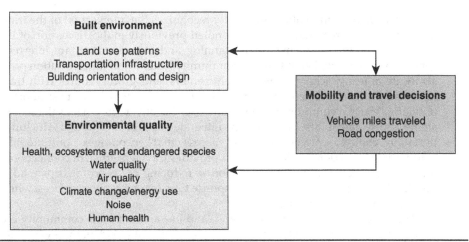

FIGURE 8.9 The transportation, development, and environmental quality relationship. (*Ref. 11.*)

offer mobility choices, thereby enhancing the livability of a community and ensuring a sustainable system that meets the needs of its users.

The transportation infrastructure has always been linked to environmental quality. The manner in which city planners develop communities directly impacts how citizens travel throughout that community and how those trips impact the environment. As illustrated in Fig. 8.9, the layout of the built environment includes land use patterns, transportation infrastructure, and building orientation and design.[16] They layout of that built environment impacts mobility and travel decisions and directly affects the number of miles traveled by a community's citizens and the amount of congestion on the transportation network. Consequently, the built environment and the related mobility and travel decisions impact all facets of the environment. All three of these elements within a community are interrelated and require a transportation agency and its regional partners to balance needs and impacts to ensure long-term sustainability and livability for their citizens.

Transportation professionals need to consider the impacts of community development and how transportation plays into related development decisions. The practice of providing more travel options in a more compact and connected community helps reduce individual vehicle trips, improve air and water quality, and support a sustainable infrastructure and a livable community. Additionally, more compact development preserves rural lands and protects natural resources, reducing the spread of urban and suburban sprawl.[8]

As with the environment, transportation is linked to a community's health. A sustainable transportation system offers ample opportunities for users to walk or bicycle, which improves personal health.[17] Increasing opportunities for travelers to take alternate modes, including transit, also reduces vehicle trips, which reduces emissions and improves air quality. Safer facilities help reduce crashes along with injuries and fatalities. Furthermore, enhancing the safety of a comprehensive multimodal network helps build a sustainable community for all citizens, including children, seniors, and low-income populations who are likely to be disproportionately impacted by lack of access to transportation.[7]

A sustainable and livable community recognizes the intersection of the transportation network and regional land use. As noted previously in the discussion of transportation and the environment, urban planning and transportation are interrelated. In general, a community benefits when community leaders and transportation professionals locate housing, schools, employment centers, and grocery stores with transit stations and provide connectivity in the street network with facilities to support walking or biking.[18] Such a community offers numerous benefits to its citizens that support livability and sustainability. Primarily, the integrated approach to land use includes transportation choices, convenience, and access that encourages multimodal travel. Additionally, the compact development provides travelers efficient connections within the transportation network to other modes, reducing the need for trips made by car. This land use approach also reduces response time for emergency services, which saves lives and community resources.[10]

The integration of transportation and land use also supports community economic development.[19] A community that offers accessibility to its residents and values livability more easily attracts economic development. An upward trend has been seen in business choosing to locate to more accessible locations that offer such community amenities as housing choices, transportation, schools, and more. Targeting transportation investments to support livability attracts businesses, offers cost savings to those businesses through compact or mixed-use development, and realizes cost savings for infrastructure and services.[12] Another component of the transportation and sustainability equation not to be overlooked is freight. An essential function of creating a sustainable community that offers strong economic development is the ability to get goods to the people and business in a community.[20] The transportation professional can work with local communities to balance livability needs with freight access. All of these strategies help create a livable and sustainable community with transportation playing a vital mobility role in the process.

As with other livability and sustainability issues, more compact and connected communities have a positive impact on housing costs for citizens. When individuals live closer to their workplace and have numerous options for transportation, they have more disposable income and are able to reduce the overall burden of maintaining a sustainable quality of life.[21] Considering the overall livability of a community when planning transportation within the housing context increases housing affordability and helps stabilize housing values over the long term. Offering multimodal transportation choices and facilitating mixed-use development contributes to a sustainable community.

The above examples discussing the intersection between transportation and sustainability also apply to the rural community. While the definition of a rural community varies according to such factors as location, geography, and economic and resource base, transportation investments in these locales can support livability in the rural setting.[22] The investments in transportation need to focus on offering choices and connections. Examples of such investments include, but are not limited to:

- Adding infrastructure features that encourage safe pedestrian movements
- Constructing and connecting bicycling trails and networks
- Facilitating and enhancing transit options, including rural on-demand transit, ridesharing, and commuter service
- Improving transportation connections between neighborhoods, schools, community services, and regional employment

- Coordinating infrastructure investments on the regional level with growth planning and resource protection
- Incorporating all community needs as discussed above to address sustainability and livability for all residents[16]

All of these approaches addressing sustainability and livability in transportation represent opportunities for transportation agencies to leverage their investments with those of the community at large. At the federal level, a number of programs are available to help state and local agencies make progress with respect to livability. These programs within the Federal-Aid Highway Program offer flexibility to agencies in how they tackle the livability challenge. Programs such as the Congestion Mitigation and Air Quality Improvement (CMAQ) Program and Transportation Alternatives (TA) funds from the Surface Transportation Block Grant (STBG) Program help support projects addressing environmental nonattainment areas and smaller-scale projects offering mobility alternatives, respectively.[23] Other programs include, but are not limited to, the EcoLogical Grant Program, the Federal Lands and Tribal Transportation Programs, and the Recreational Trails Programs. All of the programs support investments in livability that recognize that transportation projects should address the unique needs of every community and move toward the common national goal of livability for all.[18]

Enhancing the livability and sustainability of a community results in numerous benefits, and transportation plays a key role in realizing those benefits. As noted throughout this section, key impacts of transportation systems that enhance livability include the economic benefits of lower construction and operating costs; lower costs and better value for transportation, housing, and land use; improved public health through increased walking and biking; and environmental benefits through improved air and water quality.[24] As agencies consider the impacts of community development and move toward sustainability, they need to consider the key elements of sustainability, all of which support the human needs. As illustrated in Fig. 8.10, a comprehensive and effective sustainability program needs to meet the economic, social, and environmental needs of the community and its citizens and none of which should be compromised for the other.[25]

Transportation professionals can apply sustainability concepts in a variety of ways and across all aspects of their roles and responsibilities in the community. Agencies responsible for the transportation infrastructure can work throughout each step of the project development process and infrastructure management efforts to help meet regional sustainability goals and objectives. Key elements of these processes that can affect sustainability include, but are not limited to:

- Long-range transportation planning
- Short-range transportation programming
- Project-level planning
- Project-level environmental review
- Design, land acquisition, and permitting
- Construction, maintenance, and operations[24]

At each stage, the transportation professional needs to determine how a particular project or process will impact the three legs supporting the human needs within their community.

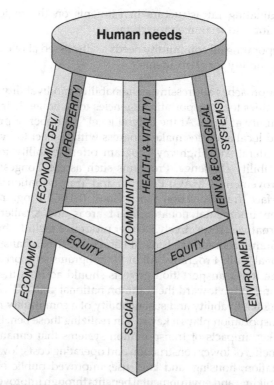

FIGURE 8.10 Principles of sustainability and the significance of equity. (*Ref. 25.*)

For a transportation agency to advance sustainability in its community, it should first establish a sustainability performance measurement framework. As noted in Fig. 8.11, this framework incorporates six steps that represent a continual improvement process for decision makers when considering transportation projects and initiatives with sustainability as a guiding principle. Brief descriptions of these steps are provided in Table 8.1, all of which support the four sustainability principles which:

1. Preserve and enhance the environment and ecological systems

2. Foster a community's health and vitality

3. Promote economic prosperity and development

4. Ensure equity among all population groups both today and over future generations[23]

When considering sustainability goals for a region, agency should select goals that can help them chart a path forward toward sustainability and be specific to the transportation infrastructure. Working with regional partners and stakeholders, an agency can select a reasonable number of goals that reflect the overall goals and objectives of the community and focus on collaboration to achieve success. Table 8.2 provides 11 categories of sustainability goals from the transportation perspective, which align with

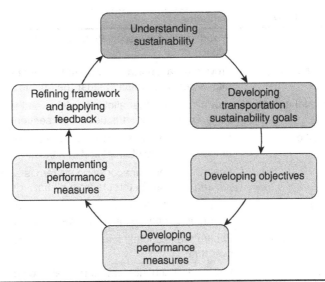

Figure 8.11   The sustainability performance measurement framework. (*Ref. 23.*)

Framework Step	Description
1. Understanding sustainability	An agency needs to understand what sustainability means for its region and can establish a definition or statement on sustainability that supports the framework and sustainability principles.
2. Developing transportation sustainability goals	An agency should establish sustainability goals that can relate sustainability principles to transportation; can be used either in their current form or be revised to align its programs with sustainability principles as well as with its current or existing goals and mission; and can frame collaborative efforts with other agencies in the region.
3. Developing objectives	An agency should develop sustainability objectives across various focus areas related to transportation agency functions and activities associated with its core business.
4. Developing performance measures	Agencies should develop performance measures that help them assess their progress toward their sustainability goals and objectives and measure outcome, output, or process and can be used to further improve performance.
5. Implementing performance measures	Agencies should integrate and implement sustainability performance measures in various day-to-day and overarching activities, including description of the measures, evaluation, accountability, decision support, and internal and external communication to stakeholders.
6. Refining framework and applying feedback	Agencies should establish an ongoing review of performance measures and processes and provide feedback to refine the framework to better address the principles of sustainability.

Table 8.1   Steps in the Sustainability Performance Measurement Framework (*Ref. 23.*)

Sustainability Goal	Definition
Safety	Provide a safe transportation system for users and the general public
Basic accessibility	Provide a transportation system that offers accessibility that allows people to fulfill at least their basic needs
Equity/equal mobility	Provide options that allow affordable and equitable transportation opportunities for all sections of society
System efficiency	Ensure that the transportation system's functionality and efficiency are maintained and enhanced
Security	Ensure that the transportation system is secure from, ready for, and resilient to threats from all hazards
Prosperity	Ensure that the transportation system's development and operation support economic development and prosperity
Economic viability	Ensure the economic feasibility of transportation investments over time
Ecosystems	Protect and enhance environmental and ecological systems while developing and operating transportation systems
Waste generation	Reduce waste generated by transportation-related activities
Resource consumption	Reduce the use of nonrenewable resources and promote the use of renewable replacements
Emissions and air quality	Reduce transportation-related emissions of air pollutants and greenhouse gases

TABLE 8.2 Transportation Sustainability Goals (*Ref. 23.*)

the four sustainability principles.[23] As with other goal-setting efforts, it is important that a transportation agency carefully selects a reasonable number of appropriate goals that can be measurable and not overwhelm the capabilities of the agency.

Another key step in the sustainability performance measurement process is the setting of objectives. Objectives establish specific actions that an agency can take to meet overarching sustainability goals. Typically, objectives and related performance measures fall into various focus areas that typically align with the core business functions of a transportation agency. As with other transportation themes, these areas as they related to sustainability include planning, programming, project development, construction, maintenance, and system operations.[23]

Key performance measures that agencies can use to assess should be driven by the capability of an agency to use the measures in a meaningful way. Issues to consider when selecting measures include understanding how the measure will be calculated; knowing what data are needed, the range of measures that can benefit from the data, and the source of the data; identifying the internal and external stakeholders that can benefit from the data; determining the responsible party for tracking and reporting the data and resulting performance measure.[23] Regardless of the performance measures selected, an agency needs to ensure that those used are reasonable in number and

SMART: specific, measurable, attainable, realistic, and time-bound.[26] With sustainability as a guiding principle, an effective sustainability performance measurement process, and effective collaboration, transportation professionals can ensure that every aspect of their job supports sustainability and livability for all system users.

8.4 Transportation System Resilience

Resilience of the transportation system is an integral component of sustainability and warrants attention from the transportation professional. Merriam-Webster defines resilience as "an ability to recover from or adjust easily to misfortune or change."[27] As discussed previously, the transportation professional is responsible for ensuring that the complex infrastructure continues to function in the most efficient manner possible and meets the needs of system users. With respect to resiliency, agencies need to consider the long-term health of the infrastructure and the extent to which extreme weather events, rising sea levels, and changes in environmental conditions impact that system.[28] For example, the impacts of Hurricane Harvey in 2017 were widespread along the Texas Gulf Coast. As illustrated in Fig. 8.12, the extreme and lengthy rainfall event associated with the Category 4 storm flooded countless roadways, many of which were major network routes throughout the region and some of which were closed for a week or more. As a result of this flooding, the integrity of facilities was compromised in various ways, including but not limited to, pavement buckling and heaving, substrate saturation, embankment erosion, and bridge scour (see Fig. 8.13). In one extreme case, the concrete barriers installed for roadway safety actually contributed to localized flooding by acting as a barrier to runoff. The Texas Department of Transportation (TxDOT) had to use explosives to destroy the barriers to help alleviate the flooding. In another

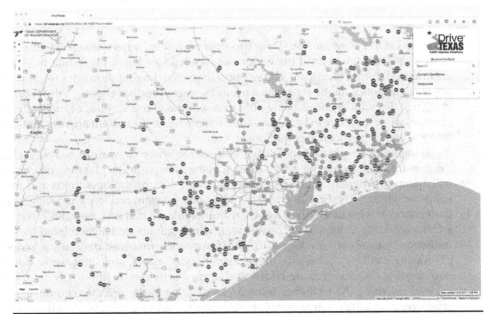

Figure 8.12 Houston area road closures due to Hurricane Harvey, August 2017. (© TxDOT.)

FIGURE 8.13 Roadway damage from Hurricane Harvey, FM 362, August 2017. (© *TxDOT.*)

location, TxDOT used an AquaDam® to hold back floodwaters along a facility to help keep it open for travel until the water had receded (see Fig. 8.14). While the flooding experienced during Hurricane Harvey was unprecedented, it illustrates the severity of impacts an agency might expect as a result of severe weather events in the future. The challenge lies with agencies being able to assess the vulnerabilities of their infrastructure and work to ensure existing and future elements of the system are resistant to such extreme and unpredictable conditions.

Transportation professionals can address resiliency in various ways, including through traditional ongoing activities such as the transportation planning process, asset management programs, project development and design, and operations and maintenance activities.[24] The first step toward addressing system resiliency is for agencies to understand to what extent their assets are vulnerable. To that end, agencies can develop a framework for vulnerability assessment, which guides decisions related to system resiliency.[29] As shown in Fig. 8.15, the framework involves defining a scope for addressing resiliency, assessing the vulnerability of assets, and integrating resiliency into ongoing decision-making efforts and agency activities. Additionally, by monitoring and revisiting the resiliency issue on an ongoing basis, agencies can develop new objectives or modify existing ones to better meet resiliency goals and objectives. Various tools are readily available for agency use to assist transportation professionals in

Figure 8.14   Use of an AquaDam to hold back Hurricane Harvey stormwater, August 2017. (© *TxDOT.*)

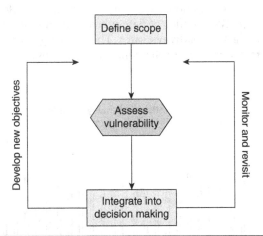

Figure 8.15   Framework for vulnerability assessment. (*Ref. 25.*)

planning for resiliency. These resources, among others, can help agencies assess the sensitivity of transportation assets to climate impacts, assess the criticality of vulnerability in planning, process climate data, and score the vulnerability assessment of assets.[30] Developing a vulnerability assessment framework and incorporation resiliency into agency activities and programs can help reduce the potential impacts of weather events and climate change on the transportation infrastructure.

8.5 Roadway Safety

Since the invention of the automobile, transportation professionals have been challenged with safety. As technology has advanced, vehicles have become safer with such inventions as seat belts, frontal air bags, and antilock brakes. Motor vehicle laws have also helped reduce roadway deaths with requirements for child restraints, graduated driver licensing, minimum drinking age laws, and distracted driving laws. Additionally, the ways in which transportation engineers design and construct the infrastructure have contributed to roadway safety. Innovations such as retroreflective sign sheeting, effective lighting, clear zones, roadside safety devices, porous asphalt pavement, and breakaway sign structures have all contributed to crash reduction and crash severity. However, safety continues to create challenges for transportation professionals as we continue to move toward zero deaths on America's roadway network.

Fatalities in motor vehicle crashes have dropped since the all-time high in 1970. As demonstrated in Fig. 8.16, overall fatalities have dropped in the past 10 years, but still rose to 37,461 in 2016.[31] The most recent number is slightly higher than the overall low in 2011 of 32,479. Additionally, the fatality rate per 100 million miles traveled has consistently dropped over time to 1.13 in 2015. While the reduction in total fatalities and rate of fatalities is great news, the fact remains that over 35,000 individuals lose their lives on U.S. roadways each year. This equates to roughly one traffic-related death every 16 minutes in the United States, and nearly every citizen can expect to be impacted in some way by a traffic crash in their lifetime.[32] This number is unacceptable and takes a significant toll on society, both in terms of human and economic loss, which must be eliminated as a public health issue.

In response to the national challenge of roadway safety, the Federal Highway Administration (FHWA) Office of Safety has as its mission to lead the highway community in making the roadways safer. The challenges associated with the mission, which every transportation professional faces, are evident in the focus areas of the

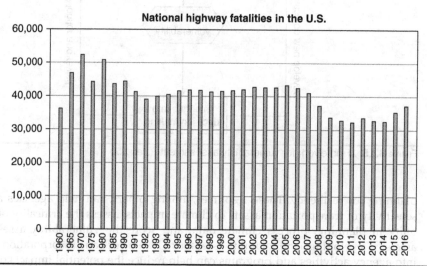

National highway fatalities in the U.S.

Figure 8.16 National Highway Fatalities in the U.S., 1960–2016. (*Ref. 31.*)

Office, including the Highway Safety Improvement Program (HSIP), intersection safety, local and rural road safety, pedestrian and bicycle safety, roadway departure safety, the Roadway Safety Data Program (RSDP), and speed management.[33] Additionally, FHWA has a series of specific initiatives that target the safety problem areas, including motorcycles, nighttime driving, older road users, and work zones, to name a few. Clearly, roadway safety is a complex challenge that should be attacked from all angles to eliminate roadway deaths.

The national conversation regarding roadway safety is growing as agencies and stakeholders highlight the problem and look for solutions. For example, *Toward Zero Deaths (TZD)®: A* National Strategy on Highway Safety emerged from a dialogue begun in 2009 between traffic safety stakeholders to bring a national vision and focus to the problem.[28] Led by a steering committee comprised of national organizations concerned with roadway safety, the TZD program serves as a clearinghouse of resources to help partners and highway safety stakeholders address the safety problem in their jurisdiction. Additionally, the Vision Zero Network is a collaborative campaign, begun in Sweden and gaining exposure in the United States, focused on promoting the concept of safe mobility and working to set a new standard for safety on the roadway network.[34] With municipalities as the primary target for this network, resources available to help transportation professionals and community leaders take on the challenge of road safety and mobility. Resources on the network include, but are not limited to, studies, reports, case studies, action plans, communications, and much more. Additional focus is brought to the issue of vision zero by the Institute of Transportation Engineers with its Vision Zero Task Force.[35] Initiated in 2016, the Task Force serves as the focal point for the organization's commitment to the ultimate goal for its members and their roles in the communities they serve to eliminate traffic deaths and severe injuries. Other efforts to bring the topic of road safety into the forefront of societal discussions include the Road to Zero Coalition[36] and FHWA's Zero Deaths program,[37] both of which reinforce the importance of transportation professionals working to reduce roadway deaths to enhance the livability of their communities. More information associated with transportation safety is provided in Chap. 5.

8.6 Disruptive Technologies and Transportation

The explosion of technology in recent years, as in the past, has begun to have a profound impact on the transportation industry in numerous ways. Frequently termed disruptive technologies, these innovations are that which may initially be considered unproven and unknown, but which eventually supersede existing technologies or applications and advance the state-of-the-art and state-of-the-practice.[38] These technologies typically advance at a rapid pace, penetrate a broad-based market quickly, and improve on existing technologies by being simpler, more reliable, and cheaper. Recent examples of these technologies and their impact on transportation are discussed in Table 8.3.

The transportation professional needs to be aware of these disruptive technologies and how they may impact their responsibilities related to the transportation infrastructure. Primarily, they may have a profound impact on the demand on the roadway infrastructure and the manner in which users interact with the transportation system. With advanced technologies, travelers are likely to change how or when they travel. Additionally, advanced technologies and data sources inherently involve the

Disruptive Technology	Description	Possible Impacts on Transportation
Mobile Internet (MI)	The combination of mobile computing devices, high-speed wireless networks, and associated applications	• Drivers' demand for more data-intensive services, such as real-time traffic conditions and advisories • Decline in travel by personal vehicle • Decreased demand for roadway capacity
The Internet of Things (IoT)	The use of sensors and data communications technologies embedded in physical objects that allow them to be tracked, coordinated, or controlled across a data network or the Internet	• Changes in how transportation agencies manage roadside assets • Increase in the amount of data available about the transportation system • Ability to provide MI-enabled travel applications or in automated vehicle operations
Advanced materials	The broad category of nanomaterials produced by manipulating matter at the nanoscale (less than 100 manometers)	• Provision of strong, ultralight materials for use infrastructure development and construction • Reduced costs in transportation infrastructure costs • Enhanced quality and safety of transportation infrastructure
Automated vehicle technologies	Technologies that allow vehicles to operate on roadways and navigate with little to no human intervention	• Changes in how drivers interact with the roadway environment • Changes in how government agencies manage the transportation infrastructure
Immersive interfaces	Technologies that involve a monitor or other view screen to view information and a keyboard or touchpad to enter information for use in interactive virtual reality environments	• New in-vehicle interfaces that display information without the need to divert attention from the roadway • Virtual reality applications that reduce the need for some trips • Virtual reality simulation to model driver behavior

TABLE 8.3 Disruptive Technologies and Transportation (*Ref. 34.*)

need to maintain both privacy and security, requiring knowledge and skills that may not be part of the traditional civil engineering curriculum. Innovative and advanced materials, such as nanomaterials, may require changes to current design and construction standards, while these technologies might also impact contracting and procurement policies and procedures for transportation projects.[34] Finally, disruptive technologies may have both a positive and negative impact on safety. For example, innovative traveler information services may shift trips to modes other than the personal vehicle, which could reduce congestion and the likelihood of crashes. Connected and automated vehicle technologies are also likely to reduce crashes within the roadway environment. However, immersive technologies and other on-board systems may actually increase driver distraction, increasing the risk of crashes. It is not known how all of these technologies—and those that have yet to be invented—will ultimately impact the transportation system and the manner in which it operates. Tomorrow's transportation professional needs to be prepared for anything.

8.7   Connected and Automated Vehicles

Connected vehicles (CVs), automated vehicles (AVs), autonomous vehicles, and their associated technologies have the long-term potential to address a myriad of challenges facing the transportation community today. To that end, transportation professionals need to develop a comprehensive understanding of these technologies and how they may impact the future of transportation. Of particular interest are such issues as legislative facilitators, incentives, challenges, consistencies, and variations that will directly impact the future success of these technologies and related initiatives. Commonly accepted definitions for these technologies are provided in Table 8.4.

The realm of issues related to CVs and automated transportation merits the immediate attention of the transportation community for several reasons. Primarily, the major commercial automakers, application developer companies, device manufacturers, and other related industries are engaged in research related to these three technological areas, and many CV technologies and applications are likely to become a reality as CV pilot projects move forward in the next few years. Furthermore, full-scale commercial introduction of truly autonomous (including driverless) vehicles will eventually become a reality as well. Components of automated transportation such as braking assist, driver warnings, adaptive cruise control, lane keeping assist, etc., are already offered commercially in cars today. As these technologies enter the marketplace in a more widespread manner, it is important for both the transportation community, including state and federal policy makers, to understand the effects that existing policy (or lack thereof) are likely to have on the development and adoption of this technology as well as the overall impact of these technologies on the transportation network and the industry as a whole.

Term	Definition
Connected vehicle	A vehicle capable of safe, interoperable networked wireless communications among other vehicles, the infrastructure, and passengers' personal communications devices to enable crash prevention and safety, mobility, and environmental benefits.[39]
Automated vehicle	A vehicle in which at least some aspects of a safety-critical control function occur without direct input from the driver, such as steering, acceleration, or braking.[40]
Autonomous vehicle	An automated vehicle that only uses vehicle sensors (as opposed to communications systems as in CVs) to control the safety-critical control functions.[41]

TABLE 8.4 Connected and Automated Vehicle Definitions

USDOT research has evolved over a decade to the current CV technologies and applications. Efforts underway within the CV technology research program include safety, mobility, environmental applications technology policy, and institutional issues. Other emphasis areas within CVs include international research, standards harmonization, and dedicated short-range communications (DSRC) technology. These technologies represent a transformation in the way vehicles will operate within the roadway environment and how agencies will manage their networks. Vehicles will send and receive information to other vehicles, the infrastructure, and personal devices, all of which exponentially increase the amount of information an agency can gather in real time about their facilities and their users. This information, in turn, can significantly enhance how an agency operates and manages its facility to optimize performance in real time and also support predictive capabilities and informational dissemination in ways that were not feasible before.

Recent accomplishments in the Safety Pilot Model Deployment and related efforts have demonstrated the technical feasibility of the core vehicle and infrastructure technologies integral to CVs. With these demonstrations showing that CVs will work as a concept, there is an increasing focus on showing how CV environments may be deployed on a broader scale and across multiple jurisdictions across the Nation. To that end, the Federal Highway Administration is providing guidance for State and local agency implementers and planners related to vehicle to infrastructure (V2I) deployment. At the same time, the National Highway Traffic Safety Administration (NHTSA) issued an Advance Notice of Proposed Rulemaking (ANPRM) to begin the implementation of vehicle-to-vehicle (V2V) communications technology. This ANPRM, related guidance on automated driving systems guidance, and companion research on V2V communications technology emphasize the importance of technical feasibility, privacy and security, and the costs and safety benefits of V2V.[42] Of particular importance is the possibility that the CV environments may need a regulatory framework and require V2V devices in vehicles in a future year, consistent with applicable legal requirements, Executive Orders, and guidance. Furthermore, once the guidance and proposed rulemaking are established at the national level, States and local agencies may need to work with their own legislatures to identify any existing laws or policies that need to change accordingly.

Automated transportation is a research initiative within USDOT that addresses the broad aspects of AVs and leverages CV technologies, infrastructure-based solutions, and other approaches.[43] As this technology matures to the point that it is approaching readiness for deployment on vehicles that will operate in public traffic, attention needs to be given to determining how it should be regulated—particularly with respect to protecting public safety—and how these technologies will impact the overall mobility on the transportation network. The USDOT is currently sponsoring the CV Pilot Deployment Program which is a national effort to deploy, test, and operationalize technologies to enable CV applications on the transportation network.[44] Three pilot projects are under development in three locations: the New York City DOT Pilot, the Tampa-Hillsborough Expressway Authority Pilot, and the Wyoming DOT Pilot. As these projects advance from planning to design and deployment, the transportation community will begin to understand how various technology applications function in the broader roadway environment. Table 8.5 provides an overview of the V2I, infrastructure to vehicle (I2V), and V2V technologies being deployed as part of these pilots.

CV Pilot Deployment	CV Application Category	CV Application
New York City CV Pilot	V2I/I2V safety	Speed compliance Curve speed compliance Speed compliance/work zone Red light violation warning Oversize vehicle compliance Emergency communications and evacuation information
	V2V safety	Forward crash warning Emergency electronics brake lights Bling spot warning Lane change warning/assist Intersection movement assist Vehicle turning right in front of bus warning
	V2I/I2V pedestrian	Pedestrian in signalized crosswalk Mobile accessible pedestrian signal system
	Mobility	Intelligent traffic signal system
Tampa-Hillsborough Expressway Authority Pilot	V2I safety	End of ramp deceleration warning Pedestrian in signalized crosswalk warning Wrong way entry
	V2V safety	Emergency electronic brake lights Forward collision warning Intersection movement assist Vehicle turning right in front of a transit vehicle
	Mobility	Mobile accessible pedestrian signal system Intelligent traffic signal system Transit signal priority
	Agency data	Probe-enabled data monitoring
Wyoming DOT Pilot	V2V safety	Forward collision warning
	V2I/I2V safety	I2V situational awareness Work zone warnings Spot weather impact warning
	V2I and V2V safety	Distress notification

TABLE 8.5 CV Pilot Deployment Technology Applications (*Ref. 40.*)

As illustrated by the breadth of technologies planned for deployment, a broad range of benefits might be realized for the traveling public, especially related to safety. The transportation professional needs to be aware of these technologies and transportation applications as they represent the future infrastructure that they will have to plan, design, build, operate, and maintain for future generations.

8.8 Smart Cities

Since the early 2000s, the concept of smart cities has emerged in the vernacular of the transportation community in response to the changing urban landscape. It is a reflection of the combination of urban population growth and economic prosperity, rapid advancement of technology, and easy accessibility to vast quantities of data.[45] Citizens have come to expect more from their communities, which remains an ongoing challenge within the context of limited resources. The smart city is one that works to provide safe, reliable, and affordable community services across the spectrum, to all citizens, by leveraging data and integrating services to optimize accessibility and performance. The stakeholders who should be engaged in the smart cities conversation include transportation agencies representing all modes; water and wastewater providers; energy utilities; community facilities and management; public services such as waste management and health; law enforcement and fire; public and private parking providers; private industry and employers; and the end users of the system.[45]

Smart cities can be considered an evolution of the integrated corridor management (ICM) concept covered in Chap. 7. Like ICM, one of the key factors in smart cities is integration across a broad range of elements of the community that are institutional, operational, and technical in nature. A description of these integration categories within the context of transportation in a smart city is provided in Table 8.6. All of these

Smart Cities Integration Category	Description
Institutional	The coordination and collaboration across agencies and local jurisdictions, such as transportation network owners and operators, in support of smart cities, including integration of responsibilities and the sharing of control across institutional boundaries and responsibilities.
Operational	The multiagency integration of transportation management strategies that frequently takes place in real-time, and promotes information sharing and coordinated operations across the breadth of transportation networks within the community in order to optimize the network as a whole.
Technical	The integration of the technical elements and systems critical to operating and managing the various components of the transportation infrastructure, including the integration of communication, data, standards, and functional systems, to foster collaborative and information decisions related to operational strategies across agencies and stakeholder partners.

TABLE 8.6 Smart Cities and Transportation (*Ref. 45.*)

integration elements are necessary for the stakeholders to optimize the transportation network so that it is part of the smart cities concept. Additionally, a smart transportation network helps leverage resources to support other infrastructure needs and services that ensure all of the needs of a community's citizens are met.

To shine the national spotlight on smart cities, the US DOT launched the Smart City Challenge in 2015. As part of the challenge, mid-size cities across the country developed innovative proposals to develop smart transportation networks that use data, applications, and technology to work to achieve the objective of safe and efficient movement of people and goods. The US DOT received 78 applications from a broad range of cities, many of which addressed a critical transportation challenge of urban mobility. Specific transportation problems that communities are facing include:

- Providing first-mile and last-mile service for transit users
- Connecting underserved communities to promote accessibility to jobs
- Facilitating the movement of freight into and within a city
- Coordinating data collection and related analysis all systems and sectors of the transportation community
- Improving the efficiency of parking systems and related payment systems
- Reducing carbon emissions and limiting the impacts of climate change
- Optimizing traffic flow on arterial street networks and freeway systems through a variety of operational strategies[46]

A review of the applications also painted a picture of how cities envision the future for their communities, residents, and businesses that technology and data have the potential to solve. Namely, the future includes such aspects as innovative travel options for travelers; efficient freight delivery in the urban core; wireless charging for electric vehicles; seamless connectivity between vehicles and infrastructure; expanded opportunity to underserved communities through connectivity and access to jobs; and integrated transportation data and analytics to enable agencies to make rapid and informed decisions on optimizing operations.

The USDOT selected the City of Columbus as the winner of the Smart City Challenge in 2016. As illustrated in Fig. 8.17, the vision for a smart Columbus centers on enabling technologies in four critical deployment districts across the city. The implementation of the Columbus Connected Transportation Network (CCTN), an integrated data exchange, enhanced human services, and an electric vehicle infrastructure enable that vision. By implementing these technologies across the four districts noted, the City of Columbus and its partners anticipated benefits including enhanced access to jobs, smart logistics in the community, connected residents and visitors, and more sustainable transportation.[46] In the coming years, residents of Columbus will be able to benefit from this investment in terms of mobility, connectivity, and opportunity. Perhaps the greatest hallmark of the Smart City Challenge to date is the fact that it spurred collaborative thinking in the transportation community. New industry and nonprofit partners became part of the dialogue surrounding transportation challenges, helping to identify innovative ways to address local problems with smart technology and data.

It is important to note that smart cities are not just about transportation, nor are they just for large communities. While large technological investments such as advanced traffic management centers and integrated data hubs are smart city tools

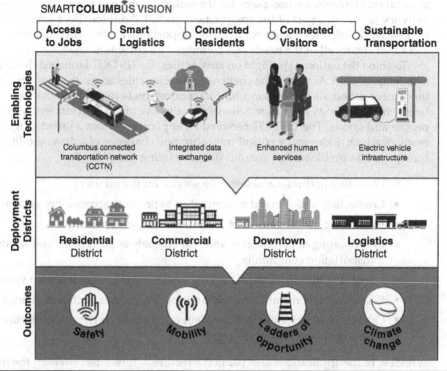

FIGURE 8.17 Columbus smart city challenge implementation vision. (© *U.S. Department of Transportation.*)

for large metropolitan areas, communities of all sizes are looking for opportunities to improve efficiencies and the overall quality of life for their citizens and businesses. Technology is a central theme in all smart city initiatives, and small communities often have the benefit of a smaller sandbox in which to experiment with and test those technologies. Smaller scale deployments offer the opportunity to identify issues and learn lessons from which larger communities can benefit. Additionally, the transportation community is only one piece of the smart cities puzzle, and it often serves as an enabler for technologies and applications that have the potential to solve non transportation-related challenges. For example, the conversion of obsolete transit vehicles into mobile grocery services offer access to fresh produce in urban food deserts. Working collaboratively with other community stakeholders, a transit agency can optimize the use of a previous investment to meet a critical need in a community that can improve the overall quality of life for a segment of the population. A sample of smart city initiatives in the United States is provided in Table 8.7. The transportation professional needs to be open to opportunities to enhance their community through innovative applications and strategies, ensuring that the right technology is used to solve the right problem in a way that benefits a broad range of stakeholders in a sustainable manner.

Location	Smart City Initiative
Pittsburgh, PA (Pop. 303,000)	• Deployment of smart traffic signal technology on major travel corridors
San Francisco, CA (Pop. 865,000)	• Implementation of CV technologies to allow the signal system to detect red light-violating vehicles and adjust timing • Deployment of personal wireless devices to prioritize pedestrian travel and safety at intersections • Pilot of a shared, electric, and autonomous shuttle
Denver, CO (Pop. 682,000)	• Upgrade of the regional traffic management center • Construction of a connected vehicle network • Installation of automated pedestrian detection at targeted sidewalks
Portland, OR (Pop. 640,000)	• Integration of shared-use mobility options into an existing trip planning application
Ketchum, ID (Pop. 2,700)	• Installation of enhanced signage for pedestrians and cyclists • Installation of smart streetlights
Madison, WI (Pop. 252,000)	• Adoption of an open source data ordinance to allows public data to be transferred and shared among agencies, private sector businesses, and the general public
Kansas City, MO (Pop. 481,000)	• Provision of Wi-Fi in key underserved areas to help improve education and job access to residents
Seat Pleasant, MD (Pop. 5,000)	• Development of a "My Seat Pleasant" mobile app to request city services and provide access to a variety of community information
South Daytona, FL (Pop. 12,800)	• Commitment to reducing greenhouse gas emissions with installation of more efficient lighting, solar water heater in the fire department, and community education on energy use

TABLE 8.7 Sample of Smart City Initiatives in the United States

8.9 Highway Automation

While much discussion and activities are moving forward in the realm of connected and AV, the transportation profession is beginning to grapple with how wholescale automation of the vehicle fleet will impact the infrastructure as a whole. Primarily, transportation agencies are unclear how vast automation will influence or change how they plan, design, construct, operate, and maintain the transportation infrastructure that provides mobility for all system users. Some likely questions include the following:

- What will happen when all of the vehicles are automated and potentially operate without a driver?
- Will passengers still need to have knowledge about the roadway network?

- How will agencies communicate that information to the passenger?
- Will vehicles need to communicate with the infrastructure?
- What information will they need to navigate the network safely?
- What elements of the infrastructure will need to provide information to the vehicle?
- How frequently does that information need to be transmitted?
- Will traffic signals still be necessary?
- Will static traffic control devices still be necessary?
- How do pedestrians and bicycles integrate into the network with automated vehicles?
- Will AVs collect information that agencies could use to better operate their systems?
- Will agencies collect data from AVs that provide information about the condition of such roadway elements as pavements, bridges, or pavement markings?
- How will be the responsibilities of TMC operators and personnel change with a fleet of AVs?
- How will agencies handle the occasional vehicle that is not automated?
- Will operating agencies prohibit those vehicles from using specific facilities?
- How do the responsibilities of law enforcement and first responders change with AVs?
- What new stakeholders need to be part of the dialogue on automation?
- What will be the new performance measures associated with highway automation?

The uncertainties are vast and present a significant challenge to transportation professionals. While the answers have yet to be determined, the transportation professional will need to recognize the future involves automation, that collaborative and creative changes are ahead, and that they need to be ready.

8.10   Case Studies

The following are case studies illustrating how state and local agencies are responding to the emerging topics impacting the transportation profession, including livability, sustainability, and resiliency.

State DOTs and Livability

Numerous states are committed to advancing livability in their communities through various tools and initiatives. For example, the Florida Department of Transportation (FDOT) developed the 2060 Florida Transportation Plan that focuses on long-term objectives to foster livable communities across the state.[47] Incorporated in that plan is a key goal to make transportation decisions that support and enhance livability by supporting local, regional, and statewide partners and coordinate investments with land use and other public and private decisions. The goal is intended to develop transportation solutions that support quality places to live, learn, work, and play.[48] California Department of Transportation (Caltrans) has taken a regional approach to advancing livability. It has developed the California Regional Blueprint Planning Program to help metropolitan planning organizations (MPOs) and rural Regional Transportation Planning Agencies (RTPAs) in their planning efforts. Through this competitive grant program, regional agencies can secure grant money to conduct scenario planning to plan a 20-year growth scenario that involves the planning of more efficient land use patterns and transportation investments that:

- Improve mobility
- Increase transportation and housing choices
- Reduce greenhouse gas emissions
- Protect natural resources
- Increase economic competitiveness
- Improve quality of life for the citizens[41]

Other ways in which State DOTs have addressed livability are described in Table 8.8. They illustrate the variety of tools, techniques, and approaches for transportation agencies to address livability through ongoing efforts.

Climate Resilience Pilot Program

In 2013, FHWA launched the Climate Resilience Pilot Program in an effort to work with state DOTs and MPOs to consider strategies to move toward resilience in the transportation network in the face of climate change and extreme weather events.[54] Over the course of 2 years, 19 pilot teams partnered on a variety of initiatives that worked to identify vulnerabilities in their respective transportation systems and determine appropriate strategies to enhance its resilience. A brief summary of each of the 19 pilot projects is provided in Table 8.9.

Throughout the 3-year pilot program, numerous success stories, best practices, and lessons learned emerged across the majority of the projects. Specific revelations and valuable lessons learned worthy of note include the following:

- Consider project budget and timeline, data availability, and near-term priorities when establishing the project scope.
- Leverage existing studies to extend project resources and potentially expand scope.
- Leverage the expertise of all stakeholders and regional partners to identify existing resources that can benefit the project.
- Consider a broad range of stressors, beyond climate-related vulnerabilities, in the assessment to reflect the interrelationships between stressors.
- Collect and utilize institutional knowledge in the assessment process to ensure issues are not overlooked.
- Engage stakeholders using visualization techniques and tools to clearly present the issues and approaches under consideration.

State	Livability Strategy	Description
Utah DOT (UDOT)	Contact sensitive solutions	Design-build project that addressed capacity, safety, and involved residents, business owners, and city officials to preserve historic and environmental characteristics and serve as an economic stimulus for the region[41,49]
Massachusetts DOT (MassDOT)	Policy and design guidelines	Developed a *Project Development and Design Guide* that encourages design flexibility, community context, integrated multimodal designs, and project development guidelines that incorporate a range of context sensitive design solutions[41,50]
Pennsylvania DOT (PennDOT) New Jersey DOT (NJDOT)	Policy and design guidelines	Developed a *Smart Transportation Guidebook* to integrate transportation system planning and design to foster sustainability and livability of communities in rural, suburban, and urban areas[41,51]
New York State DOT (NYSDOT)	Project prioritization	Established a program known as Green Leadership in Transportation Environmental Sustainability Program as a self-certification program for projects and operations that incorporate sustainable choices[41,52]
California Department of Transportation	Performance measures and scorecards	Developed a *Smart Mobility Framework and Scorecard* to evaluate options for the transportation network that meet the definition of smart mobility with respect to location efficiency, reliable mobility, health and safety, environmental stewardship, social equity, and robust economy[41,53]

TABLE 8.8   Examples of State DOTs Addressing Livability

- Exploit existing datasets and vulnerability assessment tools for efficient analysis.
- Develop and utilize criteria and benefit–cost analyses to systematically evaluate options for implementation and which reflects the viewpoints of local stakeholders and decision makers.
- Engage stakeholders as well as underserved and disadvantaged communities to ensure their needs are considered in the overall assessment process.
- Develop resources and strategies for incorporating climate information in existing engineering design processes.
- Ensure that the assessment aligns with long-range planning processes and plans as well as asset management strategies.[54]

The pilot program provided valuable insight for agencies with respect to strategies and approaches to developing resiliency in their transportation network. Working

Pilot Location	Description
Arizona DOT	• Study to identify hotspots where highways are vulnerable to associated hazards from high temperatures, drought, and intense storms • Focus Interstate corridor connecting Nogales, Tucson, Phoenix, and Flagstaff, which includes a variety of urban areas, landscapes, biotic communities, and climate zones and presents a range of weather conditions applicable to much of Arizona
California DOT (Caltrans)	• Assessed vulnerability in four counties by scoring asset criticality and potential impact. • Identified adaptation options at four prototype locations of vulnerable road segments • Formalized their adaptation methodology into a tool to assist with the evaluation and prioritization of adaptation options
Capital Area MPO	• Used a data and stakeholder-driven approach to assess risks to nine critical assets from flooding, drought, extreme heat, wildfire, and ice • Conducted a criticality workshop, developed local climate projections, and performed risk assessments for each asset
Connecticut DOT	• Conducted a systems-level vulnerability assessment of bridge and culvert structures from inland flooding associated with extreme rainfall events • Assessment included data collection and field review, hydrologic and hydraulic evaluation, criticality assessment and hydraulic design criteria evaluation
Hillsborough MPO	• Assessed the vulnerability of select surface transportation assets to sea level rise, storm surge, and flooding in order to identify cost-effective risk management strategies for incorporation into short-term and long-range transportation planning
Iowa DOT	• Developed a methodology to integrate climate projections of rainfall within a river system model to predict river flood response to climate change. • Analyzed the potential impact of the future floods on six bridges to evaluate vulnerability to climate change and extreme weather and inform the development of adaptation options
Maine DOT	• Identified transportation assets that are vulnerable to flooding from sea level rise and storm surge in six coastal towns • Developed depth-damage functions and adaptation design options at three of the sites and evaluated the costs and benefits of the alternative design structures
Maryland State Highway Administration (MDSHA)	• Developed a three-tiered vulnerability assessment methodology and GIS layers of statewide water surfaces to analyze vulnerability to sea level rise, storm surge, and flooding in two counties • Reviewed design strategies, best management practices, planning standards, and other ways to support the adoption of adaptive management solutions
MassDOT	• Combined a state-of-the-art hydrodynamic flood model with agency-driven knowledge and priorities to assess vulnerabilities of the I-93 Central Artery/Tunnel system to sea level rise and extreme storm events and develop adaptation strategies

TABLE 8.9 FHWA Climate Resilience Pilot Program, Representative Projects (*Ref. 54.*)

collaboratively with stakeholder agencies and capitalizing on expertise and available tools, agencies can identify a path forward for their communities that ensures the long-term viability of their facilities as climate change continues to shape the physical land-scape.

Summary

As discussed throughout this chapter, the transportation professional needs to be prepared to adapt the transportation infrastructure as technology evolves. History has shown that improvements and advancements in technology can be used to enhance the provision of safety mobility to transportation system users. As the demands of society change, transportation professionals must also be willing to change the way they accomplish their mission without sacrificing safety, livability, and sustainability for urban and rural communities.

Glossary of Acronyms

ASCE—American Society of Civil Engineers

AV—automated vehicles

Caltrans—California Department of Transportation

CCTN—Columbus Connected Transportation Network

CMAQ—Congestion Mitigation and Air Quality

CV—connected vehicles

DOT—Department of Transportation

DSRC—dedicated short-range communications

EPA—Environmental Protection Agency

FDOT—Florida Department of Transportation

GIS—Geographic Information Systems

HSIP—Highway Safety Improvement Program

ICM—integrated corridor management

IIHS—Insurance Institute for Highway Safety

IoT—Internet of Things

I2V—infrastructure to vehicle

MassDOT—Massachusetts Department of Transportation

MDSHA—Maryland State Highway Administration

MT—mobile Internet

MPO—metropolitan planning organizations

NHTSA—National Highway Traffic Safety Administration

NJDOT—New Jersey Department of Transportation

NYSDOT—New York State Department of Transportation

PennDOT—Pennsylvania Department of Transportation

RSDP—Roadway Safety Data Program

RTPA—Regional Transportation Planning Agency

STBG—Surface Transportation Block Grant

TA—Transportation Alternatives

TSMO—transportation systems management and operations

TTI—Texas A&M Transportation Institute

TxDOT—Texas Department of Transportation

TZD—Toward Zero Deaths

UDOT—Utah Department of Transportation

USDOT—U.S. Department of Transportation

USHUD—U.S. Department of Housing and Urban Development

V2I—vehicle to infrastructure

V2V—vehicle to vehicle

Exercises

8.1 Write a paper (no more than 10 pages) providing a comprehensive case study on a region or state that has implemented a variety of transportation programs and projects that address livability, sustainability, and/or resiliency.

8.2 Write a paper (no more than 10 pages) providing a case study of the application of connected vehicle technology or automated technology in a real-world environment and the pros, cons, and lessons learned from the deployment.

8.3 Write a paper (no more than 10 pages) discussing how the advancement of a disruptive technology has impacted the transportation infrastructure and potential impacts that might be expected in the future.

References

1. *Failure to Act: Closing the Infrastructure Investment Gap for America's Economic Future.* American Society of Civil Engineers, Washington, D.C., 2016.
2. *Infrastructure Report Card: A Comprehensive Assessment of America's Infrastructure.* American Society of Civil Engineers, Washington, D.C., 2017.
3. "Public Road Length, Miles by Ownership: 2013." Bureau of Transportation Statistics, U.S. Department of Transportation, Washington, D.C., https://www.bts .gov/content/public-road-length-miles-ownership (accessed May 2018).
4. Schrank D., B. Eisele, T. Lomax, and J. Bak. *2015 Urban Mobility Scorecard.* Texas A&M Transportation Institute and INRIX, College Station, TX and Kirkland, WA, 2015.
5. *Merriam-Webster,* https://www.merriam-webster.com/dictionary/livability (accessed October 2, 2017).

6. *Merriam-Webster*, https://www.merriam-webster.com/dictionary/sustainability (accessed October 2, 2017).

7. "Livability." U.S. Department of Transportation, https://www.transportation.gov/livability (accessed June 2017).

8. "Partnership for Sustainable Communities: An Interagency Partnership." U.S. Department of Housing and Urban Development, U.S. Department of Transportation, Environmental Protection Agency, https://www.sustainablecommunities.gov/ (accessed June 2017).

9. *Partnership for Sustainable Communities: Five Years of Learning from Communities and Coordinating Federal Investments.* Report No. EPA 231-R-14-004, U.S. Environmental Protection Agency, Office of Sustainable Communities, Washington, D.C., August 2014, https://www.sustainablecommunities.gov/sites/sustainablecommunities.gov/files/docs/partnership-accomplishments-report-2014-reduced-size.pdf (accessed October 2017).

10. "Strong Cities, Strong Communities Initiative (SC2)," https://www.huduser.gov/portal/sc2/home.html (accessed October 2017).

11. "Urban Waters Federal Partnership." U.S. Environmental Protection Agency, https://www.epa.gov/urbanwaterspartners (accessed October 2017).

12. "Livability and Sustainability." Federal Highway Administration, U.S. Department of Transportation, https://ops.fhwa.dot.gov/plan4ops/livability_sus.htm (accessed October 2017).

13. *Transportation Management and Operations.* U.S. Department of Transportation, Federal Highway Administration, Washington, D.C., https://www.fhwa.dot.gov/livability/fact_sheets/transmgtandops.cfm(accessed June 2017).

14. Grant, M., H. Rue, S. Trainor, J. Bauer, J. Parks, M. Raulerson, K. Rooney, et al. *The Role of Transportation Systems Management & Operations in Supporting Livability and Sustainability: A Primer.* Report FHWA-HOP-12-004, SAIC, ICF, and Kittelson & Associates, Inc., for U.S. Department of Transportation, Federal Highway Administration, Washington, DC, January 2012.

15. *Transportation and Safety.* U.S. Department of Transportation, Federal Highway Administration, Washington, D.C., https://www.fhwa.dot.gov/livability/fact_sheets/transandsafety.cfm (accessed June 2017).

16. *Transportation, Development, and Environment.* U.S. Department of Transportation, Federal Highway Administration, Washington, D.C., https://www.fhwa.dot.gov/livability/fact_sheets/transdevenviron.cfm (accessed June 2017).

17. *Transportation and Health.* U.S. Department of Transportation, Federal Highway Administration, Washington, D.C., https://www.fhwa.dot.gov/livability/fact_sheets/transandhealth.cfm (accessed June 2017).

18. *Transportation and Land Use.* U.S. Department of Transportation, Federal Highway Administration, Washington, D.C., https://www.fhwa.dot.gov/livability/fact_sheets/transandlanduse.cfm (accessed June 2017).

19. *Transportation and Economic Development.* U.S. Department of Transportation, Federal Highway Administration, Washington, D.C., https://www.fhwa.dot.gov/livability/fact_sheets/transandeconomics.cfm (accessed June 2017).

20. *Freight and Livability.* U.S. Department of Transportation, Federal Highway Administration, Washington, D.C., https://www.fhwa.dot.gov/livability/fact_sheets/freightandlivability.cfm (accessed June 2017).

21. *Transportation and Housing Costs.* U.S. Department of Transportation, Federal Highway Administration, Washington, D.C., https://www.fhwa.dot.gov/livability/fact_sheets/transandhousing.cfm (accessed June 2017).

22. *Transportation and Rural Livability.* U.S. Department of Transportation, Federal Highway Administration, Washington, D.C., https://www.fhwa.dot.gov/livability/fact_sheets/transandrurallivability.cfm (accessed June 2017).

23. *Federal Highway Programs and Livability.* U.S. Department of Transportation, Federal Highway Administration, Washington, D.C., https://www.fhwa.dot.gov/livability/fact_sheets/fedhwyprogandlivability.cfm (accessed June 2017).

24. *Benefits of Livability.* U.S. Department of Transportation, Federal Highway Administration, Washington, D.C., https://www.fhwa.dot.gov/livability/fact_sheets/benefits.cfm (accessed June 2017).

25. Zietsman, J., T. Ramani, J. Potter, V. Reeder, and J. DeFlorio. *A Guidebook for Sustainability Performance Measurement for Transportation Agencies.* NCHRP Report 708, Transportation Research Board, National Academies of Sciences, Washington, D.C., 2011.

26. *ATDM Program Brief: Data Needs for ATDM.* Report FHWA-HOP-16-003. FHWA, U.S. Department of Transportation, Washington, D.C., May 2016.

27. *Merriam-Webster,* https://www.merriam-webster.com/dictionary/resilience (accessed October 3, 2017).

28. "Resilience." Federal Highway Administration, U.S. Department of Transportation, https://www.fhwa.dot.gov/environment/sustainability/resilience/ (accessed October 3, 2017).

29. *The Federal Highway Administration's Climate Change & Extreme Weather Vulnerability Assessment Framework.* Report FHWA-HEP-13-005, Federal Highway Administration, U.S. Department of Transportation, December 2012, https://www.fhwa.dot.gov/environment/sustainability/resilience/publications/vulnerability_assessment_framework/fhwahep13005.pdf (accessed October 2017).

30. "Tools." Federal Highway Administration, U.S. Department of Transportation, https://www.fhwa.dot.gov/environment/sustainability/resilience/tools/ (accessed October 2017).

31. "Transportation Fatalities by Mode." Bureau of Transportation Statistics, U.S. Department of Transportation, https://www.bts.gov/content/transportation-fatalities-mode (accessed May 2018).

32. "Toward Zero Deaths," http://www.towardzerodeaths.org/ (accessed October 2017).

33. "Mission of the Office of Safety." Federal Highway Administration, U.S. Department of Transportation, https://safety.fhwa.dot.gov/about/ (accessed October 2017).

34. "Vision Zero Network," http://visionzeronetwork.org/ (accessed October 2017).

35. "Vision Zero." Institute of Transportation Engineers, http://www.ite.org/visionzero/default.asp (accessed October 2017).

36. "Road to Zero Coalition." National Safety Council, http://www.nsc.org/learn/NSC-Initiatives/Pages/The-Road-to-Zero.aspx (accessed October 2017).

37. "Zero Deaths." Federal Highway Administration, U.S. Department of Transportation, https://safety.fhwa.dot.gov/tzd/ (accessed October 2017).

38. Baker, R., J. Wagner, M. Miller, G. Pritchard, and M. Manser. *Disruptive Technologies and Transportation,* Report PRC 15-45-F, Texas A&M Transportation Institute, Texas A&M

University System, College Station, TX, June 2016, https://policy.tti.tamu.edu/wp-content/plugins/google-document-embedder/load.php?d=http%3A%2F%2Ftti.tamu.edu%2Fdocuments%2FPRC-15-45-F.pdf (accessed October 2017).

39. "Connected Vehicle Research in the United States." Intelligent Transportation Systems Joint Program Office, U.S. Department of Transportation, http://www.its.dot.gov/connected_vehicle/connected_vehicle_research.htm (accessed October 2017).

40. "Automated Vehicles." National Highway Traffic Safety Administration, U.S. Department of Transportation, http://www.nhtsa.gov/Research/Crash+Avoidance/Automated+Vehicles (accessed October 2017).

41. "Automated Vehicle Research." Intelligent Transportation Systems Joint Program Office, U.S. Department of Transportation, http://www.its.dot.gov/automated_vehicle/index.htm (accessed October 2017).

42. "U.S. Department of Transportation Issues Advance Notice of Proposed Rulemaking to Begin Implementation of Vehicle-to-Vehicle Communications Technology." National Highway Traffic Safety Administration, U.S. Department of Transportation, http://www.nhtsa.gov/About+NHTSA/Press+Releases/NHTSA-issues-advanced-notice-of-proposed-rulemaking-on-V2V-communications (accessed October 2017).

43. "Automation Research at the USDOT." Intelligent Transportation Systems Joint Program Office, U.S. Department of Transportation, http://www.its.dot.gov/automated_vehicle/avr_plan.htm (accessed August 11, 2015).

44. "Connected Vehicle Pilot Deployment Program." Intelligent Transportation Systems Joint Program Office, U.S. Department of Transportation, https://www.its.dot.gov/pilots/ (accessed October 2017).

45. Newton, D., C Vick, K. Raboy, A. Pearmine, and E. Hubbard. *Integrated Corridor Management and the Smart Cities Revolution: Leveraging Synergies.* Report No. FHWA-HOP-16-075, Federal Highway Administration, U.S. Department of Transportation, Washington, D.C., 2016 (accessed May 2018).

46. "Smart City Challenge." U.S. Department of Transportation, Washington, D.C., https://www.transportation.gov/smartcity (accessed May 2018).

47. *State DOTs and Livability,* Federal Highway Administration, U.S. Department of Transportation, Washington, D.C., https://www.fhwa.dot.gov/livability/fact_sheets/statedotsandlivability.cfm (accessed June 2017).

48. "Florida Transportation Plan (FTP) Implementation Element." Florida Department of Transportation, http://www.floridatransportationplan.com/places.htm (accessed October 2017).

49. "12300 South Design Build Project, Draper, UT." Federal Highway Administration, U.S. Department of Transportation, Office of Planning, Environment, & Realty (HEP), https://www.fhwa.dot.gov/planning/css/case_studies/12300south/ (accessed October 2017).

50. Project Development & Design Guide. Massachusetts Department *of Transportation, January 2006,* http://www.massdot.state.ma.us/highway/DoingBusinessWithUs/ManualsPublicationsForms/ProjectDevelopmentDesignGuide.aspx (accessed October 2017).

51. Smart Transportation Guidebook, New Jersey Department of Transportation and Pennsylvania Department *of Transportation, March 2008,* http://www.state.nj.us/transportation/community/mobility/pdf/smarttransportationguidebook2008.pdf (accessed October 2017).

52. "GreenLITES." New York State Department of Transportation, https://www.dot.ny.gov/programs/greenlites (accessed October 2017).

53. "The Smart Mobility Framework." California Department of Transportation, http://www.dot.ca.gov/hq/tpp/offices/ocp/smf.html (accessed October 2017).

54. ICF International. *2013–2015 Climate Resilience Pilot Program: Outcomes, Lessons Learned, and Recommendations.* Report FHWA-HEP-16-079, Federal Highway Administration, U.S. Department of Transportation, Washington, D.C., 2016.

Index

Note: Page numbers followed by *f* denote figures; page numbers followed by *t* denote tables.